HOW
TO STUDY
IN
COLLEGE

Second Edition

HOW TO STUDY IN COLLEGE

Second Edition

WALTER PAUK
Director, Reading-Study Center
Cornell University

HOUGHTON MIFFLIN COMPANY ■ Boston
Atlanta   Dallas   Geneva, Illinois
Hopewell, New Jersey   Palo Alto   London

The cover is based on a painting by Victor Vasarely enti-
tled "VEGA-KONTOSH," supplied by courtesy of the
artist.

Library of Congress Catalog Card Number: 73-14498
ISBN:0-395-17815-0

CONTENTS

PREFACE

TO THE SECOND EDITION

Over twenty years' experience with helping students develop better study skills has convinced me that any student who wants to be helped can be helped. Time and again students have told me that by learning a particular technique for taking notes, remembering what they read, reviewing for an examination, or attacking a difficult subject such as mathematics or one of the sciences, they have achieved a major breakthrough. Moreover, it often happens that improvement in one or two study techniques opens the door to the solution of a whole complex of related problems.

The second edition of *How to Study in College* is based firmly on the belief that such students are not primarily interested in theory, and most of them have little patience with merely inspirational talk. What they mainly want is straightforward, practical instruction on how to tackle and overcome their special difficulties. They want something they can readily understand and apply, and something that works. This book stresses practical study techniques which, in my experience with thousands of students at universities and two-year colleges, have been found to work.

These techniques are the product of extensive trial and experiment based on accepted educational and learning theory. But the tail is never allowed to wag the dog. Theory is always implicit, but it is never presented without specific instruction on how to apply it. After all, the person who needs penicillin is seldom cured by learning the history of antibiotics.

The chief method of this book, then, is to translate theory and the findings of research into tools which a student can grasp and use. In making the book concrete, I have relied heavily on visual examples. The student is shown economical ways of scheduling his time. He is shown facsimiles of lecture notes and the relative advantages and disadvantages of various methods of note-taking. He is shown how topic sentences and transitional expressions summarize an idea and relate the parts of a discussion. He is shown how and how not to mark the books he studies, to take notes on his reading, and to answer questions on an examination. He thus learns by vivid example to apply the principles which research in learning and education has led us to.

Among these principles is the importance of attitudes in mastery learning, both as a factor in the original motivation to improve and as a product of improvement. Some students seek help through a genuine desire to do better, while some are driven to do so by fear of what may happen to them if they don't. Whatever the drive to begin with, few can resist the lift of spirit and the deep sense of satisfaction that is the natural reward of success. And few can fail to be strengthened in favorable attitudes toward study by the mere fact of having done it well and honestly enough not only to pass examinations, but to retain their newly acquired knowledge so that it provides a solid foundation for more. For this reason I am wholeheartedly against tricks and gimmicks which overnight can fill the mind with "knowledge" which melts away after the examination and leaves everything to be done over again.

A word should be said before I close in thanks to the persons who have contributed to the book. I am deeply indebted to the following: Mrs. Jane E. Hardy of Cornell University for the chapter on writing course papers; Professor James A. Wood of the University of Texas for the chapter on how to speak effectively; Professor William G. Moulton of Princeton University for the chapter on how to study a foreign language; Professor Harrison A. Geiselmann of Cornell University for his chapter on how to study mathematics; Professor Kenneth Greisen of Cornell University for his chapter on the study of the sciences; Dr. Nancy V. Wood, Director of Study Skills and Tutorial Services, the University of Texas at El Paso, for her unpublished articles "Main Ideas" and "Organization" in the chapter on the improvement of general reading skills, as well as for certain materials originally prepared by her for the Cornell Reading and Study Skills Program; and the National Association for Mental Health, Inc., for permission to reprint most of the material in the chapter on how to keep your balance. Finally, I am eternally grateful to my many students, who have taught me so much, that I may pass a little on to others.

Walter Pauk

HOW
TO STUDY
IN
COLLEGE

Second Edition

I

THE
ACADEMIC
SETTING

1

WHAT DID YOU COME FOR?

Education is the great equalizer. Or is it? You may feel that it is really a system designed to separate geniuses from dunces, and that you come close to fitting in the latter category! College is a big, new experience, and for many students bewildering.

Consider Joe, a well-meaning guy sitting over there on a stone bench outside the student union. It is twenty minutes until his first class in freshman English, and he is scared he will never find the time to do all the assignments. The teacher has a fierce reputation. And two other courses—introduction to electronics and the math survey—sound hard, too. Maybe the course in modern American society won't be too hard, and his last course, small ensembles, should be fun because he has been playing the trumpet since he was thirteen. But all in all, he has three tough courses and he doesn't know how he will get through them.

Besides, there are a lot of other things on Joe's mind. The car pool that brings him to the campus is half an hour too late for his first class, and he'll have to find other transportation in the morning. And if he stays after 4:30 in the afternoon to use the library or the gym, he won't have a ride home. He's met a great girl named Jill that he'd like to take to a movie, but he isn't sure how much homework he'll have to do—and then there's the transport problem again. Besides, he still has to break up with his old girl at home, and he doesn't know how to do it without hurting her feelings. Maybe he should get a part-time job, so that he can buy a car.

His course schedule is a hodgepodge, he knows that. But although he has good SAT scores in math, he isn't sure what he ought to be studying. His adviser told him he would have to decide on a major by the end of the semester, and that's just one more worry. He's taking the electronics and math courses just in case he decides to major in something technical. On the other hand, even though he's good at math,

3

he also enjoys theatre, music, and reading a good book if he doesn't have to hurry through it.

What's wrong with Joe? Not too much, really. He is intelligent (you have to be intelligent to get into college these days), and he has an amiable personality, and he thinks college is the place he wants to be. But he doesn't have a clear idea of what he wants to get out of college, and he has a lot of other things on his mind besides studying. He is temporarily at sea because he lacks a sense of purpose and doesn't know which of his many problems to tackle first. Happily, he soon gets his priorities straightened out, as we shall see when we read his story in Chapter 15.

Contrast Joe with Linda, a sophomore who is intent on becoming an elementary school teacher. She knows her major career goal, and she wants to know everything she can about children and about teaching. She has a special interest in teaching children with dyslexia. In addition, she wants to learn as much about Western culture as her schedule of education courses will permit, and so she has planned to take a number of courses in history, literature, art, and environmental science.

However, Linda has trouble concentrating on her studies, even though she tries. For instance, when she discovered that her new roommate in the dorm is addicted to playing the radio during study hours, Linda lost no time in moving to the library for most of her study sessions. That was a good move, but it didn't solve all her problems. Her boyfriend has just transferred to another college two thousand miles away, and she misses him. For two weeks now she has been moping around, but she knows that she had better start working hard on her course in educational psychology. She realizes that since her primary aim in college is to become a good teacher, she must subordinate other interests and problems to that goal.

Now let's sum up. What is the difference between Joe and Linda? Here are four distinguishing characteristics of the successful college student.

1. The successful student has a clear educational goal (try writing yours down on paper).
2. The successful student recognizes that the college years offer a unique opportunity for intellectual development, and he is willing to subordinate his other concerns to take advantage of that opportunity.
3. The successful student has good study skills.
4. The successful student has the will to succeed.

"All right," you may say, "that's fine for someone who knows where he's going, but I'm here because everyone else is, and I just hope I can decide on a major before it's too late. How can I acquire a 'clear educational goal,' anyway? How can I achieve academic success when I don't know how? How can I compete with the geniuses?"

These are all good questions.

THE WILL TO LEARN

The will to learn can count more than all the techniques this book can teach you. Abraham Lincoln walked twenty miles to borrow a book, and Booker T. Washington, born in slavery, walked 500 miles to go to a high school that would give him the education he craved. But what if you don't already have this strong drive to learn all you can? What if you don't have the "passion for learning" that has been attributed to Michael Faraday, who entirely through his own efforts rose from being the untutored son of a blacksmith to be England's foremost man of science? You ask yourself, "Can I succeed when I don't have the tremendous drive that Faraday, Lincoln, and Booker T. Washington did?"

The answer is yes. Because success, even a small success, strengthens the will, and the strengthened will provides us with additional power to work even harder. This in turn helps ensure more success, and so the upward spiral begins and accelerates.

It doesn't matter which comes first, will or success. In some people, a strong natural curiosity and love of learning lead to academic success. In others, academic success brings a natural interest in the things that one is doing well.

The will to succeed provides you with the power to get up in the morning, attend classes, study assignments, rewrite a paper, hold out for long-range goals, and do many other things. If the will is to keep on providing the power, however, it must be recharged from time to time by the source of all this energy. The source is success.

This book can show you the techniques of academic success. It moves from very basic matters like maintaining your emotional balance and organizing your time to specifics on the best way to organize a research paper and how to study mathematics. It assumes that you already have the desire to learn as much as you can, but even if you lack this desire now, a little success based on the techniques described in this book will probably help you acquire it. And if you already know what you want out of college, this book can help you achieve it in the most direct and most effective way.

Achieving success through learning leads directly to improving or maintaining a healthy self image. With success comes a sense of personal dignity and pride, as well as a feeling of control over your academic environment. Success can quickly change a failure-type personality to a success-type personality.

THE POWER OF STUDY SKILLS

Don't underestimate the importance and power of study skills. Study skills are efficient ways for using your time and mind.

In a survey at a large university, the students were asked about the reasons for their success or lack of success. The two items that polled the most are as follows.[1]

Reasons given by successful students for their success		Reasons given by unsuccessful students for their lack of success	
Good Study Habits	33%	Lack of Study Habits	25%
Interest	25%	Lack of Interest	35%

[1] Henry Clay Lindgren, *The Psychology of College Success* (New York: John Wiley and Sons, Inc., 1969), p. 49.

To successful students, study skills seem even more important than their interest in a subject. That's the opinion of people who have first-hand knowledge of the power of study skills.

Experiment with Study Skills

Students usually recognize the value of study skills, but they are often slow to adopt them. This hesitancy to change old ways is a common human trait. The recommended procedure is to try some one study technique, or an entire system, for only a few weeks, to experience at first hand how these skills work. However, it takes a flexible mind to begin the process.

ARE YOU FLEXIBLE?

Some students continue to use their own homemade study methods that have, again and again, proved unsuccessful. This may be a sign of inflexibility. To test your flexibility, try to solve the problem shown in Figure 1-1.

Without fully realizing it, we all have enough creativity to get out of the rut, but to get the process of creativity started, we often need some pump-priming. This book shows how you can adapt methods, systems, and techniques of study to suit your unique needs.

The purpose of the nine-dot exercise was to have you pause long enough to realize more fully how difficult it is to break out of old grooves of thinking. As in this problem, once the method for solution is shown, we think, "How easy! Why didn't I see it myself?" Similarly, we continue using our own hit-or-miss techniques of study without realizing that there are others that may help us to work more constructively.

Now, working constructively is a very different thing from merely working hard. Most of us have seen an inexperienced driver vainly try to coax a car up a slippery slope. He spins the wheels until the tires smoke, yet makes no progress. This is undirected effort, resulting only in waste of gas, tires, patience, and time. If he redirected his efforts by spreading sand under the tires, or if he had prepared for trouble by putting on chains or snowtires, the car could move slowly but steadily forward. In the same way, time, will, and energy can easily be wasted in inefficient study. Directed systematically and intelligently, they can lead to success.

Inefficient study methods have an impact even upon able students, who, though their grades may be fairly good, express frustration over getting so little learning for so much effort. They feel they are being short-changed educationally.

Effective study methods can be learned and made habitual. One's college life should be run systematically, just as any job or profession is run. Many students have voluntarily reported that it was only when they scheduled their time realistically and used systematic study procedures that they were able to cope successfully with their assignments.

Figure 1-1 The Nine-Dot Problem. Try to connect these dots by drawing four straight lines
without taking the pencil from the paper and
without tracing any lines. The solution appears
on page 8.

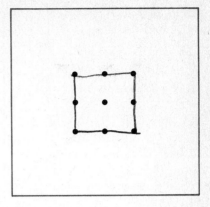

THE SECRET OF MASTERY

With almost no formal schooling, Michael Faraday, through self-education, became
Britain's leading scientist, specializing in electricity. How did he do it?

In his carefully kept diary, he tells how he mastered the material given in a public
lecture by Sir Humphry Davy, the renowned chemist.

> On leaving the lecture room I proceeded immediately homewards and in
> that and the next night had generally drawn up a second set of notes from
> the first. These second notes were more copious, more connected and
> more legible than the first.[2]

Later, when Faraday showed his notes to Sir Humphry and inquired whether he had
understood the lecture correctly, Davy was so impressed by the young man's
industry and intelligence that he offered Faraday a post as his laboratory assistant.

I am *not* advocating the rewriting of classroom notes; rather I want to point out
that the secret of Faraday's thorough learning and remembering of information was
his *mastering of the information through overlearning.*

Notice that in the same night he reworked the notes and amplified them in his
own words. To do so he had to rethink the entire lecture, probably reciting it aloud
as he rewrote it. This technique of learning and overlearning leads to mastery. This
is the secret.

To make progress in any subject or field, you must master, as soon as possible, its
basic facts or principles. It doesn't matter whether the subject is accounting,
philosophy, or welding. You must master the basics; otherwise you have nothing
on which to build, and will merely be going through the motions of getting an
education. You will be putting in time without having anything to show for it.

The Power of Mastery

Mastery converts the ideas and principles into "magnets." These magnets will then
draw the supporting facts and details around themselves naturally, like iron filings.

[2]Reproduced with the permission of the Royal Institute from Faraday's manuscript notes on a
lecture on geology delivered by Mr. Tatum, February 17, 1811.

Answer to problem in Figure 1-1.
Begin at the top left corner
and follow the arrows.

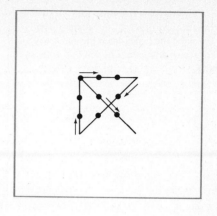

And the greater the mastery, the greater will be the magnetic field. This means that you will not only remember the material more accurately and longer, but you will also have established a magnetic center to which you can continue adding facts and details as you encounter them days, weeks, months or years to come. As Dr. Jerome Bruner of Harvard puts it, "When we learn something, the objective is to learn it in such a way that we get a maximum of travel out of what we have learned."[3]

The real reward for mastering our material is that mastery frees us to *think* with the material. We no longer need to expend our energies merely to retain it. Mastery converts us from filing cabinets into computers with brains.

STUDY SKILLS: THE GREAT EQUALIZER

By using the study skills explained and illustrated in this book, you should be able to master any assignment equal to the level of even the most brilliant student. After all, there is just so much to know about an assignment, and if you have mastered it, then you have reached the theoretical 100 percent mark. The brilliant fellow can't do any more than that. He may, however, master the assignment in half the time. Some people have, through training, run the mile in four minutes, whereas others run the mile in eight minutes; both, however, run the same distance. If you keep practicing, you, too, will cut down on the time it now takes you either to master your assignment or to run a mile. In other words, if you are willing to put in sufficient time and effort, and if you are willing to follow the study techniques presented in this book, you should be able to master your assignments equal to the best of them. These study skills are designed to help you do the very best you can with the abilities you have.

In several studies designed to test the power of mastery learning, it was found that students who were given the opportunity to study subjects until they mastered

[3]Jerome S. Bruner, "Learning and Thinking," *Harvard Educational Review* 29 (1959): 184.

them all achieved as well as the top 20 percent of the students in an average college population who studied in their usual ways.

INDEPENDENT LEARNING: THE GOAL OF STUDY SKILLS

"No one can teach you, but you may learn." This statement means that though we may hear or read the greatest words of wisdom, they will remain mere words unless we *internalize* them.

We may be able to name the courses that we have taken over the years: algebra, history, geology, French, and so forth. But unless we have internalized the subject matter or have studied it very recently, we will not recall what we have "learned."

With good study skills, you will not only learn material more thoroughly and permanently, but you will also be less dependent on your teachers. As long as you look to someone else for an "interpretation" or "explanation," you will not be a free person intellectually.

To become an independent studier, you must have the desire and courage to open a textbook, read it, study it, and ponder it. Then you must be able to get up in class the next day, or write on paper a week or so later, saying, "As I interpret the author, he says . . . ."

Eddie Rickenbacker, auto racer, aviator in World War I, and businessman, had to leave school when he was only twelve years old. Later in life, he fully realized the need for further education. To keep working, earning, and learning all at the same time, Rickenbacker decided to take a course by correspondence.

This experience, as he relates it, is a prime example of a person becoming an *independent studier.* Here is his story.

■   Then I heard of the International Correspondence School in Scranton, Pennsylvania. I wrote, and the answer came back promptly. Even then, in 1905, the ICS had exactly what I wanted, a course in mechanical engineering, complete with a special section on the automobile and internal-combustion engines.

The first lesson, I do not mind admitting, nearly finished my correspondence-school education before it began. It was tough, and I was a little rusty when it came to formal education. I had to teach myself to study all over again, and, furthermore, I had to teach myself to think. I did not realize then, as I laboriously worked away at the lessons all alone, that I was receiving a greater benefit from them than I would have received from the same courses in a classroom. As there was no teacher of whom I could ask an explanation, I had to work out the answers myself. Once I reached the answer through my own individual reasoning, my understanding was permanent and unforgettable.[4]   ■

[4]From the book, *Rickenbacker* by Edward V. Rickenbacker. Copyright © by Edward V. Rickenbacker. Published by Prentice-Hall, Inc., Englewood Cliffs, New Jersey, pp. 31-2.

You may wonder at this point, Why go to college in the first place? or What are teachers for?

Well, it is very true that you could study on your own, but you would probably do so inefficiently. Since you do not know the subject, you do not know where to start, how much of a bite to take, and so forth.

College courses are set up on the basis of years of experience. The purpose of the course is to guide you through the various steps efficiently. The teacher is there to explain and amplify your textbook—to direct your research in the library, the laboratory, and the field—to encourage and supervise your self-learning by setting limited as well as long-range goals—to stimulate thinking through classroom discussions—to measure your progress through quizzes, research papers, and examinations.

But only you can educate yourself.

WHAT THIS BOOK CAN DO FOR YOU

1. It can give you specific techniques for mastering new information, with or without a teacher.
2. If you have a strong will to succeed, it can direct and improve your efforts.
3. If you lack a strong will to succeed, it can show you the road to the academic success you need to stimulate your best efforts.

2

KEEPING YOUR EMOTIONAL BALANCE

Every stage of your life involves growth and change and decision-making and adjustment, sometimes pleasant, sometimes painful. What makes the college years unique is not their freedom from human problems, but the opportunity they offer you to devote your time and energy to becoming the person you want to be. The maintenance of a sense of balance and order in living—a healthy emotional climate—is essential for achieving success in college. It is through living each day realistically that you can best maintain your emotional health.

Most of us worry too much, criticize too much, get angry too often, and hold ourselves too tense. When we mix such a variety of emotions with studying, we become inefficient. This inefficiency then triggers a cycle of emotions: we begin to worry about our low grades and about all the work yet to be done, and we spend so much time worrying that we don't get the work done, which triggers still more worry.

ELEVEN TENSION RELEASERS

We can, however, become efficient learners by first learning how to better attain emotional balance. Try to maintain or improve your emotional health by practicing the following eleven principles set forth by the National Association for Mental Health.[1]

1. Talk It Out

When you are worried, it is a good idea to talk things over with someone. It is foolish to bottle up your worries; instead talk with some level-headed person you can trust.

[1]This material on the "eleven things you can do" is adapted from *How to Deal with Your Tensions*. Copyright © National Association for Mental Health. Used by permission.

In school you can talk to a good friend or your faculty adviser. Other sources of help include professional counseling services, provided by most colleges for students seeking help with emotional strain. If you are worried primarily about your grades, the teacher of reading and study skills can help you. Or you might go to the dean of students; he has more information on where you can get friendly help than anyone else on campus.

Other people to talk to include clergymen, people where you work (including your boss), and members of your family or family friends.

Above all, *talk to somebody*. Talking things out helps relieve strain, helps you see your worry in a clearer light, and often helps you see what you can do about it.

2. Escape for a While

When things go wrong, it is often helpful to get away from the problem for awhile, to lose yourself in some kind of activity. In school, walk over to the gym to shoot some baskets, go see a movie, or read an interesting magazine. If it is evening, take a shower and go to bed early to rest a weary body and mind.

If you cannot physically get away from your problem, try an imaginary escape to a quiet book-lined study, a small lake high in the mountains, or whatever place you find especially peaceful. Even a few moments in your imaginary retreat can refresh you.

Another way to escape is to decide that you will not face a certain problem until a specified time. "Tomorrow at nine-thirty I will consider topics for my research paper." Then you are completely free of that problem until nine-thirty tomorrow.

Making yourself stand there and suffer can be a form of self-punishment, not a way to solve a problem. It is perfectly realistic to escape long enough to recover your perspective and renew your strength. That way, you can come back and deal with your difficulty when you are in better condition emotionally and mentally.

3. Channel Your Anger

If you find that you're "blowing your top" pretty regularly, remember that while this action may give you a *temporary* sense of righteousness or power, it will probably leave you feeling foolish and sorry in the end. If you feel like lashing out at someone, try holding off for awhile until you can put your emotional energy to some good use. A good way to hold off is to hum a tune—any old tune—to yourself, or inwardly recite some poem you learned long ago, or visualize your last summer's vacation trip. Do anything to put your mental and emotional energies on another track. Whatever you do, do it calmly, because you will then have a powerful principle of psychology working for you: If you act with outward calmness, the chances are great that you will gain genuine inward calmness.

Some people control themselves in this way: They hold their tongues, but mentally rehearse how they will "tell the person off" tomorrow. Then they seldom find any need to do so actually. Frequently, the next day, they have a sheepish smile for the other person who, in turn, responds with a smile. Other people control their anger by playing a hard game of tennis or working extra hard on a tough assignment. The important principle here is to channel your "angry" energy constructively.

Sometimes there is a real problem that caused the anger. In that case, a day or two will leave you much better prepared to handle the problem intelligently.

4. Give in Occasionally

If you find yourself getting into frequent quarrels, try standing ground only on what you sincerely believe is right, but do so calmly and make allowance for the fact that you *could* be wrong. Even if you're dead right, it's easier on your system to give in once in a while on matters that are not fundamentally important. If you yield some ground, you'll usually find that others will too. The result will be a relief from tension, possibly a practical solution, and a satisfying sense of having achieved control over your emotions.

A practical way to avoid arguments is this. No matter how sure you are of a fact or idea, put yourself in a neutral corner by starting with a tentative remark like "I may be wrong, but as I see it . . ." or "Don't you think that . . . ?" Notice the difference. If you had instead said, "I believe that . . . ," you would have put yourself into a tight corner. Then if your listener confronted you by saying, "I don't agree with you," you would have had to come out fighting.

No less a person than Benjamin Franklin used this technique to avoid arguments and increase his standing with his friends. In his *Autobiography* he discusses the fact that bold assertion leads to arguments, while more modest remarks lead to discussion.

5. Do Something for Others

If you worry about *yourself* all the time, try doing something for *somebody else.* This technique will take the steam out of your own worries and—even better—give you a fine feeling of having done something worthwhile.

If you know someone who is heavy with worries, here are two things you can do to help. First, let the person know that you're interested, that you care. A person who's "fighting the whole world" will be relieved to know someone wants to be on his side. Your friendly attitude can help him to lower his defenses and adopt a more relaxed attitude toward life.

Second, be a good listener. People with worries need someone with whom they can share their troubles. Make yourself available, and when the person starts talking, listen quietly with little interruption. You don't need to criticize or give advice; just listen and let him know that you care.

6. Take One Thing at a Time

For people under tension, an ordinary work load can seem unbearable. Remember that this is a temporary condition. You can work your way out of it.

How? By tackling a few of the most urgent tasks one at a time. Once you take care of the first few items, you'll see that the rest can also be done.

Sometimes a person's obligations really do outrun the time available for them. In that case, he must leave the least important things undone, however painful that may be. Certainly it is a less painful process than collapsing from overwork. However, most people who feel that they are under too much pressure are suffering more from the *feeling* than from actual overwork. After many years of counseling, Dr. J. G. Gilkey found that one of the chief causes of breakdown, worry, and even sickness, was this feeling of pressure that many things had to be done, and that they had to be done all at once. The idea of how to help his many clients came has he watched an hourglass on his desk.

> Whenever you feel tense and hurried by the pressure of many things to do, regain your composure with the mental picture of an hourglass with its many grains of sand gathered in its "head," but with unconfused precision, handling them one by one. Visualize it so vividly that you can see each grain of sand as it falls![2]

Students, especially, can use this concept, for it seems that they constantly feel the pressure of too many things that need doing all at once. So visualize the hourglass; then take action by doing the *most important* thing first.

7. Don't Be Too Hard on Yourself

Some people expect too much from themselves and are in a constant state of worry and anxiety because they think they are not achieving as much as they should. They try for perfection in everything. Admirable as this ideal is, it is an invitation to failure, for no one can be perfect in everything. Decide which things you do well (usually they are the things you like to do best, the things that are most important to you), and put your major effort into these. As for the things you can't do so well, give them an honest effort, but don't take yourself to task if you can't achieve top honors or break records.

Don't belittle your accomplishments by comparing them with stories you hear about the accomplishments of others. Remember, you hear only about the successes, not the many failures. The other person is just as fallible as you are.

8. Go Easy With Your Criticism

Some people expect too much of others, and feel frustrated, even betrayed, when another person does not measure up to those expectations. Each person has his own virtues, his own shortcomings, his own values, his own right to develop as an individual. We are unfair to him if we try to fit him into our pattern. If you find a lot to criticize in another person, perhaps you are holding him to a standard that you would like to attain yourself. Instead of being critical, search out the other

[2]Adapted from "How to Gain Emotional Poise," in the May, 1945 *Reader's Digest*. Copyright © 1945 by The Reader's Digest Association, Inc. Reprinted by permission.

person's good points and encourage him to develop them. This will give both of you satisfaction and help you to maintain a better opinion of yourself.

9. Give the Other Fellow A Break

When you are under emotional tension, you may feel that you have to "get there first"—to edge out the other person, even if the goal is as trivial as getting ahead in a cafeteria line. Everything becomes a contest, and somebody is bound to get hurt, either physically, as on the highway, or emotionally and mentally in the endeavor to lead a full life. It need not be this way; competition is contagious, but so is cooperation. When you give the other fellow a break, you often make things easier for yourself. If he no longer feels you are a threat to him, he stops being a threat to you.

10. Make Yourself Available

Many of us have the feeling that we are being left out, neglected, rejected. Often we just imagine that others are slighting us, when in reality they are eager for us to make the first move. Instead of shrinking away and withdrawing, it is healthier and more practical to keep yourself available and to make some of the overtures instead of always waiting to be asked. Of course, it is equally a mistake to push yourself forward on every occasion. Doing so is often misinterpreted and may lead to real rejection. There is a middle ground between withdrawing and pushing. *Try it.*

11. Take Time Out for Recreation

Many people drive themselves so hard that they allow themselves too little time for recreation—an essential for good physical, mental, and emotional health. They find it hard to take time out. Such people can be helped by scheduling definite hours for some form of recreation. Some people squeeze in time almost every day for tennis, squash, jogging, or just plain walking. And almost everyone feels refreshed after working for an hour or so on a hobby or other absorbing interest. Almost everyone benefits from a change of pace from his regular work or study.

Exercise is an especially good form of recreation because it permits you to "blow off steam" in a way that is good for you and good for your friends. Not only is it good for you emotionally, but it keeps you in good physical condition as well.

THE STRESS OF LIFE

The nature of stress and the best way to deal with it have been studied by Dr. Hans Selye at the University of Minnesota since 1936. Many of his findings reinforce the eleven suggestions we have just considered.

Problems and stress.   Somehow or other many people have come to think that the ideal state of man is a relaxed body and a quiet mind. Except for isolated moments, this sluglike state is seldom achieved. Stress is unavoidable and, if controlled, it is good for you.

■ No one can live without experiencing some degree of stress all the time. You may think that only serious disease or intensive physical or mental injury can cause stress. This is false. Crossing a busy intersection, exposure to a draft, or even sheer joy are enough to activate the body's stress-mechanism to some extent. Stress is not necessarily bad for you; it is also the spice of life, for any emotion, any activity causes stress. But, of course, your system must be prepared to take it. The same stress which makes one person sick can be an invigorating experience for another.[3] ■

Your role, your life.   One source of undesirable stress, Dr. Selye found, was trying to live up to an unrealistic image of ourselves. "Most of our tensions and frustrations stem from compulsive needs to act the role of someone we are not."[4] The solution is to accept our true selves and live the life that it is natural for us to lead. In this way our energies can be directed toward our true goals, rather than into maintaining a false front.

A principle of adaptation.   Stress, as defined by Dr. Selye, is the rate of all wear and tear caused by life. Much of it is caused by our emotions, both the good ones and the bad. As we have seen, stress can be invigorating and healthful. But if it gets out of control, if we let ourselves get too keyed up for a long period of time, it can be damaging. Here is Dr. Selye's advice:

> In all our actions throughout the day we must consciously look for signs of being keyed up too much—and we must learn to stop in time. To watch our critical stress-level is just as important as to watch our critical quota of cocktails. More so. Intoxication by stress is sometimes unavoidable and usually insidious.[5]

To combat worry and reduce stress, Dr. Selye recommends the use of *deviation*. This means the turning aside of a worry, for example, by concentrating on another thought, or involving oneself in some physical activity. Many of our eleven suggestions involve different forms of this basic technique.

> Deviation is particularly important in combating purely mental stress. Everyone knows how much harm can be caused by worry. The textbooks of psychosomatic medicine are full of case reports describing the production of gastric ulcers, hypertension, arthritis, and many other diseases by chronic worry.

[3]Hans Selye, *The Stress of Life* (New York: McGraw-Hill Book Company, 1956), p. viii.
[4]Selye, p. 260.
[5]Selye, p. 265.

You must find something to put in the place of the worrying thoughts to chase them away. Nothing erases unpleasant thoughts more effectively than conscious concentration on pleasant ones.[6]

Stress in college, as elsewhere, is inevitable. Some stress is good for you, but too much stress can lead to serious worry and even sickness. Even a moderate level of worry can keep you from studying, learning, and doing well in school.

To maintain your own emotional health, try following the suggestions made in this chapter. They will help you control stress and get along better with other people, so that you can function as an intelligent and well-balanced human being.

[6]Selye, p. 268.

3

CONTROL
YOUR
TIME

Just as we may wonder what happened to the rest of a ten-dollar bill after buying only a few groceries, so we may wonder what happened to the rest of our day after attending only a few classes and looking up some references in the library.

PROGRAMMING TIME TO GAIN TIME

The way we use time—or waste it—is largely a matter of habit patterns. It is not easy to change old habits. But if they are bad habits, they put a ceiling on achievement. For example, a baseball batter, even with a poor stance that he picked up on the sandlot, can become quite good up to a point. But unless he changes the poor stance, further progress is doubtful. To change and begin almost all over again takes determination and will. But the decision to change brings the chance for a better future. If you find that you need more time for all your studies and other activities, consider programming your time. You are almost certain to "gain" extra time much sooner than you would think.

Where Does All the Time Go?

In an effort to find out more specifically how he spent his time, a student kept a diary of his daily activities for one week. He found that his "ten-minute" coffee break was nearer forty minutes. Figure 3-1 shows one page of his diary, with an analysis that demonstrated to the student how he could avoid dribbling away minutes and save hours for both recreation and study.

A study of A. A. Dole[1] showed that in a typical week, students at one university spent time in four main activities as follows:

[1]Arthur A. Dole, "College Students Report on the Use of Time," *The Personnel and Guidance Journal* 37 (May 1959): 635.

FIGURE 3-1. Record of One Day's Activities and Suggestions for Making Better Use of Time.

Time Start	Time End	Time Used	Activity - Description	
7:45	8:15	:30	Dress	Paste on mirror 3 × 5 cards: Laws of economics; psychological terms; statistical formulas — study while brushing teeth, etc.
8:15	8:40	:25	Breakfast	
8:40	9:00	:20	Nothing	Look over textbook assignment and previous lecture notes to establish continuity for today's psychology lecture.
9:00	10:00	1:00	Psychology - Lecture	
10:00	10:40	:40	Coffee - Talking	Break too long and too soon after breakfast. Should work on psychology notes just taken; also should look over economics assignment.
10:40	11:00	:20	Nothing	
11:00	12:00	1:00	Economics - Lecture	
12:00	12:45	:45	Lunch	Should re-work the lecture notes on economics while still fresh in mind. Also, look over biology assignment to recall the objective of the coming lab.
12:45	2:00	1:15	Reading - Magazine	
2:00	4:00	2:00	Biology Lab	
4:00	5:30	1:30	Recreation - Volleyball	
5:30	6:00	:30	Nothing	Use this time for reading a magazine or newspaper.
6:00	7:00	1:00	Dinner	
7:00	8:00	1:00	Nap	Not a good idea. Better finish work, then get a good night's sleep.
8:00	8:50	:50	Study - Statistics	
8:50	9:20	:30	Break	Break — too long.
9:20	10:00	:40	Study - Statistics	
10:00	10:50	:50	Rap Session	Good as a reward if basic work is done.
10:50	11:30	:40	Study - Accounting	Insufficient time allotted, but better than no time.
11:30	11:45	:15	Ready for bed	While brushing teeth, study the 3 × 5 cards. Replace cards that have been mastered with new ones.
11:45	7:45	8:00	Sleep.	

Type of Activity	Hours Spent
Sleep	49.3
Study	19.8
Class and Labs	18.7
Meals	10.7
Total	98.5

Substract this amount from 168 (the number of hours in a week), and we still have a balance of 69.5 hours unaccounted for—almost ten hours a day. But in spite of this wealth of time, college students never seem to have enough of it.

We can gain extra time in only two ways: first, by doing the job in less time than usual, and second, by using small blocks of time that we usually waste. The first way can be achieved by studying more efficiently. This book provides a great many time-saving techniques. The second way can be achieved by programming our time. This chapter offers some flexible suggestions.

Reasons for Programming Time

Some people feel that it's a waste of time to make a time schedule, and others feel that a schedule would tie them down too much. Let's consider their objections.

"It's a waste of time."   Most people try to get the most out of a vacation trip by planning sights to see, routes to follow, places to stay, things to buy, and money to spend. During the planning stage, each of these factors is adjusted and readjusted until the best possible package is assembled. It makes sense to plan the other fifty weeks of your year just as carefully. Planning is the key to efficiency.

"I want to be flexible."   Some of us are afraid that a schedule will make slaves of us. Just the opposite is true. The student with a schedule wastes less time, thus has more *free* time for personal activities. The student without a schedule has little flexibility. Disorganization and being behind can affect both your grades and your personality. If you get too far behind, you may even want to give up, because there is too much to do and too little time in which to do it.

A student may complain, "I have so many things to do that I don't know which one to do first." This kind of indecision often brings about mental conflict that keeps us from getting started on any of our tasks. Or, if we take action, we jump from one task to another, doing none well. To be decisive and to free our minds to work toward our goals, we need to schedule priorities in advance.

William James, a famous psychologist, placed a great value on programming. He said that the more details we can schedule automatically, "the more our higher powers of mind will be set free for their own proper work."

If we follow our schedules and complete our studying, we have much to gain: first, we will learn more and probably earn better grades; second, we will experience the satisfaction of being in control of ourselves and our lives. Several specific values to be derived from programming time are summarized in the following list.

The Value	*The Reason*
Gets you started	We all know how hard it is to get started. Often a well-planned schedule can be the external force that gives us a shove.
Prevents avoidance of disliked subjects	The mind can play tricks. Without actually deciding to do so, we can crowd out doing something

we don't like by occupying ourselves with favorite subjects.

Monitors the slackening off process

By looking over how our time is apportioned, we can keep ourselves from slackening as the semester wears on.

Eliminates the wrong type of cramming

If the cramming that takes place just before exams is to be *effective,* the original studying and learning must take place day by day.

Makes studying enjoyable

When done without the pressure of time, studying and learning can be intensely interesting.

Promotes cumulative review

Sandwiching in short review periods is the best way to retain knowledge, as well as to prepare for future exams. It is better to review a subject in four *distributed* 30-minute sessions than in a single *massed* two-hour session. In *massed* practice, fatigue and boredom set in. In a short unit of time, extra effort is put forth, as in a sprint.

Frees the mind

To keep from forgetting details, we may mentally cycle and recycle them. This often leads to a tense feeling of pressure and confusion. Putting the things-to-do on paper takes them off the mental treadmill.

Controls the study break

Rewarding yourself with a ten-minute break when you finish a scheduled block of study helps minimize "clock watching." During short breaks, stand up, walk around, or just stare out the window—but keep in mind the subject you're studying. Then you won't need a warm-up period when you resume studying.

Precludes overlooking recreation

It is unrealistic to omit physical and social activities from your program. They are needed for a well-balanced personality, good health, and more efficient study sessions. On the other hand, imbalance that permits extracurricular activities to outweigh studies probably accounts for more failures in college than anything else.

Helps raise your recreational efficiency

One of the saddest wastes of time and pleasure is to intermix study time and recreation time; that is, when we are studying, we keep thinking how nice it would be to be playing some game; and when playing, we think about all the studying that needs to be done. Consequently, we perform neither one of these tasks to the best of our ability, or at the highest efficiency.

Regulates our daily living

Without a plan to guide us, assignments are bound to pile up. When they do, we lose control, and our daily living is thrown into chaos. With a schedule, even weekends and holidays can be free from worry.

How To Make A Schedule

Just as there are basic rules for driving a car, no matter how long or short a trip you are taking, so there are basic rules for making a study schedule. The following list includes general principles to keep in mind for all study schedules, no matter whether they are for a single day or for a semester.

Eliminate dead hours

Make each block of one hour a productive unit. Some of the most important lessons of our lives are learned in less time.

Use daylight hours

Research shows that each hour used for study during the day is equal to one and a half hours at night.

Study before recitation-type classes

For a course in which you recite and discuss, it is an advantage to study just before class. The material will be fresh in your mind.

Study after lecture-type classes

For a lecture course, retention and understanding are aided by a review of your lecture notes immediately after class.

List according to priorities

By putting first things first, you are sure to get the most important things done on time.

Avoid too much detail

There is always the temptation to overorganize. Packing a weekly schedule too solidly and with too many details is a waste time for two reasons: first, the time it takes to make such a schedule could be better used in studying a subject directly; second, the chances of following such a schedule are very, very slim.

Know your sleep pattern

We all have daily cycles when we are naturally sleepy and when we are naturally alert. If your work, classes, and circumstances permit it, sleep when you're sleepy and study when you're naturally alert. An example: one student said he fought sleep from seven o'clock until midnight while he tried to study; and he couldn't fall asleep from midnight until almost morning while in bed. Upon hearing my suggestion, he reversed the process and achieved high grades.

Discover how long to study

The rule of thumb that you should study two hours for every hour in class is a rough guide at best. The time required per subject varies from student to student and from subject to subject. So start out allowing two hours of study for every hour in class, but start to adjust the hours according to your experience, as you find out how long it takes to master your assignment, not simply to "cover" it.

Plan blocks of time

Research studies by psychologists show that optimum efficiency is reached by planning in blocks of one hour: fifty minutes to study; ten minutes for a break.

Allow time for sleep

The necessity for eight hours sleep every night is supported by medical evidence. We should make no mistake about it, the quality of one's education depends on sufficient sleep. Sacrificing sleep to gain time for study starts a vicious circle.

Eat well-balanced meals

Take time for good meals. Living on greasy foods or other low-protein diets most of the time is no way to treat the body and brain. Dietary deficiencies result in lack of pep, irritability, and fatigue.

Double your time estimates, and start long jobs ahead of time

Most people tend to underestimate time. To avoid discovering the hard way that you cannot bang out a 1500-word paper in three hours the evening before it is due, start ridiculously early and allow more time.

Make a plan for living

Your schedule must be a plan for *living*, not merely for *studying*. After all, life, even while attending college, is many-sided, and its many sides must be recognized.

Over the years, surveys have indicated that successful students use time schedules. This relationship gave rise to a principle: schedules lead to success. However, it is important for each individual to choose the type of schedule that fits his circumstances best. Some students work better with the old-fashioned detailed schedule, whereas others work better with a brief list of things to do. And then there are modified schedules that fit in between these two types.

Circumstances as well as personality influence the type of schedule a student will choose. After all, there are on-campus students, commuting students, married students, employed students, night-class students, part-time students, and many combinations of students. It is up to each individual student to *adapt* the principles of schedule building to his personal circumstances rather than to *adopt* some ideal model which fits hardly anybody.

The schedule for *you* is the schedule that *works*. With time and experience, you can refine your schedule until you have an almost perfect fit.

The master schedule. Any plan to schedule time and activities must have at its center a master schedule, that is, a schedule of activities that is fixed. A master schedule needs to be drawn up only once a semester, unless changes occur in the basic program. Figure 3-2 shows a form that is useful for making out a master schedule. First, fill in all the required school activities, such as courses, classes, and laboratory periods. Second, add other regular activities, such as a part-time job, commuting time, sports, and regular meetings. Third, include the housekeeping chores, sleeping, and eating. With the fixed activities accounted for, the remaining blank spaces on the uncluttered chart are free for use on a weekly or day-by-day basis. Such a schedule on a 5 x 8 card, scotch-taped over your desk or carried in your notebook, unclutters your mind. More important, it enables you to visualize the blank boxes as actual blocks of time into which you may fit necessary activities.

With the master schedule as your base, you can devise any type of schedule that fits your unique combination of courses, your part-time or full-time job, and your personality.

A detailed weekly schedule.   Some people work best when guided by a detailed weekly schedule that is an expansion of the master schedule. If the demands on your time are both heavy and predictable, then you may need a detailed weekly schedule like the one shown in Figure 3-3. This kind of schedule needs to be made out only once, early in the semester. Below are some principles of scheduling which were used to set up the schedule.

Some Principles of Scheduling

Monday through Friday/Saturday

7– 8 A.M.   Avoid the frantic dash and the gobbled (or skipped) breakfast by getting up on time.

12– 1 P.M.   Take a full, leisurely hour for lunch.

5– 6   Relax before dinner—your reward for a day of conscientious work.

7– 9   Keep up with current notes and assignments by systematic studying.

9–10   To forestall cramming at quiz and examination times, give some time every day to a review of previous assignments and ground covered to date.

10   A "cease-study" time of ten o'clock is an incentive to work hard during the day and early evening.

10–12   You should devote some time every day to reading books that truly interest you. Recreational reading and conversation help you "unwind" for a good night's sleep.

Figure 3-2 A Master Schedule.

	MON.	TUES.	WED.	THURS.	FRI.	SAT.	SUN.
7-8	←————————Dress + Breakfast————————→						
8-9	Economics		Economics		Economics	Dress + Breakfast	
9-10	English		English		English		Dress + Breakfast
10-11		Statistics		Statistics		Statistics Lab	
11-12	Business Law		Business Law		Business Law	↓	
12-1	←————————LUNCH———————————————————→						
1-2	Accounting		Accounting		Accounting		
2-3		Phys.Ed.		PhysEd.			
3-4							
4-5							
5-6							
6-7	←————————DINNER———————————————————→						
7-8							
8-9							
9-10							
10-11							
11-12	←————————SLEEP————————→						

Monday–Wednesday–Friday

9–10 A.M.   Use the free period after history (a lecture course) to study your lecture notes.

10–11   Since French (at 11) is a recitation course, prepare by studying during the free period that precedes class.

2– 3 P.M.   In math class (1–2) problems are usually discussed and worked out on the blackboard. Take very brief notes on both discussion and blackboard work. Then, because math problems can quickly

Figure 3-3   A Detailed Weekly Schedule Based on a Master Schedule. Assume that this schedule is your own, and study it in the light of the analysis on the opposite page.

Time	Mon.	Tues.	Wed.	Thurs.	Fri.	Sat.	Sun.
7-8	← Dress & Breakfast →						↑
8-9	History	Study Chem.	History	Study Chem.	History	Study Chem.	
9-10	Study History	Phy. Ed.	Study History	Phy. Ed.	Study History	Phy. Ed.	Church, Recreation, Conversation, Recreational Reading
10-11	Study French	Chem.	Study French	Chem.	Study French	Chem.	
11-12	French	Study Chem.	French	Study Chem.	French	Study Chem.	
12-1	← Lunch →					↑	
1-2	Math	Film-making	Math	Film-making	Math		
2-3	Study Math	Library: Theme	Study Math	↑	Study Math	Conversation, Special Proj., Extra Work on Difficult Subject	
3-4	Study English	"	Study English	Chem. Lab.	Study English		
4-5	English	"	English	↓	English		
5-6	← Recreation →						
6-7	← Dinner →						↓
7-8	Study English	Study Math	Study English	Study Math	Study English		English Theme
8-9	Study French	Study History	Study French	Study History	Study French	Recreation, Conversation, Reading, Thorough Review.	English Theme
9-10	Review English	Review French	Review History	Review Math	Review Chem.		Study History
10-11	← Recreational Reading →						
11-12	← Conversation, Sleep →					↓	

	become "cold," use the free period from 2–3 to go over the work covered in class during the preceding hour.
3– 4	English (4–5) is often a discussion period. Use the free hour to study and warm up in advance.
7– 8	Your evening study time begins. Start with English, your last class, so that any notes you have taken can be reviewed before forgetting takes place.
8– 9	Study French, giving priority to the notes and assignments of the day.

Tuesday–Thursday–Saturday

8– 9 A.M. Since chemistry (10–11) is your "hard" subject, you build your morning study program around it. An hour's study before class will make the class period more meaningful.

11–12 Another hour's study immediately after chemistry class will help you to remember the work covered in class and to move more readily to the next assignment.

Special

Tuesday 2–5 P.M., library: theme

Sunday 7–9 P.M., English theme
For some assignments you will need to schedule blocks of time in order to do research or to develop and follow up ideas.

Saturday from noon on is left unscheduled—for recreation—for special projects to which you must devote a concentrated period of time—for extra work on difficult subjects—for thorough review.

Sunday is your day until evening. Study history before you go to bed, because it is the first class you'll have on Monday morning.

An assignment-oriented weekly schedule. Another type of weekly schedule is based primarily on specific assignments, rather than on time available. It is a supplement to the master schedule and can be used whenever you face unusual or long-term assignments. Since it schedules specific assignments, it covers only one specific week.

Figure 3-4 shows a weekly assignment schedule. The format is simple: draw a horizontal line to divide a lined sheet of paper approximately in half. Use the upper portion to list your subjects, assignments, estimated study times, and due dates. Then, using the due dates and estimated times as control factors, check your master schedule for hours available. Choose enough available hours to do each job, and write them on the appropriate line on the bottom portion of the weekly schedule sheet. *Then stick to your schedule.* Give study hours top priority. As long as you do, the remaining free hours will be really free.

Your daily schedule. You will probably want to have a daily schedule that you can carry around with you. A 3 x 5 card is just the right size. It will fit perfectly into your shirt pocket or handbag so that it will be at hand when you need it.

Every evening before leaving your desk, look at your master schedule to determine your free hours and courses for the next day; then jot down on the card a plan for the next day: the subjects you plan to study, the errands, appointments, physical exercise, recreation, and any other activities you want to do, with their corresponding times. The five minutes so spent are vastly important for two reasons: first, you will have a written record to which you can refer, thus uncluttering your mind; and second, you will have mentally thought through your day, thus putting into action a psychological time clock.

Figure 3-4   A Weekly Schedule Based on Assignments. To provide a time dimension, this schedule is being made out on Saturday, November 11, for the coming week.

Subject	Assignment	Estimated Time	Date Due	Time Due
Electronics	Chap. V – 32 pp – Read	2 hr.	Mon. 13th	8:00
English	Paper to Write	18 hr.	Mon. 20th	9:00
Math	Problems on pp. 110–111	3 hr.	Tues. 14th	10:00
Industrial Safety	Make shop layouts	8 hr.	Fri. 17th	11:00
Graphics	Drawing of TV components	6 hr.	Fri. 17th	1:00
Electronics	Chap. VI – 40 pp – Read	2½ hr.	Wed. 22nd	8:00

Day	Assignment	Morning	Afternoon	Evening
Sun.	Electronics – Read Chap V English – Find a Topic			7:30–9:30 9:30–10:30
Mon.	English – Gather notes Math – Problems		2:00–6:00	7:00–10:00
Tues.	English – Gather Notes Industrial Safety	8:00–10:00	3:00–6:00	7:00–10:00
Wed.	English – First Draft Graphics		2:00–6:00	7:00–10:00
Thurs.	Industrial Safety English–Paper Graphics	8:00–10:00	3:00–6:00	7:00–10:00
Fri.	English – Final Copy Electronics		2:00–6:00	7:00–9:30
Sat.				

By studying Figure 3-5 you will notice that the daily schedule is organized on the basis of *blocks of time,* rather than on fragments of time. By assigning a topic to a block of time, you work as efficiently as you can within it. With just a little experience, you will be able to set a pace that is best for you in studying and getting other things done.

Long-term assignments.   A father gave the following advice to his daughter: Do your assignments every day and you will succeed!

Halfway through the semester, this freshman found her father's advice hard to follow because most assignments were not portioned out in bite-sized, day-by-day units. Some assignments spanned a week; some a month; and some, like research

Figure 3-5   A Daily Schedule.

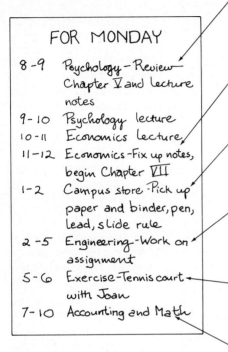

FOR MONDAY

8-9   Psychology – Review Chapter V and lecture notes

9-10   Psychology lecture

10-11   Economics lecture

11-12   Economics – Fix up notes, begin Chapter VII

1-2   Campus store – Pick up paper and binder, pen, lead, slide rule

2-5   Engineering – Work on assignment

5-6   Exercise – Tennis court with Joan

7-10   Accounting and Math

Review: Just before class is a good time to review the high points of chapters previously studied. Also review the previous lecture so that you'll have continuity with the current lecture.

Fix up notes: The very best time to fix up lecture notes, and review them simultaneously, is immediately after the lecture.

After lunch: This is a good time to give yourself a semi-break from academic work and do some necessary errands.

2-5 Block: This is a valuable block of time during which you should be able to read the assignment and work out the assigned problems without losing continuity.

Exercise: After an entire day with the books, some exercise and a shower will help to put an edge on your appetite, as well as making a definite break between study during the day and study during the evening.

After dinner: Both subjects need unbroken time for efficient production. Use the block of three hours to do a balanced amount of work for each, depending on the assignments.

Breaks: Breaks are not listed. You judge for yourself when a break is best for you. Also, the break should be taken when you arrive at a good stopping point.

papers and projects, an entire semester. Though it paid to study every day, this freshman realized that some long-term planning also had to be done.

You are likely to have one or two long-term assignments at all times, and it is possible to get confused by having too many separate schedules. It is best to keep a record of the full assignments and their due dates in your notebook for the particular subject. Plan to get started on these assignments early by allotting some time to them on your daily 3 x 5 card schedule. If you still have trouble remembering to do them, you may need to make out a weekly assignment schedule like the one shown in Figure 3-4.

A busy graduate student once illustrated excellent long-term planning. He mentioned that, in addition to four other courses, he would be examined at the end of ten weeks on the contents of a 560-page book in statistics. In answer to my look of amazement, he said "It isn't much. All I need to do is read eight pages a day."

Students With Jobs

Students who hold full-time or part-time jobs usually have less time and less energy to use for studying than regular full-time students; consequently, they must use both time and energy very carefully. The main difference is that the full-time student can use big blocks of uninterrupted time for studying, whereas the job-holding student must devise ways for using scattered pieces of time.

There are two main ways in which the working student can use time wisely. First, the daily study schedule should be simply a list of things to do in the order of priority. Assigning specific times is likely to lead only to frustration. Second, his study materials should be in a form that permits him to carry them about to use whenever he finds a piece of spare time.

List of things to do.   The 3 x 5 card with a list of things to do does not need to refer to specific times. To be successful, however, you should have some sense of urgency about studying whenever an opportunity presents itself. Figure 3-6 shows a typical daily list for a working student.

Preparing notes for study on-the-run.   To take advantage of pieces of spare time, study materials must first be in a form that is readily available. One way to make materials available is to write or type notes on small cards; another way is to record notes on cassettes.

After reading an assignment or attending a lecture, select from it only the information that you believe is important enough to master. Using your own words, write or type this information on 3 x 5 or 5 x 8 cards. The same notes, or a portion of them, could then be recorded on cassettes.

If you have time to use only one of the means for recording information, I would strongly suggest using the notes on 3 x 5 or 5 x 8 cards.

How to study on the run.   Here are some ways to study in time that is ordinarily only half-used.

1. Paste or tack small metal or plastic clips near mirrors and on walls, at eye level. Place in these clips a note card. While shaving and combing your hair, or while washing dishes, for example, you could read aloud or silently the notes on the cards. Cards placed in clips can be easily changed, whereas pasting or taping them to walls is not so practical.
2. To vary the routine and to use the sense of hearing, you could listen to a cassette or two while going through your morning routine.
3. When you drive your car to work, listen to several cassettes, instead of music on the radio. Or, if you have only cards, recite aloud from memory (not verbatim) some of the ideas, formulas, or definitions that are on the cards. After you stop driving, read the cards to check on your accuracy.

Figure 3-6 A Things-to-Do Schedule for a Working Student.

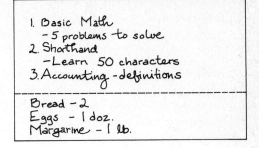

1. Basic Math
   - 5 problems to solve
2. Shorthand
   - Learn 50 characters
3. Accounting - definitions

Bread - 2
Eggs - 1 doz.
Margarine - 1 lb.

4. As you walk from the parking lot to your place of work, flip through several of your note cards, or listen to a cassette.
5. At lunch, while munching a sandwich in your place of work, you could, for example, work a problem or two in math; or, if you prefer, you could listen to a cassette.

Making good use of small pieces of time will enable you to devote more time to your family, job, and school without scrimping on sleep.

Get Things Done

As we grow older, most of us become more and more skilled at putting things off; and no matter how clever our excuses, each time we put something off, we lose a bit of self-respect. We also lose a double dose of time: first, we lose the time spent in the original thinking and making of a schedule; and second, we lose the time we would have gained had we followed our well-laid, well-planned plans. If not carried out, the best schedule is no more than a scrap of paper.

Whether we like it or not, all of us tend to pick up various delaying actions. We sharpen pencils, get another coke, make that phone call, see Bill for a "minute," watch just one more TV show, take a "short" nap before studying, think about plans, and so on and on.

Such action-delaying techniques are not new. We readily recognize them in this passage from *Dead Souls,* by the Russian novelist Nikolai Gogol (1809-1852).

He was not a bad sort: he was simply a sky-gazer. By way of a sample, here is one day from his life.

He was late of waking in the morning and, propping himself up in bed, he sat there for a long while rubbing his eyes. At last he would get out of bed, wash himself, put on his dressing-gown and proceed to drink his tea, coffee, and his steamed milk, sipping a little of everything. There he would sit for two hours over his breakfast.

Before dinner [meal at noon] he used to retire to his study for a couple of hours in order to apply himself seriously to a work he was engaged on, a work intended to embrace the whole of Russia from every angle—civil, political, religious, and philosophical. However, this colossal undertaking was restricted to thinking about it: the quill pen would get nibbled, doodles would make their appearance on the paper in front of him, and then all this would be pushed aside, a book would find its way into his hands and there it would remain until dinner time.

A schedule, like an alarm clock, represents a plan. Just as the buzz of an alarm clock is the signal to get up, so sitting down at your desk should be a signal to begin to study. It all depends on your attitude. If you make a habit of getting started immediately and then studying vigorously, you will accomplish a great deal. Your achievement will make it much easier to get started next time.

This vigorous, aggressive approach must become a way of life in the classroom, the laboratory, the library, and elsewhere. Get what you came for! During a lecture, for example, you must be alert and work hard to capture the lecturer's ideas and get them down on paper.

In the library, some students wander about aimlessly or spend most of their time looking around and watching other students coming and going. If your purpose is to gather data for your research paper, then move on to the card catalogue, gather your references, secure the books, begin reading and taking notes. Get something done according to plan!

The intelligent use of time is a large part of academic success. Plan your time wisely and then be sure to follow the plans that you make.

II
THE SUPPORTIVE SKILLS

4

THE
ABILITY TO
CONCENTRATE

Stated in simple terms, concentration is thinking. And during our waking hours we are, with varying degrees of intensity, thinking all the time. Actually, our supply of things about which to think and worry never runs out. William James, the famous Harvard philosopher and psychologist, said that some thought or idea tries to gain the focus of our attention every two or three seconds. These thoughts and ideas bang, rattle, and knock on the door of our consciousness, trying to gain entry! It is no wonder, then, that it is so difficult to keep our minds on the job in hand.

Concentration is a slippery quality, because it is not a product or a process; rather it is a by-product. Concentration happens only when we don't think about concentration. For example, if you were thinking deeply about the principle of magnetism and suddenly realized that you were concentrating, then, at that moment of realization, you would have broken your concentration on the subject of magnetism. In the words of William James, trying to seize concentration is "like seizing a spinning top to catch its motion, or trying to turn up the gas light quickly enough to see how the darkness looks."[1]

We all agree, I believe, that concentration is elusive. What do you see in Figure 4-1? You will probably find your visual focus shifting every few seconds, so that you first see a goblet and then two profiles, and then the goblet again. It is difficult to focus visually on just one of the images and ignore the other. Similarly, it is hard for the mind to focus on just one idea at a time.

Concentration is one of the keys to success. A person who can focus his total thinking on the task before him has an infinitely better chance of completing the task more quickly and accurately than a person who divides his attention, focusing

[1]William James, *Psychology* (New York: Holt, Rinehart, and Winston, Inc., 1893), p. 161.

Figure 4-1   A Goblet or Two Profiles?

only 25 percent of his thinking on the task, while the other 75 percent is concentrated on a television program that he watched the night before.

Even in physical tasks, concentration is the key. Take bowling, for instance. A good bowler takes his position, stares at the pins, tries to shut out the noise and people, and then when he has gathered and concentrated all his thinking on the pins at the end of the alley, he makes his move. After a short measured run, he arcs the ball smoothly onto the runway. With the ball rolling down the alley, his thinking is still so concentrated that he tries to control the ball with "body English." That's concentration!

Imagine reading your text so intensely that you speak out to the author: "That's not proof enough," or "Other writers explain it differently," or "I never thought about the problem that way before." That's concentration!

Trouble in concentrating may come from many causes, often interrelated. For example, many students are so afraid of failing that the dread specter of failure takes more of their attention than their study assignments. Anxiety causes them to do poor work, and this in turn intensifies the fear they started with. Some students never get off this treadmill. But many do, and nearly all can, if shown the way.

Fortunately, the ability to concentrate can be improved by learning to recognize the causes of poor concentration and by learning to control them as a matter of habit. The causes can be external or internal distractions, physical or mental fatigue, or lack of interest in the work to be done. All these, once recognized, can be overcome.

EXTERNAL DISTRACTIONS

College study halls and libraries are full of external distractions, ranging from blue eyes to banging doors. Select your place of study carefully. Distraction can be minimized by following these suggestions.

A Place to Study

Some of us study whenever we have the chance. Itinerant preachers read their bibles on horseback as they traveled from village to village. Abe Lincoln read by the light from the fireplace. Most of us, however, need something more stable. We need a workbench or desk—a place of our own where pens, pencils, paper, and dictionary are at our fingertips, a place where we can leave books open and papers ready for our next study session. As a student, I had a plain-faced door supported by two saw-horses—a wonderful space on which to work.

Psychologists emphasize that a conditioning effect is created between the desk and you: If you nap or daydream a lot while sitting at the desk, then the desk can act as a cue for napping or daydreaming. To avoid this type of negative conditioning, always use your desk just for studying. When you want to nap or daydream, leave the desk and nap or daydream elsewhere.

Equipment for Studying

More ink and more words have been wasted extolling the virtues of a straight-backed, hard-seated hickory chair than any other single piece of equipment. I would like to consign this cure-all chair to the same place where now resides that old hickory whacking-stick. Instead, use a comfortable, well-cushioned chair.

Keeping awake or falling asleep does not depend on the type of chair; rather, it depends primarily on the method of study, as well as on one's attitude, self-discipline, light, and room temperature. A hard, straight-backed chair can hardly be expected to take the place of these basic requirements.

An extremely practical piece of equipment is a book stand. I don't mean a book shelf or bookends; rather, I mean a stand that is placed on your desk to hold the book in a tilted position with the pages held down so that they do not flip over. It can work for you in many ways: first, and very important, it can give you a feeling of readiness to study—a feeling of being a scholar in the traditional sense. This alone is worth many times the price of a stand. Second, the stand provides physical freedom. It eliminates the strain of continually holding the book open, pressing down on two sides to keep the pages from flipping over, tilting the book to avoid the glare, and trying to find something heavy enough to hold the book open as you free your hands to make notes. It permits you to sit back with arms folded, to contemplate and reflect on the meaning of what you are reading.

Other basic equipment should include an up-to-date dictionary and other reference tools such as books, slide rule, clock, and calendar. Some students struggle along without small-but-necessary items like paper clips, cellophane tape, rubber bands, erasers, an ample supply of note cards, and so on. Keep your desk well stocked so that you don't have to make unplanned emergency trips to obtain small items.

How About Light?

The quality of the light by which you study is of crucial importance. Researchers report that a poor quality of light can cause eye strain, general tension, dull headaches, and sleepiness. Worst of all, these irritations interfere with concentration.

Lighting engineers find that there are three steps in creating a good quality of light.

1. Eliminate glare.   Glare may come from the bulbs themselves or from shiny surfaces that reflect the light. So cover the bulb with a good shade, and put a light-colored blotter on your desk. An important way to reduce glare is to use indirect light. Indirect lighting is almost as good as daylight, which is, of course, best. Indirect lighting is light that is bounced down onto a lower reflector which, in turn, directs the light to an upper reflector or ceiling which, in turn, bounces the light down onto your desk. Two researchers found that studying by the light of an unshaded lightbulb for three hours can cause an 81 percent loss in clear vision. Glare must be eliminated!

2. Eliminate contrasts between light and dark areas in the room.   Contrasts and shadows on your book or paper also tire your eyes. Indirect light on your work area helps, but the best way to eliminate shadows is to have two light sources in the room. This can be done quite easily by having a floor lamp or a ceiling fixture to supply general light, and a desk lamp to light your study area.

3. Eliminate flicker.   An incandescent light (regular bulb) is a steady and constant light source, but it may flicker because of a loose connection. A fluorescent bulb has a constant flicker (strobism), but by using a double-bulb fixture, the sychronization of the two bulbs eliminates visual flicker. With a single bulb, flicker cannot be eliminated.

What kind of desk lamp should you use? Most people like fluorescent lights. I swear by them. Single-tube fluorescent lamps, however, are not adequate. They flicker so badly that I tire within a few minutes; but with two-tube fluorescent lamps, I've worked many times for a straight twenty hours without undue tiring effects to the eyes.

My fluorescent lamp is a draftsman's type with extension arms that permit me to position the light exactly where I want it. In this way, I just about eliminate all glare, and at the same time regulate the intensity of the light by bringing it closer or farther away. A good investment! I bought it as a freshman 25 years ago.

A few people prefer incandescent light. If you are one of them, make sure that the bulbs are shaded from your direct view. You can diffuse the light somewhat by using "soft-white" bulbs, but even these should be shaded. Draftsman's lamps are available that take incandescent bulbs instead of fluorescent. And some companies manufacture study lamps with an intricate arrangement of reflectors and filters, so that even with an incandescent bulb you get a high quality of indirect light.

Finally, if you have tried to study under good light, and your eyes still bother you, it would pay to have them examined by an oculist or ophthalmologist. Clear and comfortable vision is essential to good studying.

Noise

If you are a person who needs a quiet spot for efficient study, do your utmost to find such a spot. If the library is the right place for you, then always go there. Nothing is more wasteful than going over the same paragraph again and again because there is too much noise for you to absorb what you are reading. Noise in your living quarters is one of the most serious single obstacles to effective study.

Many students rationalize that it takes too much time to walk to the library, but two or three hours of efficient study in quiet surroundings does more good than ten hours in near bedlam. Many students find the walk to the library refreshing, and report that they can even concentrate on their studies and get something done as they walk. Unless you make a firm decision about finding the quiet spot, you might become psychologically trapped, like the student who reported,

> I am failing several of my courses because I just cannot study in the noisy dormitory; yet, though I know I should, I don't feel like going to the library. I kid myself by saying, "Maybe it'll be different tonight," but it never is.

One sure way to avoid being trapped in a noisy dormitory: study in the library beginning with the *first* day of classes.

Background Music

This external distraction will be dealt with at some length because so many students use the radio or stereo as background music for studying. The big question is: Does background music help the learning process or interfere with it? In this section, some evidence and an opinion are presented.

Background music in industry.   Soft, wordless, nonstrident background music in industry provides a pleasant atmosphere that is often effective in maintaining productivity. The music helps overcome drabness, boredom, and monotony of jobs in assembly lines, supermarkets, and similar places. We must bear in mind that these tasks are routine and manipulative; they do not involve higher conceptualizing, *learning* tasks.

Background music in education.   In a review of thirteen experiments on the effect of music on learning ability, the following results were gleaned.

1. In seven experiments, groups *without* music in the background achieved higher scores on a quiz than groups *with* music.
2. In five experiments involving some groups *with* and some groups *without* music in the background, tests showed that there were no significant differences in achievement.
3. In one experiment in which a bell was struck intermittently, a group of college students taking a thirty-minute intelligence test gained *slightly. The more intelligent students in the group, however, made more mistakes with the bell striking.*

The box score for music in the background is: one win, not really by music, but by the bell; five ties, and seven losses. A very poor record!

Dr. M. T. Henderson found that students who prefer to study with soft, background music get *less* out of their reading than students who read without background music.

The author's opinion.   Click off the radio or stereo. In this business of studying, music is *noise*. Some students report that all through high school they studied successfully with music in the background. Success in passing high school courses is no proof that background music is, therefore, a noninterfering factor. These students should be asked: How much better could you have studied without music? How much more could you have learned during the same period?

By exerting extra energy when the music is playing, you may be able to keep your mind on your studies 75 percent of the time. Then the music captures only the other 25 percent of your attention, but your mind and body are being bombarded by the relentless sound waves 100 percent of the time. Such bombardment is physically tiring. Why voluntarily introduce interference when you are studying? It is hard enough to concentrate as it is.

INTERNAL DISTRACTIONS

To minimize internal distractions, the following suggestions have worked for many, many students.

1. *Indecision*. Indecision about when to study and about which subject to study first is not only a great time-waster but also a sure way to create a negative attitude toward studying. You can hurdle this psychological barrier by planning ahead. This is such an important part of good study habits that an entire chapter has been devoted to it (Chapter 3).

2. *Daydreaming*. One of the worst time-wasters is daydreaming. Daydreaming is a way of escaping from hard work. Pleasant as it is, it can become a vicious habit since daydreaming can use up precious time in which you could be working toward the goals you really want to achieve. It is far better to get back to the job and establish the positive habit of plunging directly and efficiently into your work. *This* is a habit which will stand you in good stead all your life.

3. *Personal problems*. Each person must develop ways of dealing with personal problems that distract him from his work. The suggestions in Chapter 2 are designed to help you cope with various emotional problems. If you cannot study because your mind is clogged with personal worries, positive action must be taken.

For example, if a problem intrudes on your thoughts while you are studying, make it a firm habit to write it out on a sheet of paper to deal with after you have completed your work. If you begin entertaining problems while studying, you may get in the habit of solving personal problems as a device for escaping the hard work of studying, just as one uses daydreams.

After you have completed your work, attack the problems directly. If you cannot solve them yourself, get the help of friends or counselors. Decide on a plan of action, and follow it.

4. *Bothered by a course*. It is not unusual to have one course almost every semester that bothers you for one reason or another. It is surprising how quickly an initial feeling of discontent spreads into a general anxiety that interferes with all your studies. One way to dispel anxiety in this situation is to talk the matter over with the instructor. There is a good chance that he will be able to help you.

For example, one student who came to me first reported that she liked the instructor and the course. About four weeks later, she said, "The instructor is too brusque; and, in his lectures, he doesn't stick to the topic." About five minutes later, almost as if it were an after-thought, the real reason for discontent surfaced. "And he is requiring everyone to lead a class discussion." Then she added, "I'll be home for the holidays, but I won't enjoy a minute of it thinking about having to get up in front of the class as soon as I get back." Almost to herself, she trailed off saying, "Maybe I'll drop the course."

Realizing that for some students who haven't had some formal training in speaking such a venture could be traumatic, I suggested, "Go to the instructor, and sincerely put the cards on the table." By the time the student left my office, no decision or promise of action had been made; but, at least, an alternative had been presented to her to think about.

About two weeks later, the student re-entered my office, smiling and self-assured.

"Well? What happened?" I asked.

"The prof said that he understood, and as an alternative assignment, I could write a paper on the topic that I had chosen."

"I can see that you accepted the alternative assignment," I said.

"You bet I did. The prof even suggested a few up-to-date references. One of the references was an article written by him. Actually, we were kidding each other before I left."

5. *Set realistic goals.* Set up realistic goals for study. If a student has hardly been studying at all, it is not realistic for him to announce suddenly: "Tonight I plan to study for six hours." The chances are that so much sustained effort will be too much for him, and he will only experience another discouraging failure. To succeed, the change in habits must be gradual. If that same student were to study for only two hours on that first evening, he would have a far better chance of achieving his goal.

6. *A reminder list.* To avoid worrying about the possibility of missing personal appointments, write them down on your daily 3 x 5 reminder card (this technique is discussed in Chapter 3). If an appointment is several days away, write it on a desk calendar which is ideal for this purpose. Having made a written reminder, you no longer need to clutter your mind with these details.

The following list summarizes other techniques that have helped students concentrate. Try one or two at a time to see whether they are for you.

Positive attitude	Try to look upon studying as an opportunity to learn, rather than as an unpleasant task to complete. Also, since you may be spending a great deal of time in your room, do not make it a prison; rather look to your room as a sanctuary. Remember, you are always free to take a well-earned break.
Why does attention shift so often?	It is quite natural for your attention to shift frequently. Probably this is an inheritance

from our caveman ancestors who had to be constantly aware of what was going on around them. There will be shifts in attention, but try to confine these shifts within the subject matter at hand.

The spider technique

A vibrating tuning fork held close to a spider's web will set up vibrations in the web itself. After the spider makes a few hurried but flyless investigations, it learns to ignore the vibrations.

The next time that you are studying in the library and the door opens, don't look up. Controlling your impulse to look up will disturb your concentration on your work for the first few times. But very soon, like the spider, you'll learn to ignore these external disturbances.

Becoming annoyed by noise around you

There will always be some noise around us. Avoid disturbances if you can; but do your best to ignore the noise you cannot avoid. By all means do not let yourself become annoyed. The internal irritation that you create has a more devastating effect on concentration than the external noises themselves.

Make sure you have everything

Before sitting down to study, make sure you have everything. Sharp pencils, fresh paper and cards, necessary books. Then stay in your chair until you have studied an hour or so. In that way, you'll remain in the driver's seat; that is, in control.

The no-room principle

Imagine that certain pathways of your mind are completely filled with thoughts about the subject in front of you. Then there will be no room for extraneous thoughts, and they will be turned away.

The check-mark technique

Have a sheet of paper handy by your book; then when you catch yourself not concentrating, put a checkmark on the sheet. The mere act of checking will remind you to get back to work. Students report that when they first tried this system, they accumulated as many as twenty checkmarks per textbook page; but, after one or two weeks, they were down to one or two checkmarks per page.

Will power!   Will power alone can't make you
                       concentrate. You will be breaking concentration
                       whenever you remind yourself, "I must use
                       will power to concentrate!"

Hunger   Hunger is such a basic and persistent state
                       that there is no sense trying to overcome it.
                       Give in! Feed yourself, then go back to work.

PHYSICAL FATIGUE

There is little doubt that our general health affects our brain, consequently, our ability to concentrate and learn. Our general health, it seems, depends mainly on the following three factors: diet, sleep, and exercise.

How's Your Diet?

Nutrition experts remind us that *we are what we eat.* We often interpret this principle in physical terms, but the experts go beyond this. They say that nutrition determines whether we are grumpy or cheerful, radiant or dull, even young or old. And on the mental side, they say that nutrition determines the quality of thinking: whether it will be clear or confused. Nutrition, then, affects our whole being.

Breakfast is most important. There is nothing wrong with a doughnut and coffee as a snack, but it is hardly enough food to sustain you from last night's dinner at about 6:00 until lunch today. The hours from dinner until lunch the next day add up to about 18 hours—and only a cup of coffee and a couple of doughnuts during that long span of time! Yes, I know, there probably was a midnight snack of pizza, a treat to the taste buds, but a gooey mass to the stomach.

Nutrition chemists continually emphasize the importance of maintaining a proper level of sugar in your blood. If you've been feeling groggy all morning, maybe this excerpt will help explain why.

> Research in nutrition reveals that energy is produced in cells of the brain
> and nerves only from sugar. When the amount of sugar in the blood
> available to the cells decreases below a certain level, thinking slows down
> and becomes confused, and nerves become tense. These conditions often
> lead to irritableness, depression, and disorientation. In some cases where
> the blood sugar level drops abnormally low, blackouts or fainting may
> result.[2]

However, eating sugar alone will not give you a proper level of sugar in the blood. Sugar or starches alone can leave you in a worse state than before taking them. The important point is the *slow* release of sugar in digestion, which occurs only when protein and fat are being digested along with the sugar.

In one experiment several different breakfasts were fed to volunteers, and the

[2] E. Orent-Keiles and L. F. Hallman, "The Breakfast Meal in Relation to Blood Sugar Values," U.S. Department of Agriculture Circular No. 827 (1949), pp. 1-24.

level of blood sugar measured afterwards. For example, "after black coffee alone, the blood sugar fell below the pre-breakfast levels, and the volunteers experienced lassitude, headache, weakness, and hunger."[3] Here is an account of the coffee and doughnut routine: "After two doughnuts and black coffee, there was a rapid rise in blood sugar followed by a plunge to below the pre-breakfast levels, resulting in fatigue and general inefficiency."[4]

None of the breakfasts effectively maintained blood sugar, not even the "basic breakfast" of orange juice, two strips of bacon, toast, jam, and coffee with cream and sugar. Even when oatmeal was added to the basic breakfast, the level of blood sugar rose at first, then plunged in only an hour or so. Finally the experimenters hit on an effective combination, as reported here.

> It was not until eight ounces of whole milk, fortified with two and one-half tablespoons of nonfat powdered milk was added to the above basic breakfast that the blood sugar rose and remained above the baseline throughout the entire morning, thus raising the subjects to a prolonged sense of well-being and satisfaction. In another combination, the basic breakfast was used, and two eggs replaced the fortified milk. Here again, the blood sugar rose and remained above the baseline throughout the morning.[5]

The lesson we draw from these experiments is that we must include some protein in our breakfasts, such as milk and eggs (meat is okay, too), but remember that bacon is very low in protein. Without protein, we short-change our entire system, especially by drastically diminishing the thinking power of the brain.

The following account, describing the same series of experiments, carries us right on through lunch; thus, you will be able to see the effect that breakfast has upon your brain throughout the whole day.

■ **The bonus-effect of a breakfast that includes eight ounces of fortified milk or two eggs is that it provides a strong foundation of well-being not only for the morning, but also for the entire day. At noon, the volunteers who had eaten the various breakfasts were given the same lunch: a cream-cheese sandwich on whole-wheat bread and a glass of whole milk. Blood samples were taken every hour. Those volunteers who had fortified milk or eggs for breakfast showed not only an immediate increase in the blood sugar level directly after lunch, but also maintained a high blood sugar level all afternoon. Those volunteers who did not have milk or eggs for breakfast, and whose blood sugar levels became low during the morning showed the following effects: the blood sugar level increased directly after lunch for only a few minutes, then fell to a low level and remained at a low level all afternoon.[6] ■**

---

[3]Orent-Keiles and Hallman.
[4]Orent-Keiles and Hallman.
[5]Orent-Keiles and Hallman.
[6]Orent-Keiles and Hallman.

How About Sleep?

Reports have it that Thomas Edison, Winston Churchill, and Napoleon got along with a minimum of sleep, yet put out a prodigious amount of work. It is true that they seldom slept for eight consecutive hours, but what is not reported is that they were free to nap at various times. An examination of the records shows that their catnaps often added up to about eight hours for every sixteen that they worked.

Everyone needs to sleep, no matter how important the task he is working on. Even astronauts sleep. The physiological reasons for sleep are not fully known, but it is obvious that sleep relaxes and refreshes both mind and body.

How long do you need to sleep each night?   That is a matter for each individual to determine, but most people need to sleep seven to nine hours out of every twenty-four. You probably know how much you need to feel at your peak.

Insufficient sleep can produce unpleasant effects, from loss of memory to muscular weakness. Experiments on sleep deprivation conducted at the Walter Reed Army Medical Center have shown the following:

1. After prolonged visual activity, the eyes tend to wander; we call this effect *visual attention fatigue.*
2. Brief periods of extreme drowsiness occur between midnight and dawn, and these interrupt any chain of mental operations.
3. Acquisition of new information is impaired.
4. A person "listening to a conversation may progressively lose his grasp of the situation, being dimly aware that people are talking but not of what they are saying. During this time, he is unable to comprehend the real situation, and he confuses external and internal events."[7]

What conclusion can we draw from these observations? Obviously, it is that prolonged wakefulness, as in staying up all night to study, seriously impairs mental processes. You can't stay up all night and expect to function well the next day.

A regular day-night rhythm is essential to health. If you normally are awake during the daytime and early evening, it would be difficult for you to go to bed at either 3 P.M. or 3 A.M. The mind and body come to depend on a stable rhythm of waking and sleeping. Changing your schedule disrupts you both physically and mentally, a statement that is borne out by scientific investigation. So if you normally go to bed at midnight, do so regularly. Otherwise you will have to pay the price.

Some students get so tense during the day that they are still tense when they go to bed. Then they have trouble going to sleep. This is especially true of very sensitive people who carry their arguments, their defeats, and their disappointments in their minds, playing and replaying the episodes over and over again. These replays simply heighten your feelings and emotions, causing you to get keyed up even more, and this stress-reaction may carry over into the night. Here is the way Dr. Hans Selye explains it:

[7]G. O. Morris, H. L. Williams, and A. Lubin, "Misperception and Disorientation During Sleep Deprivation," *A.M.A. Archives of General Psychiatry* 2 (1960): 247-54.

Keep in mind that the hormones produced during acute stress are meant to alarm you and key you up for peak-accomplishments. They tend to combat sleep and to promote alertness during short periods of exertion; they are not meant to be used all day long. If too much of these hormones is circulating in your blood, they will keep you awake, just as a tablet of ephedrine would. (Incidentally, ephedrine is chemically related to adrenaline.) Your insomnia has a chemical basis, which cannot easily be talked away after it has developed; and *at night in bed it is too late* to prevent it from developing.[8]

Is there anything you can do about insomnia? The ideal, of course, is to avoid getting into those super-stress situations in the first place. But if you are already in bed and you just can't sleep, try this advice from Professor Walter Rudolf Hess, Swiss mental specialist and Nobel Prize winner:

If you cannot sleep, resign yourself to it, arrange your limbs comfortably and enjoy the feeling of their relaxed heaviness. Occupy your mind with pleasant thoughts and memories, without worrying about the passage of time. Then sleep, too, will come.[9]

This recipe is short, but it is distilled from years and years of experience with insomniacs. Notice that he does not say, "Go to bed determined to fall asleep." Rather he says, "Accept the fact that you don't and possibly won't fall asleep, but be comfortable in the meantime. Enjoy the physical feeling of rest, and give your mind the pleasure of pleasant thoughts."

This is the simplest, most direct prescription that I have encountered. Try it, but gently.

Conclusion.   It is reasonable to conclude that when we deprive ourselves of sleep in order to study, we enter into a losing game for at least two reasons: first, with thinking disorganized and memory impaired, very little if anything can be really learned and retained during the study process. Second, with little or no sleep, when we attend class for recitation or examination the following day we arrive incapable of performing even adequately either mentally or physically.

In summary, here are three things you can do to improve your studies and your health.

1. Get enough sleep, seven to nine hours a night.
2. Have a regular bedtime.
3. If you can't get to sleep, at least rest, relax, and think pleasant thoughts.

Resist the temptation.   We have just finished exploring all the reasons why you should not rob your sleep time for purposes of studying. Now I will emphasize that

---

[8]Selye, *The Stress of Life,* p. 271.
[9]Thomas Kirk Cureton, *The Physiological Effect of Exercise Programs on Adults* (Springfield, Illinois: Charles C Thomas, Publisher, 1969), p. 19.

you not sleep when you are supposed to be studying. During study time, you're suppose to fight sleep to get the job done.

Most students find sleepiness one of their greatest problems. Sleepiness can result from real fatigue or from a subconscious desire to avoid a dull task. One way to fight sleepiness is to take frequent five-minute breaks. Another is to pace the floor slowly while reading a book or reciting a lesson aloud. Still another is to schedule recreation or academic assignments involving physical activity (such as rearranging your lecture and reading notes, writing in key words and phrases, or doing some of the errands that you have been putting off) at hours when you ordinarily find it hard to study. Psychologists find that each person's sleepy period occurs at about the same time every day or evening. One word of warning: too many students rationalize that it is better to give in to the urge to sleep and that when they wake up they will be refreshed. Few students report this happy result. Rather, they awake to a formidable pile of work undone. It is far better to combat the desire to sleep, get the work done, and then go to bed at the usual time with a clear conscience.

Then, after a good productive evening of study, you have earned the right to a good night's sleep.

And Then There is Exercise

A good workout promotes a keen appetite, keeps the brain and body in tone for alert studying and thinking, and triggers the organic clock when our regular bedtime rolls around. Then, after our night's sleep, we wake up alert for the day's academic work.

Exercise has these beneficial effects because it improves the circulation of the blood. Some people become mentally stale and physiologically old at a relatively young age. And why? Research unmistakably indicates that health, endurance, nutrition, and general well-being all depend on one thing—circulatory fitness. And the only way to achieve this is through *regular exercise.*

Dr. Paul Dudley White, special physician to President Eisenhower, focused the attention of the world on the importance of regular exercise to improve circulation and thus guard against heart attacks. Interest zoomed and is still high in programs emphasizing regular jogging, walking, swimming, calisthentics, and many other activities. All these exercises, many quite vigorous, are designed to do one thing: through regular exercise, to attain *circulatory fitness.*

Researchers report that physical exercise not only makes us feel better, but it is also *the only way* that our body chemistry can be kept in good condition.

The kind of exercise you get in college depends partly on the facilities available. Your school may not let you use the gym unless you are in an organized class or on a school team. Tennis courts may be available for casual play only during specified hours.

You have to be a detective to find out what kinds of exercise are open to you. Perhaps you can schedule a course in basketball or swimming. Find a partner or two who can meet you for squash. Find out what the local "Y" and other community agencies have to offer. Even vigorous walking and bicycling can supply your need for exercise.

Don't settle for the required physical education courses. You will meet those requirements long before you are out of college, but you will still need exercise.

One thing you can do while you are in college is try out a number of different sports. One or two are bound to give you more pleasure and satisfaction than others, and they may well become your lifetime sports. Dr. Eric Weiser, a German doctor, recommends that we choose a sport that we can continue playing well into old age. For example, King Gustaf of Sweden continued to play an active game of tennis well into his 80's. Dr. Weiser recommends taking up gymnastics, walking, tennis, swimming, rowing, or bicycling.

MENTAL FATIGUE

Research has shown that it is all but impossible to develop mental fatigue by studying, even by studying hard. We get "tired" readily enough, but this happens because we are bored with the subject, not because bodily wastes accumulate in the brain, or even in the muscles. You may push away a textbook with the comment, "I'm exhausted! I can't read another word," then casually pick up a magazine or newspaper and read avidly, without any signs of fatigue, for an hour or so. Obviously, we have confused *fatigue* with *boredom*.

Erle Stanley Gardner, the mystery story writer and creator of Perry Mason, finds that he can best use his time and energies by working on three stories at one time. He finds that he is more refreshed by switching from one story to another than by simply taking a rest break. Often, when we think that we're tired, we are actually "tired" of the subject; consequently, switching from the subject provides the "break" we need.

There are three lessons to keep in mind here: First, stay in good physical condition with the right kind of food, sleep, and exercises. Second, schedule your different subjects so that you don't study any one subject so long that you get bored with it. Third, be interested, or create interest in the subject in hand, so that you can keep working beyond the first symptoms of tiredness.

The American philosopher and psychologist William James developed this insight years ago. Basing his ideas partly on his background in medicine, he believed that most people do not use their mental energies in sufficient depth. He said that our reserves of energy are stored layer upon separate layer. In the physical (muscular) sense, after using up most of the energy in the top layer through working or running, signs of fatigue relay the message for us to stop; but in cases of necessity when we do not stop to rest, a surprising thing happens:

> The fatigue gets worse up to a certain critical point, when gradually or suddenly it passes away, and we are fresher than before. We have evidently tapped a level of new energy.[10]

We have, in other words, gotten our *second wind*, and continue to work or run almost effortlessly until we approach a third layer. We become tired again, but if we continue we can pierce through the resistance to gain a third and a fourth

[10]William James, *On Vital Reserves* (New York: Holt, Rinehart and Winston, Inc., 1911), p. 4.

"wind." William James said that in this process, there is an exact parallel between physical energy and mental energy.

The feeling of "tiredness" *occurring well before quitting time* may very well be a sign that you are *approaching* the second layer of mental energy. It is, however, *not* a sign that you are actually fatigued. At this point, William James might say, "Don't stop! Keep going! You are on the verge of tapping a new layer of reserved mental power that heretofore you never realized you had. Keep going, and you will attain the energy of your mental 'second wind' enabling you to continue studying not only at a higher mental level, but also with relative effortlessness."

Most of us find it particularly hard to concentrate on a "boring" or "difficult" subject. The difficult subject is often the one that we are not interested in; consequently, we do not care to read and think about it. Frequently, the subject remains "boring" and "difficult" simply because our knowledge remains meager. Worse still, it pulls down our grades and upsets our composure and self-confidence. When we make the effort to break through this barrier, we are almost always pleasantly surprised. Once we read and think about any subject, we soon find in it something of interest and value.

In the following excerpt, William James describes graphically the delaying action taken by a person who tries to avoid grappling with a "detested" subject.

■   There are topics known to every man from which he shies like a frightened horse, and which to get a glimpse of is to shun . . . One snatches at any and every passing pretext, no matter how trivial or external, to escape from the odiousness of the matter in hand. I know a person, for example, who will poke the fire, set chairs straight, pick dustspecks from the floor, arrange his table, snatch up the newspaper, take down any book which catches his eye, trim his nails, waste the morning anyhow, in short, and all without premeditation—simply because the only thing he ought to attend to is the preparation of a noon-day lesson in formal logic, which he detests. Anything but that!¹¹   ■

The following suggestions will help you take a more kindly attitude toward the "detested" subject and overcome your burden. They may even help you gain a true education.

Small group sessions.   Find two or three other students who are interested in meeting with you to discuss briefly each assignment in the particular subject that is "boring" to you. During the give-and-take of the discussion you are bound to learn a great deal and the subject may become "alive" to you. Also, the enthusiasm of some of the members might rub off on you. Once you begin to

¹¹James, *Psychology,* pp. 225-26.

know something about the subject, your interest level will rise, and the vicious circle will have been broken. The only prerequisite for a group meeting is that every member should do his homework. Only then can each person become an active contributor as well as a receiver.

Individual tutoring. Don't just "hang in" there knowing less and less, while almost every one else is learning more and more. When you see that you are going to have trouble, find a classmate who is mastering the subject and arrange, for a modest fee, to be tutored. The tutor will probably be able to supply the understanding that will make it possible for you to be on your own in a short time.

Alternative textbooks. The writing in some textbooks is more difficult to grasp than in others. Often it is the style of the author that causes the difficulty, not the abstruseness of the topic itself. In the library you will find many other books in which other authors discuss the very same topics. From personal experience, I know how helpful an alternative textbook can be. After reading the alternative textbook, however, it is important to go back to your regular textbook to read the assigned chapters. You will understand them now.

Workbooks and programmed instructional materials. There are many supplementary materials on which to practice and to learn. These materials force you to take action. In the programmed materials, especially, each step is a small problem that has to be solved on the basis of information presented in the previous steps. The on-going sequence of problem-solving, continually putting you on the spot, forces you to concentrate and hold in mind the previous steps in order to find solutions. Your solutions are immediately compared with the correct answers. In this way, wrong solutions are straightened out in your mind before they become embedded, and correct solutions are reinforced. These learning-by-doing programmed materials virtually ensure understanding; once you grasp the basics of your subject through such materials you will understand your "boring" subject much better.

THE SECRET TECHNIQUE: THE PENCIL

I have saved the best for last.

A technique that has never failed any student over the past twenty years is the simple, humble *pencil technique*. The technique is this: *Whenever working to learn, always study with a pencil in hand.* For example, if you are taking notes on a textbook chapter, stop after reading several paragraphs and very briefly, in your own words, write the key points made by the author. If, after reading several paragraphs, no words come to you, then you have no other recourse than to go back and read the passage again. This time, read with determination and concentration, to make sure that you learn the key points. The secret: activity promotes, almost ensures, concentration. The pencil provides the activity!

After reading this chapter, you can appreciate the immensity and complexity of the job of *concentration*. Our objective, based on the evidence, should be: don't waste your energies trying to achieve continuous concentration. Rather, stay in good physical condition, and then use techniques to bring your attention back to the job in hand quickly every time your thoughts wander.

5

FORGETTING: THE RELENTLESS FOE

Forgetting happens to all of us. It is an almost irresistible process that destroys a great deal of what we have labored to learn.

To overcome this "relentless foe," we need to know more about it. How powerful is it? What different forms does it take? How does it operate? In this chapter, we investigate the enemy. In the next chapter, we shall map out a strategy for victory.

THE STRENGTH OF FORGETTING

During every moment of our waking hours, a constant stream of thoughts and impressions flows into our consciousness from all our senses. A series of tests by the famous psychologist Robert S. Woodworth revealed that in only four weeks' time, we lose 98 percent of the total sum of these ideas, both the important and the unimportant ones. See Figure 5-1.

Wanting to find out how much forgetting took place during the summer vacation period, on their return for the fall semester, E. B. Greene tested students in psychology, zoology, and biochemistry. Fifty percent of the material had been forgotten!

Testing students' retention of elementary algebra after one year of non-use, E. T. Layton found that they had lost, on the average, two-thirds of their algebraic knowledge.

Forgetting is the biggest single problem faced by most students. The entire process of learning depends on *decelerating* forgetting and *accelerating* learning. We must develop powerful techniques and systems of study to overcome the devastating process of forgetting.

The Memory Trace

The mere fact that we do have memories of previous experiences demonstrates that the nervous system does somehow retain a record. This record laid down in the brain is called a *neural trace*. It is analogous to the molecular change that takes place in a magnetic recording tape. Unfortunately, like the traces on a recording tape, the brain traces can be erased.

Time and Forgetting

Unless reviewed periodically, what we have learned in the past fades with the passage of time; consequently, we often assume that there is a cause-effect relationship between time and forgetting. This conclusion, however, is erroneous. As Ian Hunter, a British psychologist, points out, "Iron rusts *in* time," but rust is not caused *by* time. The rust is caused by oxidation. Similarly, time itself does not cause forgetting; rather, it is what happens in time that does. In the following sections, we shall turn mainly to research to identify the "what" that happens in time.

Research Studies Using Meaningless Syllables

A great deal of interesting research has been done using meaningless syllables (GEP, NAW, XOL, YOX, HUZ, and so on). Such syllables were chosen to eliminate, as much as possible, a person's use of previous memories. Consequently, the general laws based on these experiments cannot be applied to much college studying. Nevertheless, in a specific way, these experiments show how rapidly forgetting can and does take place.

The famous Ebbinghaus experiment.   The German psychologist Hermann Ebbinghaus was the first to use meaningless syllables in research. Using himself as a subject, he would memorize, for example, a list of syllables by reading the list over and over until he could recite it once perfectly. Then twenty minutes later, after some forgetting inevitably took place, he would relearn the list and record the time required for the relearning. He then calculated the percentage of time saved at the relearning when compared to the original learning time. He then would learn other

Figure 5-1 In only four weeks' time, we loose 98% of the total sum of ideas entering the mind.

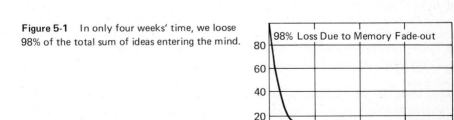

lists, and relearn them at longer and longer intervals of time. The results of his various experiments are shown in Table 5-1.

TABLE 5-1   THE RATE OF FORGETTING MEANINGLESS SYLLABLES

Time from first learning to relearning	Percent of material remembered (savings)	Percent of material forgotten
After 20 minutes	53%	47%
After 1 day	38%	62%
After 2 days	31%	69%
After 15 days	25%	75%
After 31 days	22%	78%

From his experiments, Ebbinghaus concluded that:

1. The greatest amount of forgetting occurs directly after finishing the learning task.
2. After the initial loss, forgetting slows down.

After years of experimenting and gathering statistics, Ebbinghaus constructed the first curve of forgetting (see Fig. 5-2). Regardless of the type of material used in experiments, no matter whether it was nonsense or full of meaning, researchers have invariably found rapid initial forgetting, then the gradual slowing down of forgetting.

Evaluation.   Research studies on meaningless material cannot tell us the whole story about forgetting what we study in college.

Ausubel has suggested that "plausible reasons exist for believing that rotely and meaningfully learned materials are organized much differently in consciousness and hence conform to quite different principles of learning and forgetting."[1]

Meaningless materials (MEB, YUX, YIL, and so on) are isolated bits that do not relate to previously learned materials; they do not "anchor" to existing clusters of knowledge. Floating freely in the mind, such isolated bits of "information" are especially susceptible to rapid forgetting. We need to know more about the retention of meaningful material.

Research Studies Using Meaningful Material

In this section, we explore the many different kinds of forgetting that take place in an academic situation. Since psychologists have studied nearly every aspect of this problem, we will look at many of their results.

The form of meaningful material.   It was easy to predict that meaningless syllables (like JUK, FOV, KEV) would be difficult to memorize and retain; but it is

[1]David P. Ausubel, "A Subsumption Theory of Meaningful Verbal Learning and Retention," *The Journal of General Psychology* 66 (1962): 213–24.

not so obvious that single meaningful words would be vastly more difficult to remember than meaningful words in sentence form. From their experiments, Binet and Henri concluded that memory for connected sentences is approximately 25 times as good as memory for separate, discrete words.

Textbook reading.   A considerable amount of forgetting takes place even after reading material in which ideas are developed quite fully. Dr. J. N. Moore found that the average reader recalls only about half of the ideas in a textbook chapter that has just been read.

It is logical to assume that by the time a student reaches the end of a chapter, some of the facts and ideas encountered at the beginning and middle of the chapter would have been forgotten. However, forgetting does not begin only after the last word of the last page of the chapter has been read. The erosive power of forgetting is constantly working to erase the memory traces of learning, even as the process of learning itself is going on.

The classic Spitzer study.   In a famous study on the retention of meaningful material over time, H. F. Spitzer divided 3605 students into ten groups: eight experimental and two control. All ten groups read two articles. Then a test was administered, but only to Groups I and II. Groups III through VIII took a test at the same time, but their test had little relation to the content of the articles. These tests were given to keep Groups III through VIII from expecting a test later. Later, however, the real test was given to them, each group being tested at a different time interval: 1, 7, 14, 21, 28, or 63 days. (The way in which the two control groups were used will be described in the next chapter, "How to Build a Strong Memory.")

To establish a realistic baseline for calculating forgetting, it was necessary to establish first how much was comprehended at the beginning of the testing. The

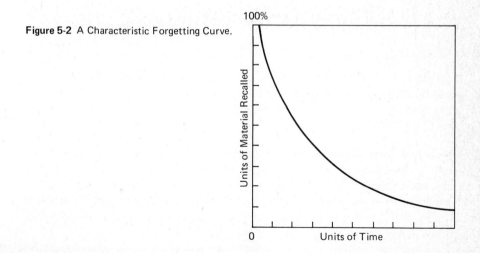

Figure 5-2 A Characteristic Forgetting Curve.

baseline was established by using the scores attained by Groups I and II. These groups took the test immediately after reading, and their average score was 53. Henceforth, this score would be considered the highest score attainable—it would be the 100 percent baseline. The percentages given in Figure 5-3, therefore, are based not on the highest score theoretically possible, but on the score actually achieved by the first two groups.

From the graph we can see that on the test administered only one day after reading the articles, the students in Group III remembered only 54 percent of the amount of material learned by Groups I and II the day before. For Group V, the amount retained after 14 days was only 21 percent.

Notice the similarity between this curve and the one developed by Ebbinghaus (Figure 5-2). Forgetting, even of meaningful material, takes place terribly fast and in wholesale lots after a single reading.

Forgetting: spaced and unspaced memorizing.   K. Gordon tested the effectiveness of spaced and unspaced memorizing by reading the "Athenian Oath" (containing 115 words) to Class 1 six times in succession, allowing one-half minute between readings. The students just listened. At the end of the sixth reading, they were asked to write down all they could remember of the oath. Four weeks later, they were again asked to write what they could recall.

To Class 2, K. Gordon read the Oath three times in succession. Three days later, she read it to the same class three more times in succession. At the end of this sixth reading, the students were asked to write out their recollections. Four weeks later, they were again asked to write what they could remember.

The results for the two classes in immediate and delayed recall are listed in Table 5-2.

TABLE 5-2 EFFECTS OF SPACED AND UNSPACED MEMORIZATION

	Number of readings	Type of drill	Average score in percent of recall	
			Immediate	4 weeks later
Class 1	6	Unspaced	70%	32%
Class 2	6	Spaced	66%	42%

They indicate that unspaced memorization is slightly more effective than spaced memorization for immediate recall (short-term retention). But spaced memorization is more effective for delayed recall (long-term retention). Other researchers have reached similar conclusions.

Forgetting controversial material.   Long before experimental studies were made on this subject, people were aware of the tendency to forget material that conflicts with our attitudes. When Charles Darwin was collecting evidence for his theory of evolution, he made a very special effort to write immediately into his notebook any evidence that was contrary to his theory, for he knew that otherwise he would forget it.

A great many studies and observations have supported his views. For example,

Figure 5-3 Curve of Forgetting Meaningful Material.

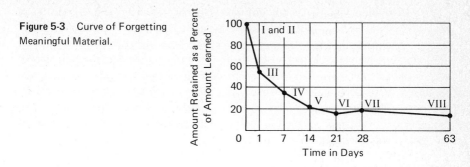

Adapted from H. F. Spitzer. "Studies in Retention," *Journal of Educational Psychology,* Vol. 30, 1939, pp. 641-656. Copyright 1939 by the American Psychological Association. Reprinted by permission.

in a controlled experiment, Levine and Murphy found that students who expressed anti-Communist feelings remembered anti-Communist arguments, and the students who expressed pro-Communist feelings remembered pro-Communist arguments.

When you are reading a textbook or researching for a term paper, be aware of these human weaknesses. Since hardly anyone is fully aware of all his own attitudes and emotions, follow Darwin's example of objectively writing down both sides of a problem.

Listening and forgetting. Remembering what you have *heard* is usually more difficult than remembering what you have *read*. In reading, you can slow down, pause, reflect, and even re-read. But in listening, you usually hear material only once, and you have to take notes, mental or written, to retain it. The Leon-Clyde episode illustrates this point very well.

The Leon-Clyde Episode
(100% True Story)

Characters:		Setting:
Leon	— Psychologist	Faculty lounge, enjoying
Clyde	— Philosopher	coffee after lunch
Walter	— Author of this book	

Clyde: Did you hear last night's lecture?
Walter: No, I was busy.
Clyde: Well, you missed one of the best lectures in recent years.
Leon: I agree. The four points that he developed were gems.
Clyde: I never heard anyone make his points so clear.
Walter: I don't want you to repeat the lecture, but what were those four points?
Leon: (Long silence). Clyde?
          (Passage of 2 or 3 minutes. Seemed like an hour.)
Leon: Well, I better get back to the office.
Clyde: Me too!
Walter: Me too!

Both Clyde and Leon were brilliant men. Neither, however, was able to recall even a fragment of any point made in the lecture they had heard. The four points were forgotten because they did not transfer them from the short-term memory to the long-term memory by rehearsing them. They did remember that the speaker was clear, forceful, wise, and that he made four points; after the speech, they rehearsed these generalities. However, they did not rehearse the four points by specifically thinking through them. In other words, they remembered their own thoughts and evaluations of the four points; but they did not recall the contents of the *four* points made by the lecturer.

Forgetting when listening to a discussion.   The amount of forgetting that takes place in a general discussion is even greater than that which takes place when listening to an organized talk. J. Blackburn and E. J. Lindgren, two Cambridge University psychologists, demonstrated the amount and kinds of forgetting that took place in one discussion.

> Without the knowledge of the people present, they made a recording of the discussion which followed a meeting of the Cambridge Psychological Society. Two weeks later, they wrote to all those who had attended and asked them to write down all they could recall about this discussion. When the reports were received, they were checked against the recorded version and it was found that the average number of specific points recalled by an individual was only 8.4 percent of the total recorded. Moreover, 42 percent of the recalled points were substantially incorrect. A large variety of errors and confusions appeared. Happenings were reported which had never taken place at all or which had taken place on some other occasion. Thus a person might report a colleague as having made a remark which he knew this colleague habitually made but which he did not happen to make on this particular occasion. There were also elaborations, as when some casual remark was expanded into a fairly lengthy contribution to the discussion or when a point was reported as having been made explicitly, whereas it had only been hinted at. In short, what was recalled was not only fragmentary but also distorted, and much was recalled which, in fact, had never happened.[2]

Pseudo-Forgetting

The word "forgetting" is an umbrella under which is grouped many kinds and degrees of forgetting. Two types are not really forgetting at all, so let's dispose of them before turning to the causes of real forgetting.

"You never had it" forgetting.   The word "forgetting" implies that a person has something to forget. But you cannot forget something that you never did have in the

---

[2]Ian M. L. Hunter, *Memory: Facts and Fallacies* (Baltimore: Penguin Books, 1957), p. 83. Copyright © 1957 by Ian M. L. Hunter. Reprinted by permission of Penguin Books Ltd.

Figure 5-4   Retroactive Interference.

12 ideas with details Jan 10	Jan 11	Jan 12	Jan 13	Jan 14	Jan 15	3 ideas and 2 partial ideas Jan 16

On Jan. 10 you learned 12 ideas with details, and you did not review them later.

During these 5 days you were busy attending lectures, reading books, talking, etc. All this intervening knowledge and information acted to mask the recall of the 12 ideas learned on Jan. 10.

On Jan. 16 you were able to recall only 3 complete ideas and fragments of 2 others.

first place. For example, during an introduction a name may be mumbled and garbled so that it is never heard and learned in the first place; yet we often ascribe our not remembering such names to forgetting.

The mental blur.   Akin to the "you-never-had-it-in-the-first-place" situation is the almost certain forgetting that goes along with incomplete learning. For example, an idea or fact is read and noticed in such general terms that no clear image is formed. Only a mental blur is recorded, similar to a blur of landscape on the film of a swiftly moved camera.

If an idea or fact is to be retained in the memory, it must be impressed on the mind clearly and crisply at least once. A neural trace must be laid down in the brain. You cannot retain something that is not there in the first place.

WHAT CAUSES FORGETTING?

Of the various theories of forgetting, we will discuss only one; the *interference theory*. This theory has gained ascendancy because it seems to dovetail with reality and because it can be demonstrated.

The first part of the theory deals with *retroactive interference,* which means that new learning interferes with, or masks, old learning. Figure 5-4 gives an example of retroactive interference.

It is not simply the passage of time or the disuse of material that causes forgetting; rather it is the accumulation of additional knowledge that acts as a barrier for the full recall of previously learned material. It is this type of activity (learning—more learning—forgetting) that makes pursuits so difficult for many students. No wonder we have heard: the more you learn, the more you forget!

Proactive interference is the other part of interference theory. It is bad enough that new learning interferes with the recall of old learning, but there is additional bad news: earlier learning interferes with the recall of later learning. This process is also called *proactive inhibition.* Figure 5-5 shows how the process works.

In the experimental situation represented in Figure 5-5, Group B remembered 32 percent more ideas and details than Group A. Why should this be so? Both groups

Figure 5-5   Proactive Interference.

	Stage 1 30 Minutes	Stage 2 30 Minutes	Stage 3 30 Minutes
GROUP A	READ Article on "Arctic Exploration"	READ Article on "Training Chimpanzees"	EXAM 50 Questions "Training Chimpanzees"
GROUP B	REST Close eyes and rest	READ Article on "Training Chimpanzees"	EXAM 50 Questions "Training Chimpanzees"

read the article on chimpanzees at the same time, and both groups were tested at the same time.

Apparently the difference between the scores is due to the different activities during Stage 1. Group B rested, while Group A read an article. Then when both groups read the article on chimpanzees, the earlier article evidently interfered with Group A's learning of the chimpanzee material.

Thus in interference theory, there seems to be interference both coming and going.

CONCLUSION

In this chapter, we have seen the power of the forgetting process. We have traced the development of the forgetting curve, which shows the universal tendency to forget new material rapidly at first, more slowly later on. Interference theory, which describes how new and old learning masks the very facts we want to recall, is not an optimistic appraisal of the learning process.

Nevertheless, it is possible to learn—thoroughly learn—academic material. The next chapter describes the techniques that will work to strengthen your memory and defeat the processes of forgetting.

6

HOW TO BUILD A STRONG MEMORY

Almost all the scientific studies and experiments on memory conclude that we can improve our memory only by *learning our material thoroughly* in the first place. It all comes back to the primary law of laying down a clear, crisp, strong neural trace at the time of original learning; without a neural trace, there is nothing to remember. William James made this point by saying, "All improvement in memory consists in the improvement of one's habitual methods of recording facts."[1] Before going on to specific techniques for building a strong memory, however, let's look at some of the forgetting processes that the memory techniques are designed to overcome.

1. The moment learning ends, forgetting begins immediately.
2. The greatest amount of forgetting is caused by interference; that is, what we learn today weakens the memory of what we learned yesterday.
3. Failure to *use* our learning precludes the *practice* or *rehearsal* of it. All this weakens the memory trace.
4. The *bulk* of forgetting occurs within a short time after learning ends. After the initial onslaught, forgetting is more gradual and at a decelerating pace.

EIGHT LEARNING PRINCIPLES

There are ways to combat every one of these processes. By applying the principles described in this chapter, you *can* learn to remember.

[1]William James, *Psychology* (New York: Holt, Rinehart, and Winston, Inc., 1893), p. 298.

61

The Principle of Motivated Interest

Psychologists agree that to learn something thoroughly, one must have *interest* in the material being studied. It is almost impossible to remember anything that does not interest us in the first place.

Some experiences, even though they occur but once, are so clear that we tend to remember them for the rest of our lives. Other things, learned without interest, tend to be forgotten rapidly.

In Chapter 1 we saw how interest in learning could be stimulated by a little academic success. In Chapter 4, we mentioned a few specific techniques for building interest in a distasteful subject. Here we simply point up the power of motivated interest.

■ I once interviewed a feeble-minded man who had been committed to an institution because he could not earn a living or function satisfactorily in the community. This man had a remarkable memory in one small area of knowledge. He could tell the day of the week for any date within a period of about twenty-five years. We could trace this ability back to an occasion when, as a boy, he had surprised his teacher by telling her that Lincoln's birthday would come on a Thursday. She praised him, and it was a rare thing for him to be praised for any mental accomplishment. He began to study the calendar, and soon he was able to amaze his classmates with day-and-date stunts. He continued to develop this ability, devoting all his spare time to it. In the institution he was regarded as a mental magician and was given the less unpleasant jobs for that reason. There was nothing miraculous about his ability; it was based on memory developed by intensive and prolonged effort—because he had a highly motivated interest in the feelings of success that his efforts brought him.[2] ■

The wizard of batting averages. In my home town, a young man achieved a town-wide reputation for remembering every baseball player's batting average on a day-by-day basis in both the American and National leagues. Motivated interest: he was continually the center of enjoyable light-hearted attention.

8000 names. Charles Schwab, when general manager of the Homestead Mill of the Bethlehem Steel Corporation, knew by name all his 8000 employees. Motivated interest: he believed in the dignity of the common working man; consequently he showed his respect by learning and using each man's name.

A college president. Charles W. Eliot, who was president of Harvard for forty

[2]James D. Weinland, *How to Improve Your Memory* (New York: Barnes and Noble Book Division of Harper and Row, Publishers, 1957), p. 6.

years, year by year knew the names of all the students and faculty. Motivated interest: at one time he was so embarrassed by his inability to remember the name of one of his colleagues that he determined never to suffer the embarrassment again.

Motivated interest and studying. If you could study every one of your subjects with motivated interest, you would not have to worry about your final grades.

Here's how to get this powerful principle to work for you. If you are naturally interested in a subject, then you have no problem. If, however, you are not naturally interested, then create an artificial interest and enthusiasm. (Read again the techniques described at the end of Chapter 4.) The trick is that when you begin to learn something about a new subject, the chances are great that you will find it genuinely interesting.

The key point to remember: use the power of *interest* to work for you, not against you.

The Principle of Selectivity

To pare the job of learning down to manageable size, you must decide which facts to master and which ones you can safely ignore. This is a very difficult principle to follow, because of the tiring effect of constant decision making. But the deciding and selecting must be done if real learning and remembering are to be achieved.

It is impossible to learn and remember any subject with all its details; and any person who tries to do so will become bewildered and will end by remembering less than if he had tried to master less material in the first place. This sad situation is exemplified by the over-conscientious student who sets out to "learn everything in the book." In trying to do so, he actually sabotages his own efforts because he runs directly into some unyielding laws: In addition to the general laws of forgetting discussed in the previous chapter, there is the law of memory-capacity for discrete items.

Hermann Ebbinghaus demonstrated this law when he recorded the number of trials that it took him to memorize six nonsense syllables. He then counted the number of trials needed to memorize twelve such syllables. He found that the number of trials required to learn the list of twelve syllables was fifteen times as great as that required to learn six syllables! One would speculate that memorizing the twelve-syllable list would take approximately twice as long as the six-syllable list; but we now see that the time and effort must be calculated not arithmetically, rather, exponentially. This is why a student should be selective: overloading the memory slows down learning to a drastic extent.

Perhaps once again William James has said it best: "The essence of genius is to know what to overlook."

Selecting and rejecting. When urged to be selective, students often say, "What if I select the wrong ideas, facts, and details to memorize?" The answer to this question has six parts.

1. Have the courage to select and reject. You know that to memorize everything in a chapter will surely lead to failure.
2. As you evaluate and judge the relative importance of each item, you will be thinking actively and consciously, thus learning. This is the great bonus of this system.
3. With only a little practice you will become quite proficient in selecting the important ideas, facts, and details. Unless you begin using selectivity, you will be at the mercy of undifferentiated masses of material.
4. If, with the book open before you, you cannot select the important points, think how much more difficult it will be to formulate an answer in the classroom or on an examination, *without* the book in front of you. So, while you still have a chance, read thoroughly and make the best decisions that you can.
5. You have context on your side. In a new course, you have already listened to a lecture or two, heard general discussions, and perhaps, skimmed the first and second chapters. So the subject matter and the course are not totally new. Now, when studying Chapter 3, you have a general background that will help you from going too far astray when making a choice among ideas, facts, and details.
6. Some students use this variation: They go through a chapter the first time to select only the main ideas, thus establishing a strong framework. They then go through the chapter a second time and work into the framework the necessary details; thus, ending up with the information in organized form.

This system has an inherent strength in that general principles and main ideas are easier to remember because they involve understanding; your mind can associate them with all kinds of information already stored in your brain. The supporting details are more difficult to remember because they involve memorization through repetition. Try hard, therefore, to establish a general principle as the magnetic center around which to cluster the supporting details. A unit is easier to remember than many separate details.

The Principle of Intention to Remember

Without an intention to remember, it is doubtful that any worthwhile learning takes place. Many people have personally experienced the truth of this principle without realizing it. For example, many of us have helped a child memorize a poem or a speech by correcting his errors and prompting him when he forgot his lines. Yet, after spending as much time on the poem or speech as did the child, we knew hardly any of it, but he had mastered it. The explanation: He *intended* to remember; we didn't.

The intention to remember is well illustrated by waiters in restaurants who exhibit a remarkably good memory for what customers order up until the moment they have paid their bills. Once the order has been filled and the bill fully calculated, the waiter jettisons the entire transaction from his mind so that he can give full attention to his next customer. In this case, just as he intends to remember, he can intend to forget.

This concept of the intention to forget, so that one has room for new material, is succinctly put forth by Dr. Hans Selye in the following excerpt.

> It seems that to some extent *newly learned facts occupy the place of previously learned or subsequently learnable ones.* Consequently there is a limit to how much you can burden your memory; and trying to remember too many things is certainly one of the major sources of psychologic stress. I make a conscious effort to forget immediately all that is unimportant and to jot down data of possible value (even at the price of having to prepare complex files). Thus I manage to keep my memory free for facts which are truly essential to me. I think this technique can help anyone to accomplish the greatest simplicity compatible with the degree of complexity of his intellectual life.[3]

The *intent to learn,* of course, is an overall positive attitude that automatically triggers several subsidiary attitudes, such as paying attention, getting a fact right the first time, and striving to understand.

Attention.   Attention is the mental set of giving yourself fully to the task at hand. Unfortunately, inattention is common in reading textbooks, especially when an idea in the book starts your mind dreaming down another road. Then your eyes move along the printed lines without comprehending them at all. Our chapter on concentration (Chapter 4) tackles this problem directly.

Getting it right the first time.   We have learned that all remembering depends on forming an original, clear neural trace in the brain in the first place. These initial impressions are vitally important because the mind clings just as tenaciously to incorrect impressions as it does to correct impressions. Then we have to unlearn and relearn. Incorrect information is so widespread that Mark Twain once wrote, "Education consists mainly in what we have unlearned."

One helpful aid in getting it right the first time is to be attentive and cautious when it comes to learning new knowledge. Go very slowly at first. Place your emphasis on accuracy, not speed.

Striving to understand.   First and most important, you must make sure that you understand new material before trying to remember it. A good technique to ensure understanding is to recite or write the author's ideas in your *own words.* If you cannot, then you do not understand them. The conclusion: You cannot remember what you do not understand. In other words, you cannot form a clear and correct memory trace from a fuzzy, poorly understood concept.

In the classroom, do not hesitate to ask the instructor to explain further a point that is not clear to you. If the point is unclear to you, there is a good chance that

[3]Hans Selye, *The Stress of Life* (New York: McGraw-Hill Book Company, 1956), p. 269.

it is unclear to others; so you will not be wasting anyone's time. Furthermore, most instructors appreciate the opportunity to slow down a lecture to answer questions.

The Principle of the Basic Background

Our understanding of what we *hear,* what we *read,* what we *see,* what we *feel,* and what we *taste* depends entirely upon what we already know—upon the knowledge and experience we have in our background. When listening to a speaker, we understand the successive points that he is making as long as we can interpret those points in terms of what we are already familiar with. But the moment he refers to a concept like the "Zeigarnik effect," or to a word like "serendipity"—a concept or a word that we do not have in our background, then we are lost. This concept and this word stand alone as isolated sounds; we cannot attach an accurate meaning to them. At this point, we may need to stop the speaker and ask him to explain. Experienced speakers, however, usually know when they are putting forth concepts and words that are not popularly known, and they provide the audience with an example or analogy.

(To satisfy your curiosity, the Zeigarnik effect is the tendency to remember uncompleted tasks better than completed tasks. Serendipity is the faculty of making fortunate discoveries by accident.)

Many students make the mistake of thinking that the basic courses taken in their freshman year are a waste of time. These courses create the background essential for all their later courses. The budding technician or engineer should realize that when he starts studying these basic courses, he has already begun his career. The upper-level courses do not convey all the secrets of being a technician or an engineer. Your professional life begins with your freshman courses. And if you want to become a good technician or engineer, you will have to remain a student all your life.

Figure 6-1   Lists of Words and Non-Words.

List 1	List 2	List 3
GIH	WHY	THE
WUK	ONE	BOY
NAF	THE	RAN
SIJ	TOO	TO
HUQ	CAN	THE
MAV	TEN	STORE
TIZ	HOW	TO
YEM	LET	BUY
NOL	NOW	A
LIW	ASK	CAN
DOF	OUR	OF
KAG	AND	MILK

The Principle of Meaningful Organization

When it comes to remembering large masses of material there is no better method than the *personal organization* that you impose on the material. In other words, cluster the facts and ideas into categories that are meaningful to you. The importance of organization is illustrated in Figure 6-1.

After inspecting these lists, you were quickly able to see, no doubt, that List 1 would be most difficult to memorize because it contains groups of letters that simply don't make sense. List 2 would not be so difficult to memorize since each word is meaningful, even though the words are unrelated. List 3, however, could be memorized easily because all the words fit into a sentence, and they make sense.

The category system.   When reading or taking notes, first gather the facts and ideas. Then look them over with an eye toward clustering them under categories. For example, if you were asked to buy at the market the following items, you would have a difficult time remembering them.

hamburg	celery	butter
lettuce	eggs	pork chops
milk	steak	carrots

But if you rearranged the items under natural categories, you would find very little difficulty in remembering.

Meat	*Vegetables*	*Dairy*
hamburg	lettuce	milk
steak	celery	eggs
pork chops	carrots	butter

The category system of organization is very simple, but it has been of practical use to mankind for a long, long time. Over two thousand years ago, the Greeks depended heavily on memorized knowledge and information. A great deal of the ancient knowledge and wisdom was stored in the minds of scholars who transmitted it by word of mouth. To remember so much, the Greeks most often used the category system of *general heads* and *sub-heads*.

In the following excerpt the speaker, Critias, refers to details ("particulars") clustered under general categories ("heads"):

> And now, Socrates, to make an end of my preface, I am ready to tell you the whole tale. I will give you not only the general heads, but the particulars, as they were told to me.[4]

The magical number seven theory.   Recent experiments have revealed the exciting possibilities of remembering vast quantities of materials when organized into categories or blocks. One researcher, G. A. Miller of Harvard, found that the immediate memory span of an adult appears fixed at approximately seven

[4]"Timaeus," *The Dialogues of Plato* (Oxford, England: Clarendon Press). Translated into English by B. Jowett (New York: Random House, 1937), Vol. II, p. 10.

separate "bits" of information. This limitation—seven in number—holds true also for larger "chunks" of information. Miller observed that it was probably not by chance that we have *seven* days in the week, *seven* wonders of the world, *seven* seas, *seven* primary colors, *seven* notes of the musical scale, *seven* deadly sins, and so forth.

Miller says that we can get around the limitation of seven by leaving the number of chunks constant, but adding numerous *bits* of information to the chunks. There is no limit to the number of bits we can add to the limited number of chunks. In this way we dramatically increase the amount of information we can retain.

In order to make these larger chunks cohesive, they must always be put in our own words and then rephrased in our own words so that the seven chunks together form a continuous story in our mind. You are sure to find words that will bring together the seven chunks. As Miller says, "Our language is tremendously useful for repackaging material into a few chunks rich in information."[5]

Magnetic centers.   This is another way of remembering material, somewhat different from the category system. John Livingston Lowes observed that once he learned a brand new word, fact, or idea, he would soon encounter it again and again, in such places as a newspaper or magazine. He postulated that the "new" words or facts have appeared previously, too, but that the eye and mind had blithely glided over them. But now that these previously unfamiliar items are familiar, we tend to notice them when we see and hear them.

Once such unknown items are learned, they create a so-called magnetic center in the mind. Then additional bits of information that we notice day-by-day seem to be attracted to the magnetic centers and cling there like metal filings on a magnet.

The practical implication of Lowes' magnetic construct seems to be that when we learn something new, we should take great care to learn it accurately and well, since it will become the center around which will cluster a whole constellation of additional information.

The power of association.   William James told his secret for developing a good memory in these words:

> The secret of a good memory is thus the secret of forming diverse and multiple associations with every fact we care to retain. But this forming of associations with a fact, what is it but *thinking about* the fact as much as possible? Briefly, then, of two men with the same outward experiences and the same amount of mere native tenacity, the one who *thinks* over his experiences most, and weaves them into systematic relations with each other, will be the one with the best memory.[6]

[5]G. A. Miller, "The Magical Number Seven, Plus or Minus Two: Some Limits on Our Capacity for Processing Information," *Psychological Review* 63: 81-97.
[6]James, *Psychology*, p. 294.

He elaborates by saying that when we have committed a new idea to memory, "Each of its associations becomes a hook to which it hangs, a means to fish it up by when sunk beneath the surface."

To carry out the prescription by William James successfully, we need an already existing background. The richer the background, the easier and the better will be our diverse and multiple associations. Thus a good background not only helps us understand new material, as we saw in a previous section, but it also helps us organize and remember it.

The Principle of Recitation

There is no principle that is more important than *recitation* for transferring material from the short-term memory to the long-term memory.

What is recitation?   Recitation is simply saying aloud the ideas that you want to remember. For example, after you have gathered your information in note form and have categorized and clustered your items, you recite them. Here's how: You cover your notes with a blank sheet of paper, expose only one category title, then recite aloud the material under that category. After reciting, expose the notes and check for accuracy. You should not attempt to recite the material word for word; rather your reciting should be in the words and manner that you would ordinarily use if you were explaining the material to your roommate. When you can *say it,* then you *know it.*

Recitation may be used while reading a textbook. After reading through a headed or sub-headed section consisting of a page or two, it is wise to stop reading and test yourself on what you have just read by reciting aloud the key ideas. Having recited, thus showing that you understand the ideas thus far in the chapter, you will read and recite the subsequent portions with greater understanding and efficiency. Additional uses of recitation in your college work will be mentioned in succeeding chapters.

Dr. Schweitzer and reciting.   Dr. Albert Schweitzer, the great missionary doctor who set up a large hospital and leper colony in Africa, used the technique of recitation when prescribing pills and medicine to his patients in the Congo. He would have a patient repeat the instructions for taking the medicine ten times before permitting the patient to go back to his native village.

Recitation and the ancient Greeks.   In several of the dialogues of Plato we find reference to the reciting technique. Here Critias is speaking to Socrates:

> I thought that I must first of all run over the narrative in my own mind, and then I would speak.[7]

[7]"Timaeus," *The Dialogues of Plato,* Vol. II, p. 10.

In the next paragraph, Critias continues:

> I listened at the time with childlike interest to the old man's narrative; he
> was very ready to teach me, and I asked him again and again to repeat
> his words, so that like an indelible picture they were branded into my
> mind. As soon as the day broke, I rehearsed them as he spoke them . . .[8]

How recitation works.   Recitation transfers material to the secondary memory.
While you are reading the words in a sentence or paragraph, the *primary memory*
(short-term memory) holds them in mind long enough for you to gain the sense of
the sentence or paragraph. However, the primary memory has a very limited
capacity, and as you continue to read, you displace the words and ideas of the
initial paragraphs with the words of subsequent paragraphs. This is one reason for
not remembering everything in the first part of the chapter by the time we reach
the end of the chapter when we read continually without pausing to recite.

It is only when we *recite* or contemplate the idea conveyed by a sentence or
paragraph that the idea has a chance (not guaranteed) of moving on into the
secondary memory (a long-term storage facility).

All verbal information goes first into the primary memory (short-term memory).
When it is rehearsed (recited), part of it goes into our secondary (long-term)
memory. The rest of it, usually the part we are least interested in, returns to the
primary memory and is then forgotten. Figure 6-2 illustrates the entire process.

Whether new information is "stored" or "dumped" depends, then, on our
reciting it out loud and on our interest in the information.

The power of review.   In the last chapter, we promised to tell how H. F. Spitzer
used the two control groups in his famous experiments on retention and
forgetting. You probably remember that he had ten groups of students for his
experiment. All ten groups read two articles. Groups I and II were tested on the
material immediately, and their average score was considered 100% of the
material learned. Then each group, III through VIII, was tested after a certain
interval of time. Their forgetting curve is shown by the solid line in Figure 6-3.

Groups IX and X, the control groups, were given three review tests, one
immediately after reading the articles, one after seven days, and one after
sixty-three days. Their rate of remembering shown by the dashed line in Figure
6-3, was far higher than that of the students who did no reviewing.

After this number of days	The amount remembered by students who did no review was	The amount remembered by students who reviewed was
7	33%	83%
63	14%	70%

The practical lesson to be learned from the Spitzer experiment should be clear.
If you want to remember the facts and ideas gained from a lecture or a textbook

[8]*Ibid.*

Figure 6-2 The Primary and
Secondary Memory Systems.

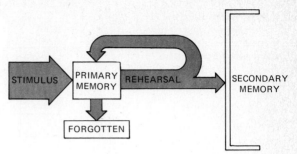

This figure is taken from Nancy C. Waugh and Donald A. Norman, "Primary Memory," *Psychological Review,* Vol. 72, No. 2, March 1965, p. 93. Reprinted by permission.

chapter, it pays to review your notes immediately upon completion. Later, review again from time to time. If you use this technique, the amount you remember will follow the path of the retention curve (upper curve) in Figure 6-3. If, however, no review is done, the amount of forgetting will follow the lower curve.

Why recitation works.   Recitation is far more effective than merely reading for the following reasons.

1. Since you know that you will stop to recite after reading each headed section within a chapter, you will be more motivated to understand.
2. Recitation lets you know how you are doing. A correct recitation is an immediate reward that helps keep motivation high. An incorrect recitation is punishment that motivates a student to avoid future punishment by studying harder.
3. Recitation deepens or makes more indelible the original memory trace, because your mind must actively think about the new material. Recitation is a form of immediate review.
4. The physical activity of thinking, pronouncing, and even hearing your own words involves not only your mind but also your body in the process of learning. The more physical senses you use in learning, the stronger the neural trace in your brain.

Importance of physical activity.   To promote recall, it is important to make outward, physical motion a part of the learning process. Students who silently read their assignments, no matter how diligently, often wonder why they remember so little after several days have passed. They do not realize that using the eyes alone as a means of absorbing information is an inefficient and ineffective method. Reciting aloud or writing the information even sketchily, is better by far.

In an experiment to test short-term and long-term memory, three groups of students were given new material to learn. The first group was told to write down

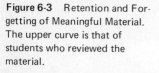

Figure 6-3 Retention and Forgetting of Meaningful Material. The upper curve is that of students who reviewed the material.

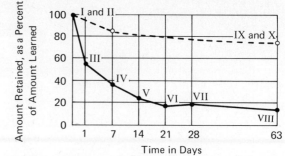

Time in Days

Adapted from H. F. Spitzer. "Studies in Retention," *Journal of Educational Psychology,* Vol. 30, 1939, pp. 641-46. Copyright 1939 by the American Psychological Association. Reprinted by permission.

answers to certain questions; the second group was told to "mentally compose" answers to the same questions; and the third group was told to simply read the correct answers, which were supplied for them.

On a test given immediately after this the three groups showed no significant differences. However, another comparable test was given two weeks later. The group that had made the written responses had significantly higher scores than either the silently thinking group or the reading group. The muscular activity of writing down information had helped engrave it on their minds.

Muscular learning.   We all know that once we have learned to swim or skate, the muscles never completely lose these skills. True, we may become "rusty," but we can still function more or less adequately.

Another example is the skill of typewriting. In this case, the muscles seem to "know" and retain the skill even better than the conscious mind. For example, it is difficult to visualize mentally the exact location of the letter "L" on the keyboard; but place the fingers on the keyboard and the appropriate finger will peck out the letter "L" unerringly. The muscles seem to "remember" better than the mind in such cases.

The lesson for studying is to trust and use your muscles as powerful aids to the memory.

How much recitation?   Students often ask: "How much time should I spend reciting?" The answer depends on the type of material you are studying. If much memorizing has to be done, for example, of lists of dates, names, experiments, principles, or formulas, then recitation should take about 95 percent of your study time.

On the other hand, in subjects like sociology and history, in which the primary concern is with ideas and events, then recitation should take about 30 percent of your study time.

In such subjects as economics and psychology, which have a high density of ideas, data, and theories, your recitation should take up about 50 percent of your study time.

The Principle of Consolidation

Dr. Robert S. Woodworth, a professor of psychology, relates this personal experience in his book, *Experimental Psychology:*

> A young man doing a little mountain climbing with friends falls on his head, being knocked unconscious for a moment and left in a dazed state for a couple of hours. We could not expect him to remember what happened during the dazed state, but the curious and psychologically significant fact is that his memory for the 15 minutes *preceding* the accident was blank and permanently so.[9]

Numerous records kept on automobile accidents reveal that this kind of blank period is common in people who have been knocked unconscious by a blow on the head.

The conclusion that psychologists have drawn from these cases is that the neural traces in the mind need some time—from four or five seconds to about fifteen minutes—to jell or consolidate. A sharp blow evidently permanently disrupts this settling-down process, but it does not noticeably affect memory of earlier events that have had time to consolidate.

Experiments with rats and hamsters offer concrete evidence that information needs to be harbored in the mind for a period of time before a temporary memory can be converted or consolidated into a permanent one. In rats, the neural trace must persist in the brain for at least 90 seconds. Perhaps for the conversion of the temporary memory into a permanent one in human beings, the neural trace must persist for only a few seconds, perhaps four or five.

This principle of consolidation may well be at work when you *recite* or *write* the ideas and facts that you read. As you recite or write you are holding each idea in mind for the four or five seconds that are needed for the temporary memory to be converted into a permanent one.

Another practical application of the principle of consolidation is to review your notes immediately after class. If the reviewing is done by recitation you will be not only consolidating the new information but also strengthening the neural trace made in your brain.

A. M. Sones's experiment on the value of review is illuminating. One group of students had no review immediately after a class meeting; a second group had only a five-minute review test. Yet with only this 5-minute advantage, the second group recalled one and a half times as much material as the group that had no immediate review, when both groups were tested six weeks later.

William James indirectly suggested the principle of consolidation when he said

[9]R. S. Woodworth and H. Schlosberg, *Experimental Psychology*, rev. ed. (New York: Holt, Rinehart and Winston, Inc., 1954), p. 773.

that we learn to ice-skate in the summer and to swim in the winter. It seems that consolidation, once accomplished, ensures long-term remembering.

The Principle of Distributed Practice

Is distributed practice more effective than massed practice? First, to explain our terms: in *distributed practice* the student uses relatively short study periods broken up by rest intervals. In *massed practice* the student studies continually until the task is completed. The answer: Many experiments show that, in general, there is an advantage to distributed practice. The length of the study period, of course, varies with different individuals, as well as with the nature of the material being studied.

Why it works.   There are three apparent reasons why distributed practice is more efficient than massed practice:

1. Both physical and emotional fatigue are prevented.
2. Motivation is higher when working within short blocks of time.
3. The neural processes of learning, once energized, seem to continue working during the rest period.

There is an interesting comment regarding this third point. Some psychologists claim that a person is going over the task in his mind (rehearsing) during the rest periods. However, distributed practice results in increased learning in animals, too, and it is highly improbable that the increased learning in a rat, for example, would be due to any rehearsing that it might do while resting. So the increased learning in rats must be due to distributed practice, not to rehearsing.

A practical application.   A practical application of the principle of distributed practice would be the use of small blocks of time (often only ten minutes) that occur between classes. When the classroom lecture ends, while walking to the next class, try to recall the entire lecture, or as many of the ideas as possible.

Immediate and long-term gains.   In an extensive experiment, Irving Lorge found that with the introduction of distributed practice, students immediately improved their performance. However, if distributed practice was stopped while the students were still working on the experiment, their performance decreased. There was an immediate reaction to both the injection of and the withdrawal of distributed practice.

Bertram Epstein experimented to find out whether or not distributed practice had an effect on retention; so he tested his groups immediately after learning, then retested them two weeks and ten weeks after the original practice. He found distributed practice to be superior to massed practice for both immediate and long-term retention.

Use of massed practice.   In some cases, massed practice is superior to distributed practice. In work such as the writing of a paper, massed practice is often essential.

For example, the exact locations of the little stacks of notes spread over the desk are held in mind with precision; the discrete bits of information are precariously suspended in mind to be fitted in like a jigsaw puzzle piece at the appropriate time; and, the organizational pattern, though dimly perceived, is beginning to take shape. To stop at this point would be disastrous. The entire effort would collapse. So, in creative work, or work which needs to be overviewed at one sitting, it is far more efficient to over-extend yourself—to complete that stage of the process —than to take a break or otherwise apply the principle of distributed practice.

QUESTIONS STUDENTS ASK

What is the difference between *recognition* and *recall?*

Recognition is an easier stage of memory than the *recall* stage. For example, in an examination, it is much easier to *recognize* an answer to a question if five options are listed, than to *recall* the answer without the options listed.

Do fast learners remember better?

Dr. Ian M. L. Hunter of the University of Edinburgh says: "The slow student who works out his lesson until he is more than thoroughly familiar with every aspect of it, remembers more than his faster colleague who barely masters it and no more."[10]

Do women have better memories than men?

Numerous studies on memory show that there is no consistent difference between men and women when it comes to the retentive abilities.

Why are separate items, rotely learned, more difficult to retain than meaningful ideas?

Separate, discrete items (such as lists of terms or facts) learned by rote are especially difficult to retain for the following reasons: (1) it is hard to fit them into a category; (2) it is hard to associate them with other ideas already in mind; (3) since they are isolated, meaningless items, they must be "parroted," and such drudgery is distasteful. Unfortunately, some material, like languages and scientific formulas, must be learned by rote. Whenever possible, try to comprehend the material first. Do not learn by rote what can be learned by reasoning.

Is memory affected by age?

Yes! As far as learning ideas and facts is concerned, people over 30 are slower, especially in formal, academic situations; but the older people make up for this relative slowness by their retentiveness, since they have more accumulated experiences to which they can associate the new material.

[10]Ian M. L. Hunter. *Memory: Facts and Fallacies* (Baltimore: Penguin Books, 1957) pp. 49-50. Copyright © Ian M. L. Hunter, 1957. Reprinted by permission of Penguin Books Ltd.

Does overlearning lead to better retention?	Yes! After you have recited a lesson long enough to say it perfectly, if you continue reciting it a few times more, you will overlearn it. Ebbinghaus said that each additional recitation engraves the mental trace deeper and deeper, thus establishing a base for long-range retention.

Actually, overlearning follows the first principle of remembering: *learn the material accurately and thoroughly in the first place.*

For many people, overlearning is difficult to practice because, by the time they achieve bare mastery, they are eager to drop the subject and go on to something else.

When we forget, is all the previous effort wasted?	All is not lost when you forget material which you earlier studied thoroughly. Forgetting almost inevitably takes place when you do not rehearse or use such material. You will be surprised, however, when you begin to relearn the "forgotten" material. Such material will be relearned in just a fraction of the time that it took to learn it originally. This is true even after years of disuse.

It is generally agreed among psychologists that the ease and rapidity of relearning some "forgotten" material is a function of the original number of recitations of that material. This is a basic law of learning.

MEMORY SYSTEMS

To combat forgetting, some students take memory courses given by commercial enterprises. Many others invent (or inherit) *mnemonic devices*—words, sentences, rhymes, and other formulas that associate a complex principle or body of fact with a simple statement that is easy to remember. Both the memory courses and the mnemonic devices have serious drawbacks.

How Commercial Memory Courses Work

The first step of most memory systems involves the memorizing of a master list of words called "pegs." Each word is numbered, and a strong association is made between the number and the word; for example, number one may be an *alarm clock,* number two a *revolving door,* and so forth. So when you need to remember a list of such items as butter, sugar, and so forth, you form a bizarre image associating the first peg word and the first item on the list to be memorized. For example, for *butter* you may visualize a pound of butter atop a fiercely ringing metal alarm clock. For sugar, you visualize dropping a pound of sugar in the revolving door of a busy post office, almost hearing and feeling the crunching of the sugar as people stomp on it and the revolving door grinds it on the cement floor. Later, on entering the supermarket, to recall the grocery items, it is only necessary to recall the well-memorized peg words in numerical sequence, and almost automatically, with each peg word will come to mind the item associated with it. The next day, however, you may have to associate a pound of sugar with the alarm clock, and yesterday's butter might interfere with today's sugar. In other words, interference caused by using the same symbols for many different things makes the system unworkable. Such systems are fun at parties, but hardly applicable for serious studying and learning.

Mnemonic Devices

A classic example of a mnemonic device is the old jingle by which most of us learned the irregularities of our calendar.

> Thirty days has September,
> April, June, and November
> All the rest have thirty-one
> Except February alone—

Another is

> i before e except after c
> or when pronounced a
> as in *neighbor* and *weigh*.

One or two simple rules like these, or even half a dozen, won't hurt anyone. They may even help you retain certain dull but necessary facts. But except for purely mechanical matters, like the number of days in the months or problems in spelling, mnemonic systems are of doubtful utility. Their chief fault is that they side-step the intrinsic meaning of the material being learned. It then remains a compartmentalized parcel of data which is mechanically taken out of the mnemonic context only when needed. The student may learn a sequence of names and dates this way, but the chances are he does not learn much about them. If, on the other hand, he learns the same list directly and meaningfully, he can integrate it into his general knowledge for use in relation to other facts and ideas.

If for example, you had to learn the names of all the cranial nerves, you could repeat a jingle such as medical students have devised for associating the names and the order of the nerves with the initial letters of the words:

> On Old Olympus' Towering Tops
> A Fat Angelic Girl Viewed Spanish Hops.

(The nerves are Olfactory, Optic, Oculomotor, Trochlear, Trigeminal, Abducent, Facial, Auditory, Glossopharyngeal, Vagus, Spinal Accessory, and Hypoglossal.) But a more effective procedure would be as follows:

1. Look up each word in the dictionary to learn more about it. Learn its Latin or Greek derivation. The more associations you can make, the better you will remember.
2. Study a diagram showing the nerves as they enter the base of the brain. With such a mental picture in mind, you will be able to identify them in order and name their functions.

Artificial mnemonic systems have two additional faults. The slightest error in the jingle or anagram can throw you off completely. And the time spent in memorizing it is rarely justified by the result.

Students often use mnemonic devices in preparing for examinations, usually in desperation, hoping somehow to "get by." But facts so learned—if they really *are* learned—are usually retained for a relatively short time. Students who resort to cramming in this fashion, realizing that they are gearing for an examination only, often promise themselves afterwards they will restudy the material and "really learn" it. Such restudying is rare, since the kind of student who has to cram for examinations is rarely the kind who has time for extra tasks.

THREE RULES OF MEMORY

To help you remember the important steps in building up your memory, here is a list of rules. You will see that it is a very brief summary of all the principles we have discussed in this chapter.

1. Create a positive mental set. Create, either naturally or artificially, an active interest in what is being said or read so that you will get the information accurately in the first place.
2. Think actively by listening, observing, talking, selecting, and organizing. All with the intention to remember.
3. Recite and review facts, names, and ideas, so that consolidation and transference to the long-term memory can take place.

III

THE BASIC ON-GOING SKILLS

7

BUILD A PRECISE VOCABULARY

To be good, a vocabulary need not be large, but it needs to be *precise*. If it is both large and precise, that's all the better. But precision stands first.

Numerous research studies, both in the academic and business worlds, show a close relationship between a good vocabulary and success.

A survey in an eastern engineering college showed that the students who improved most in vocabulary during their freshman year averaged three or four places nearer the top of their class in academic standing during the sophomore year; those who did not improve at all in vocabulary averaged 7.5 places nearer the bottom.[1]

The Human Engineering Laboratory, a company that specializes in testing business executives, found a highly significant correlation between high vocabulary scores and success at the top executive level. These and similar findings demonstrate that a good vocabulary is a valuable asset both in college and after.

WHAT'S SO MAGICAL ABOUT WORDS?

Words, of course, are the coinage of communication, and they have far-reaching effects.

In Speaking

It is easy enough to talk about the weather; but it is not so easy to talk about ideas and concepts. How many times have you heard, "I know what I mean, but I just

[1]Cited in *Word Study*, Copyright © 1958 by G. & C. Merriam Co., publishers of the Merriam-Webster Dictionaries.

can't express it." This is an outright confession of an inadequate vocabulary, at least, at the higher level. To transmit ideas, Plato said that a speaker must paint pictures in the minds of his listeners through use of precise words.

A man who can explain a job process clearly to a machinist is more valuable to his company than a man who cannot. At higher levels in business, the person who can present ideas at a staff conference clearly will almost naturally emerge as a leader. In college, a good oral report or a clear, precise contribution to a class discussion has far more impact than vague generalities. And the knowledge that you have something to say and that you are saying it well can do wonders for your sense of self-worth.

In Reading

Especially in reading, it is easy to make one wrong interpretation after another because of an imprecise vocabulary. Take the word *fulsome,* for example. As the eyes glide along the printed lines, very few people would stop to use the dictionary upon encountering this sentence: "The mayor spent considerable time giving *fulsome praise* to the chairman of the finance committee."

Such words as *fulsome* are extremely deceptive, because the parts are familiar. Many people leap to the conclusion that *fulsome* is merely an elaborate way of saying *full*; consequently, *fulsome praise* is erroneously interpreted as "full of praise."

The dictionary meaning of *fulsome,* however, is:

> **ful·some** (fool' səm) *adj.* **1.** Offensively excessive or insincere.
> **2.** Offensive to the senses; loathsome; disgusting.[2]

A person with an imprecise vocabulary could totally misinterpret an author's presentation. Obviously, a reader who misconstrues several paragraphs cannot put such a fuzzy conglomeration into the thinking machine and hope to grind out crystal clear concepts.

In Learning

Without an adequate vocabulary, mastery of important principles and ideas is not possible. The fundamental building blocks of learning and knowledge are words—words with precise meanings.

A student lacking a functional vocabulary will have to work harder until he overcomes this temporary limitation. An inadequate vocabulary can limit a student's ability to conceptualize; that is, though he may hear and recognize individual words, he will have difficulty seizing the sequence of concepts being developed by a speaker or an author.

The spoken word is but a sound; the written word is but a symbol. The listener or the reader must clothe the sound or the symbol with meaning. The word

[2]*The American Heritage Dictionary of the English Language* (New York and Boston: American Heritage Publishing Co., Inc., and Houghton Mifflin Company, 1970), p. 532.

lantern, in the following quotation, for example, though readily understood as a word, does not have much meaning unless the student already knows the historical incident with which this word is precisely associated.

> And not long ago I was able to lay by my lantern, for I found an honest man.[3]

The specific reference in this case is to the lantern carried by Diogenes, the ancient Greek cynic philosopher who went about the streets of Athens in the daytime with a lighted lantern to satirize the difficulty of finding an honest man.

In Thinking

J. B. Watson, a noted psychologist, said that thinking is silent speech. This means that when we think, we do not use some mysterious fluffy "thinking-stuff." Rather, we use actual words, either silently or not so silently. Thinking is usually accompanied by tiny movements of the speech muscles and organs. The words are not audible, nor do the lips move; nonetheless, the subvocal monologue sends words racing through the mind.

Our thinking can hardly be more precise than the vocabulary we use. The stark implication (just as in reading) is that we cannot expect to put hazy, nebulous, and imprecise words into our thinking process and hope to come forth with clear, logical thoughts. In other words, a student with a limited or imprecise vocabulary is limited in the scope and clarity of his thought.

Since the processes of learning and thinking must go on with the vocabulary that you already have, it is important to study with a dictionary close at hand to insure more accurate understanding of what you read and hear. In order to think, read, listen, and speak more clearly and easily, you may need to embark on a vigorous program of vocabulary building, using some of the suggestions in this chapter. If you need to improve your vocabulary, begin immediately.

WHERE DO YOU STAND?

As a warm-up exercise, test yourself on the vocabulary quiz *(page 84)*. The phrases on this list were actually taken from books, magazines, and newspapers that are now in general circulation. It is true that most of these words are seldom heard in general conversation, but they are often used in good writing.

Most students achieve a relatively low score on this quiz, so don't be discouraged if you do. The purpose of the quiz is to demonstrate the necessity for using a dictionary when you read your assignments. Another reason for choosing this difficult test is to wake you up to the realization that perhaps you should take some positive steps to improve. All of us need to work continually to make our vocabularies more precise.

[3]Robert Louis Stevenson, *Virginibus Puerisque* (New York: Charles Scribner's Sons, 1905), p. 12.

Test Your Vocabulary

Directions: Circle the one of the four word choices that most nearly expresses the meaning of the italicized word in the phrase in the left-hand column. (Answers are given on pg. 72.)

	1	2	3	4
1. An *inscrutable* face	jovial	inexpressive	frightened	distinguished
2. *Bemused* by his message	dazed	threatened	instructed	disturbed
3. To *deride* a suggestion	make	discuss	adopt	ridicule
4. *Perjured* testimony	judicial	forceful	objective	false
5. A *diminution* of tensions	decrease	stabilization	creation	increase
6. *Turbid* water	limpid	sterilized	cloudy	lukewarm
7. A *turgid* stream	rippling	roaring	swirling	swollen
8. *Mundane* affairs	religious	illegal	business	worldly
9. A *burgeoning* population	growing	hungry	discontented	bilingual
10. Exposed to *calumny*	disease	hardships	slander	treatment
11. *Somnolent* students	intelligent	youthful	drowsy	forgetful
12. *Redoubtable* advisors	respected	senile	weak	international
13. A *maladroit* candidate	astute	awkward	studious	experienced
14. A *sententious* oration	clever	spellbinding	fascinating	pompous
15. A *nocturnal* march	military	tragic	stirring	night
16. The *saturnine* doctor	comforting	trustworthy	rambling	gloomy
17. To view with *equanimity*	alarm	approbation	misgiving	calmness
18. *Insouciance* of colleagues	optimism	warning	indifference	attitudes
19. *Myriad* uses of wood	constructive	common	particular	numberless
20. An *ineffable* quality	indescribable	manly	measurable	transparent
21. A *whimsical* taxi driver	odd	reckless	talkative	stolid
22. The science of *ornithology*	trees	living	insects	birds
23. *Fecund* plant life	parasitic	prolific	decaying	aquatic
24. An *invidious* comparison	truthful	offensive	clever	silly
25. Carefully *effaced* inscriptions	copied	written	erased	preserved
26. A *fortuitous* resemblance	family	natural	faint	chance
27. An *arch* foe	foreign	cunning	arrogant	enervated
28. A *saline* solution	logical	salty	satisfactory	medical
29. To participate in *chicanery*	debate	frivolity	athletics	deception
30. An *evanescent* thought	fleeting	pragmatic	farcical	reverent
31. A *droll* expression	simple	trite	comforting	amusing
32. Men given *kudos*	scholarships	recognition	commissions	honors
33. To establish *rapport*	contact	policies	understanding	credit
34. To give *succor*	relief	assurance	awards	satisfaction
35. An African *safari*	emperor	expedition	aborigine	native
36. *Furtive* glances	bold	loving	respected	sly
37. A *sardonic* look	triumphant	wan	immaculate	scornful
38. He spoke *fatuously*	tirelessly	impartially	sensibly	foolishly
39. A *phlegmatic* disposition	sanguine	dejected	calm	violent
40. *Dilatory* behavior	dogmatic	puerile	wise	delaying
41. *Exigent* problems	omnipresent	critical	extra	domestic
42. A *chimerical* undertaking	expensive	complicated	unnecessary	visionary
43. A *paragon* of patience	model	quality	lack	surfeit
44. Incredibly *gauche*	impolite	powerful	awkward	intelligent
45. To *avert* a strike	arbitrate	end	prevent	foment
46. A *rubicund* man	ruddy	fat	gluttonous	elfish
47. To eye *truculently*	slyly	endearingly	obtusely	fiercely
48. A *tacit* admission	boastful	sworn	guarded	unspoken
49. The *temerity* of youth	skillfulness	pessimism	optimism	rashness
50. *Fulsome* praise	unusual	fanatic	insincere	unexpected

Adapted by permission. From Vocabulary Quiz, copyright 1957 by G. & C. Merriam Co., Publishers of the Merriam-Webster Dictionaries.

SOME VOCABULARY SYSTEMS THAT DON'T WORK

The following four systems are widely used by teachers to help develop students' vocabularies, but they all have serious limitations. We mention them here only because you may have run into one or more of them.

Natural Growth

Vocabularies do not grow naturally as time goes on. In fact, many studies show an actual decrease in vocabulary strength with the passage of time. To continue to grow in vocabulary, a person must make a direct effort to learn words.

Reading Books

Another widespread notion is that vocabulary will increase automatically if a person reads books. This notion is true if the reader would stop to look up words in a dictionary, but very few people expend the time and effort to do so.

Word Lists

In theory, learning five words a day adds up to approximately 1825 words a year. In practice, however, no such results take place. Word lists have too many strikes against them: first, memorizing is a chore; second, forgetting is rapid; third, learning someone else's list is nonmotivating; and fourth, words lists are artificial since words do not exist in isolation, except in crossword puzzles and quizzes. The nonrewarding results of the word-list technique soon make themselves felt. Enthusiasm plummets, and the project is abandoned.

Prefixes, Roots, and Combining Forms

The prefix-root approach has been used over the years with varying degrees of success. At first thought, it would seem that this system has great potential because an estimated 60 percent of the English words in common use are made up partly or entirely of prefixes and roots derived from Latin and Greek.

Unfortunately, the system does not work well except for those who already have a strong vocabulary. Here are the reasons: First, memorizing lists of prefixes and roots is not much different from memorizing impersonal lists of words—it is boring and nonmotivating. Boredom is not eliminated by placing actual words, composed of prefixes and roots, in artificially contrived sentences. Second, forgetting is rapid because these word parts are separate, noncluster-type items. Third, only students who are already strong in vocabulary show improvement.

This last point needs to be explained. It appears that the student whose vocabulary is on the weak side can best learn new words *inductively*. He builds his vocabulary on the basis of learning individual words that he locates in a meaningful context. After looking up the word in a dictionary, he may then add precision to the definition by studying the prefix and the root.

On the other hand, the student already strong in vocabulary can see how the prefixes and roots apply to the words he already knows, thus making it easier for him to apply them to specific new words.

BECOME INTERESTED IN WORDS

The first step in improving your vocabulary is to develop a genuine interest in words. Probably it happens in a different way for each person.

For me, the critical incident was a remark I heard when I was very young. While talking about the perennial topic of weather, a man said, "It will stop raining by this afternoon, and we'll have sunny skies. I'm an optimist." I suddenly became aware that one's thoughts and personality could be expressed in interesting, thoughtful, and precise terms. Although I did not know the definition of *optimist* until later that day when I looked it up in a dictionary, I knew immediately that here was a man who was not perfunctorily uttering clichés. This man was thinking as he was speaking. And to think well, I realized, a person had to have a good vocabulary.

One of the most successful techniques for engendering interest in words is through the use of a book like *Interesting Origins of English Words*. This book was used in experiments with high school junior and senior students in a special six-week course in study skills at Cornell. Improvement in vocabulary consistently ranged from 35 to 65 percent for the class average.

The following excerpt points up the fascination in learning the history of words.

■ To the man who knows its origin, every word presents a picture. Not only do these stories make interesting reading, but to know them will give you an effectiveness in speaking and writing that can come in no other way. When you know the origins and the essential meanings of words, your own use of words will become more forceful, accurate, and colorful.

Back of almost every word in the English language there is a "life story" that will come to many as a fascinating revelation. Our words have come to us from a multitude of sources. Some of them have lived for thousands of years and have played their parts in many lands and many civilizations. They may record ancient superstitions. They may be monuments to customs dating back to classical antiquity. They may reveal our ancestors' manners and beliefs, shrouded in the mists of ancient history. Words that you use today may have been the slang of Roman soldiers twenty centuries ago or the lingo of savages. They may have been used by an Athenian poet or by an Anglo-Saxon farmer.[4]   ■

Figure 7-1 gives a specific example of a vivid and memorable word.

[4]By permission from *Interesting Origins of English Words,* Copyright © 1959 by G. & C. Merriam Co., Publishers of the Merriam-Webster Dictionaries.

In Old English, *nēah* meant "near" and *gebūr* meant "dweller," "farmer." These two words were combined into *nēahgebūr*, meaning, literally, "a nearby farmer." The word appears in Middle English as *neighebor* and in Modern English as *neighbor*. Its meaning, changing with the evolution of civilization, no longer applies particularly to neighboring farmers but refers to all persons living near each other. Even nations in the modern world are called "neighbors" — an interesting development of a word that means, literally, "nearby farmers."

Figure 7-1   An Interesting Word History.   Reprinted by permission from *Picturesque Word Origins,* Copyright 1933 by G. & C. Merriam Co., Publishers of the Merriam-Webster Dictionaries.

BE DICTIONARY-MINDED

Many scholars and business executives attribute their interest in words to the old-time "vest-pocket" dictionary.

Eddie Rickenbacker, who left school when he was only twelve, nevertheless made it a habit to carry a small dictionary in his pocket. Here is his own account.

> Though much of my association was with mechanics and other drivers, I also had the opportunity to converse with men in higher positions, automotive engineers, and company officials. . . . I listened carefully and marked well the way such men constructed and phrased their thoughts. I carried a dictionary with me always and used it. I have never slackened in the pursuit of learning and self-improvement.[5]

Here is the way to use one of these small pocket dictionaries. Instead of reading the print on cereal boxes, advertising placards on buses and subway trains, or just staring into space, whip out the thin dictionary; it will provide interesting "reading" material for years. Though it provides "definitions" in terse synonyms, its value lies in fostering a life-long interest in words, as well as providing many delightful serendipitous excursions. It does not, however, provide enough information for the serious student.

[5]From the book, *Rickenbacker* by Edward V. Rickenbacker. Copyright © 1967 by Edward V. Rickenbacker. Published by Prentice-Hall, Inc., Englewood Cliffs, N.J.

Every college student should own a good desk dictionary for ready reference. Especially recommended are the following.

The American College Dictionary (Random House)
The American Heritage Dictionary of the English Language (American Heritage Publishing Company and Houghton Mifflin Company)
Webster's New Collegiate Dictionary (G. & C. Merriam Company)
Webster's New World Dictionary of the American Language (World Publishing Company)

Keep your dictionary within arm's reach as you study, and develop the habit of consulting it.

For intensive word study there is no substitute for an unabridged dictionary. Locate the unabridged dictionaries in your library—normally you will find them in the reference room—and use them to supplement your own abridged desk dictionary. An unabridged dictionary gives more definitions, more about the derivation of words, more on usage. Good one-volume unabridged works include Webster's New International Dictionary of the English Language (G. & C. Merriam Co.), in either the second or the third edition; and the New Standard Dictionary of the English Language (New York: Funk and Wagnalls). The Oxford English Dictionary or "OED" (Oxford, England: Clarendon Press), in ten volumes and supplement, is indispensable for the historical study of words, but more detailed than you will need for most purposes.

The reference librarian can also help you find specialized dictionaries on various subjects. They list technical terms not always found even in unabridged dictionaries. However, your textbooks are the best sources for such definitions.

Prefixes and Roots

The prefixes and roots listed in Tables 7-1 and 7-2 illustrate how a knowledge of them can help you understand definitions more precisely. Whenever you use the dictionary, take time to ponder the ancestry (Latin, Greek, French, Anglo-Saxon) of the prefixes and roots, and to see how each word-part makes its contribution to the definition. Remember! Surrounding a word with as many associations as possible will help you remember it better.

As you work to make your definitions more precise, you will appreciate more and more the value of prefixes and roots. Soon, some of them will become old friends, and you will recognize them almost daily as you read and listen. And when you recognize these word-forms as parts of new words, you will already know half the meaning. With one well-understood root word as the center, an entire "constellation" of words can be understood better. Figure 7-2 shows such a constellation, based on the root duct, from the Latin ducere (to lead). You will notice that it makes use of other prefixes and combining forms as well as various suffixes, or word endings. It does not exhaust all the possibilities, either; you will surely encounter other words growing out of duct.

TABLE 7-1 EXAMPLES OF COMMON PREFIXES

Prefix	Meaning	Example	Definition
ante-	before	antebellum	*Before* the war; especially in the U.S., before the Civil War
anti-	against	antitank	Weapons used *against* tanks
auto-	self	automatic	*Self*-acting or self-regulating
bene-	good	benefit	An act of *kindness*; a gift
circum-	around	circumscribe	To draw a line *around*; to encircle
contra-	against	contradict	To speak *against*
ecto-	outside	ectoparasite	Parasite living on the *exterior* animals
endo-	within	endogamy	Marriage *within* the tribe
hyper-	over	hypertension	*High* blood pressure
hypo-	under	hypotension	*Low* blood pressure
inter-	between	intervene	Come *between*
intro-	within	introspect	To look *within,* as one's own mind
macro-	large	macroscopic	*Large* enough to be observed by the naked eye
mal-	bad	maladjusted	*Badly* adjusted
micro-	small	microscopic	So *small* that one needs a microscope to observe
multi-	many	multimillionaire	One having *two or more* million dollars
neo-	new	neolithic	*New* stone age
pan-	all	pantheon	A temple dedicated to *all* gods
poly-	many	polygamy	Having *many* wives
post-	after	post bellum	*After* the war
pre-	before	precede	To go *before*
proto-	first	prototype	*First* or original model
pseudo-	false	pseudonym	*False* name; esp., an author's pen-name
retro-	backward	retrospect	A looking *back* on things
semi-	half	semiannual	*Half* a year
sub-	under	submerge	To put *under* water
super-	above	superfine	*Extra* fine
tele-	far	telescope	Seeing or viewing *afar*
trans-	across	transalpine	*Across* the Alps

THE FRONTIER VOCABULARY SYSTEM

Most vocabulary improvement systems are based on a body of words or word forms (prefixes, roots, and suffixes) chosen by an expert who then commends the system to all people. In such procrustean systems, the individual must conform; yet we all know that individuals are at different stages of intellectual development, with different interests and abilities, and different personalities.

Wouldn't it be logical, then, to start the other way around? Wouldn't it make more sense to have a vocabulary development system that lets each individual choose his own words? You might say, "Fine! But how could anyone develop such an individual system?" Well, here's a very specific suggestion.

The frontier vocabulary system developed by Johnson O'Connor is based on

TABLE 7-2 EXAMPLES OF COMMON ROOTS

Root	Meaning	Example	Definition
agri-	field	agronomy	*Field*—crop production and soil management
anthropo-	man	anthropology	The study of *man*
astro-	star	astronaut	One who travels in interplanetary space (*stars*)
bios-	life	biology	The study of *life*
cardio-	heart	cardiac	Pertaining to the *heart*
chromo-	color	chromatology	The science of *colors*
demos-	people	democracy	Government by the *people*
derma-	skin	epidermis	The outer layer of *skin*
dyna-	power	dynamic	Characterized by *power* and energy
geo-	earth	geology	The study of the *earth*
helio-	sun	heliotrope	Any plant that turns toward the *sun*
hydro-	water	hydroponics	Growing of plants in *water* reinforced with nutrients
hypno-	sleep	hypnosis	A state of sleep induced by suggestion
magni-	great, big	magnify	To enlarge, to make *bigger*
man(u)-	hand	manuscript	Written by *hand*
mono-	one	monoplane	Airplane with *one* wing
ortho-	straight	orthodox	Right, true, *straight* opinion
–pod	foot	pseudopod	False *foot*
psycho-	mind	psychology	Study of the *mind* in any of its aspects
pyro-	fire	pyrometer	An instrument for measuring temperatures
terra-	earth	terrace	A raised platform of *earth*
thermo-	heat	thermo-electricity	Electricity produced by *heat*
zoo	animal	zoology	The study of *animals*

natural learning processes.[6] We know that before a child can run, he must first learn to walk, and before walking, he must learn to toddle, and before toddling, he must learn to crawl.

We know, too, that a child can pronounce the letter *P* at age three and one-half; the letter *N* at age four and one-half; but, the letter *R,* is usually not pronounced clearly until age seven and one-half.

There are many other skills that develop in tune with physical growth and general maturation. In all these processes, we find these four characteristics.

1. Skills proceed from the simple to the complex.
2. Each skill is developed in an orderly sequence of steps.
3. Each step is at a different level of difficulty.
4. No significant step may be skipped. It seems that each step develops the muscle or brain pattern that makes the next step possible.

[6]Much of the discussion in this section is based on an article by Dean Trembly, "Intellectual Abilities as Motivating Factors," *Japanese Psychological Research,* Vol. 10, No. 2, July, 1968, pp. 104-108.

From his analytical research over the past thirty years, O'Connor has concluded that learning new words is much like any other skill. We proceed from simple words to more difficult ones in an orderly sequence. The difficulty or ease of learning a word does not depend on

its length	teachers
its frequency of use	books
its geographic origin	parents
its pronunciation	

Instead, the difficulty of a word depends on the complexity of the *idea* that it stands for. Defining words with simple synonyms does not provide the learner with a background sufficient to think with the words. Since words stand for ideas, the ideas behind them should also be learned.

S. I. Hayakawa, the noted semanticist, agrees with this view. He questions the old-fashioned notion that the way to study words is to concentrate one's attention exclusively on words. Hayakawa suggests that words should be understood in relationship to other words, not only other words on the same level, but also words at a higher level (more abstract) and words at a lower level (more concrete).

Principles Governing the Learning of Words

The following specific findings by O'Connor form the basis for the frontier vocabulary system:

The easier words are learned first, then the harder ones.

At the forward edge of the mass of all the words that have been mastered, is the individual's *frontier*. Only a very few words *beyond the frontier* have already been mastered.

Figure 7-2   A Constellation of Words from One Root.

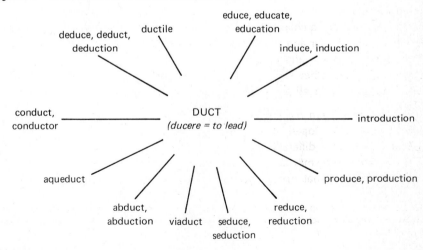

The greatest learning takes place in the frontier area (Edgar Dale calls it the "twilight zone") that lies between the line where all the words have been mastered and the line where no words are known. (See Figure 7-3.)

The most significant characteristic of the words in the twilight zone is that they are, to some extent, *familiar*. The maximum advancement in our own mastery of words takes place in the twilight zone, where hundreds of almost-known words need only a slight straightening out to make them familiar.

Learning becomes extremely inefficient, and actually breaks down, whenever a person skips the twilight zone and tries first to learn totally unknown words.

Your familiarity with words on the frontier means that you already have a piece of the word or its definition. You may, for example, know how to pronounce the word and know its general meaning. Or you may know only one facet of its several meanings. The important point is this: By singling out a frontier word and learning its specific meaning, or its several definitions, you can master the word with a minimum of time and effort.

By working continually on the frontier, you will be making rapid progress in mastering words, thus extending the forward edge of your frontier into the twilight zone. At the same time, you will continually be creating new frontier words to conquer. As the process continues, the frontier will enter into the area that was formerly the zone of totally unknown words.

The key principle to remember is that your frontier words are always the easiest and the most natural ones to master. Best of all, you will never run out of frontier words.

Examples of Frontier Words

On the following pages we have listed a great many frontier words. (Of course, they may not be your own personal frontier words, but they are typical of the breed.)

Answers to Vocabulary Quiz				
1. (2)	11. (3)	21. (1)	31. (4)	41. (2)
2. (1)	12. (1)	22. (4)	32. (4)	42. (4)
3. (4)	13. (2)	23. (2)	33. (3)	43. (1)
4. (4)	14. (4)	24. (2)	34. (1)	44. (3)
5. (1)	15. (4)	25. (3)	35. (2)	45. (3)
6. (3)	16. (4)	26. (4)	36. (4)	46. (1)
7. (4)	17. (4)	27. (2)	37. (4)	47. (4)
8. (4)	18. (3)	28. (2)	38. (4)	48. (4)
9. (1)	19. (4)	29. (4)	39. (3)	49. (4)
10. (3)	20. (1)	30. (1)	40. (4)	50. (3)

Figure 7-3 The Concept of Frontier Words.

ZONE OF KNOWN WORDS

These are the words already mastered. They are used in reading, writing, listening, and thinking.

The Edge of the Frontier

TWILIGHT ZONE

The words in this zone are the frontier words. They are somewhat familiar.

ZONE OF TOTALLY UNKNOWN WORDS

An occasional word, like an island in an unknown sea, might have been discovered and made one's own because of necessity.

From these examples you will readily see why frontier words are the easiest to master. They already provide a "handle," a meaning or an association. A person may have already brought a great deal of interest and imagination to the word. All he needs is to straighten out some of the irregularities and he will have a precise, full-blown word-concept of his own.

Sound somewhat alike.   In the following pairs of words, the person mistakes one of the words for the other. For example, students have written, "The man was arrested for the *elicit* use of drugs."

illicit   = Not permitted; improper; unlawful
elicit   = To draw out; as, to *elicit* truth by discussion
bizarre   = Odd, extravagant, or eccentric in style or mode
bazaar   = A fair for the sale of fancy wares, toys, etc.
magnet   = An iron bar having the power to attract iron
magnate   = A person prominent in the management of a large industry; as, an oil *magnate*
criterion   = A standard of judging
centurion   = A captain in the Roman army

Look somewhat alike. The following pairs of words are frequently confused because they look so much alike.

posterity	=	All future generations
prosperity	=	Success, good fortune
psychic	=	A person apparently sensitive to nonphysical forces
physique	=	One's body or a type of body
derelict	=	Given up by the owner; abandoned
dialect	=	A local or provincial form of a language
marital	=	Pertaining to marriage
martial	=	Pertaining to war, as *martial* music

Used together. Like a chameleon, one word takes on the color of the other. There are many words frequently used in pairs and in the same context. These words are so strongly associated as pairs that when they are separated from their usual context, many people still attribute to each word (the ones in italics below) the meaning of the pair.

Pair	Incorrect Meaning	Correct Meaning
prodigal son	wandering	wasteful expenditure; a spendthrift
anonymous donor	generous	name kept secret
exotic flower	beautiful	introduced from a foreign country
capital crime	important	punishable by death

Suggest an embedded word. Some words often incorporate a smaller, more common word which, in itself, has a definite meaning. So it is quite natural to guess or attribute to the new word the meaning of the small, embedded common word.

Word	Incorrect Meaning	Correct Meaning
succulent	To suck up like a vacuum cleaner	Juicy; having juicy tissues, most cacti do
ramify	To butt, as with a long log	To divide or spread out into branches, or ramifications
longevity	Tall	Length of life; long-lived
strident	Having a long stride	Harsh-sounding; shrill
archaic	Having arches	Old-fashioned; antiquated

Prefix-root trap. If only a prefix or root is known, one can occasionally infer the wrong meaning for an unfamiliar word.

Word	Incorrect Meaning	Correct Meaning
sublime	Underneath the ground	Elevated or exalted; noble
biweekly	Twice a week	Occurring every two weeks
ingenious	"in" equals not; not a genius; not very bright	Having high mental powers, clever
preponderance	To ponder, to think beforehand	Superiority of weight, influence
expound	To flatten out	To set forth; as, to *expound* a theory

Right church, wrong pew. Some words are one-directional. For example, *infer* means "to draw out," whereas *imply* means "to put in." Also, some words are used with the correct meaning but in the wrong context.

Word	Correct Definition	Wrong Use
dwindle	To diminish; decrease	The money *dwindled* in slowly.
senility	Old age, usually people	The chair is an antique because of its *senility*.
affable	Pleasant; gracious; courteous (people)	We had an *affable* trip.
prolific	Multiplying fast	Ralph gets A's in arithmetic because he's *prolific*.

Slightly more than a case of spelling. These pairs of look-alikes and sound-alikes can lead to humorous consequences if mixed up.

The town's *Hysterical* Society held its regular meeting in the museum.
  Historical: based on history; former events and people.
  Hysterical: wildly emotional

The bride and groom were happy and *contentious*.
  Content: happy and satisfied
  Contentious: quarrelsome

They found the mountain air clear and *accelerating*.
  Exhilarating: enlivening
  Accelerating: gathering speed

The prize was awarded *posthumorously*.
  Posthumously: occurring after one's death
  Posthumorously: no such word

The *pastoral* colors made the room bright and gay.

Pastel: a soft, delicate hue

Pastoral: relating to rural life and scenes

Many stories have come out of Tibet about the *Abdominal* Snowman.

Abominable Snowman: A manlike creature, reportedly seen on the high slopes of the mountains of Tibet.

Abdominal: relating to the belly

How to Find Your Frontier Words

Here is how to find your own frontier words: first, be aware of your daily speech, and make a list of the more unusual words you use. It will be a most rewarding experience when you look them up in an unabridged dictionary. Almost always you will gain a sharper definition. Furthermore, you will find (and now you are ready for them) one of two additional meanings that will truly turn the words into full-blown concepts, thus enabling you to communicate your ideas to others more easily and accurately.

Second, there are many words that you recognize in reading, but that you do not use in speaking and writing. From this source choose carefully *only* the words that appeal to you, that is, the words which fit your personality. These will be easy to learn because you already recognize them, you know the approximate meaning from constant context, and best of all, you want to learn them. They are your type of words.

Third, listen attentively while other people speak. The chances are great that you will recognize and know the general meaning of all the words you hear. Choose from this stream of speech the words that appeal to you—words that you feel are your type, and that you could easily incorporate into your own speech pattern.

Fourth, after writing out the definition for your frontier word, look for its opposite. If it interests you, learn that word too. Learning pairs of contrasting words creates the strong force of spontaneous suggestion—either word suggests the other. For example, when you think of *genuine* you also think of *artificial*; the word *happiness* suggests *sadness*; you may associate *apathetic* and *animate*, *haphazard* and *orderly*. Each word brings instantly to mind two concepts, and we can juxtapose these concepts for lively thinking, speaking, and writing.

Making the Frontier Vocabulary System Work

Use the 3 x 5 card plan. Here is how this flexible plan works.

1. When a word is encountered that cannot be precisely defined, copy on a 3 x 5 card the entire sentence in which the word occurs. Underline the word so that it stands out.

2. When a small number of these cards have accumulated, look up the words in an unabridged dictionary.

3. On the same side of the card that bears the excerpted sentence, the word with its syllables and diacritical markings should be printed so that accurate pronunciation is possible. You will find it much easier to use the word in conversation if you practice saying it out loud. Nothing else should be placed on the front of the card, unless you wish to footnote the source of your sentence, phrase, or word.

4. Now use the reverse side of the card. If the word has been made up of a prefix and a root, record this information on the card. Knowing the derivation of the word and some of its ancestry will help you learn the word with greater precision.

5. Write the several definitions, or variations of the definitions, on the reverse side. Place an asterisk beside the definition that best fits the word as it was used in your original sentence. Figure 7-4 shows two typical cards.

6. Carry about a dozen of these filled-out cards in your shirt pocket or hand bag, so that they will be handy to review whenever there is a spare moment. You could look at them when standing in a cafeteria line, waiting for a bus, sitting in someone's outer office, and so on.

Figure 7-4 These two cards happen to show a pair of words that are opposite, or complementary. Such words studied side-by-side are bound to take on more precise meaning. Notice that the front of each card shows the new word underlined in a complete sentence. It also shows how to pronounce the word and its variations. The reverse of each card defines prefixes and roots and gives important dictionary definitions of the word. An asterisk is placed beside the definition that most nearly matches the use of the word on the front of the card. Brief synonyms are also given.

FRONT

His silence implied that he, at least, did not disagree with my statement.

im-ply   (ĭm-plī´)
im-plied´ (ĭm-plīd´)

REVERSE

[im = in] [plicare = fold]
[implicare = to fold in; to involve]

1. To express indirectly; to suggest; to hint or hint at.
*2. To involve when not expressly stated in words or by signs.
syn: Involve

FRONT

From his silence and manner, I inferred that he agreed with my statement.

in-fer´   (ĭn-fûr´)
in-ferred´ (ĭn-fûrd´)
in-fer´ring (ĭn-fûr´)

REVERSE

[in = in] [ferre = to bring(out)]

1. To derive by reasoning; to conclude from facts or premises.
*2. To surmise; to guess

syn: deduce, conclude

7. Always look at the front side of the card. The word should be pronounced correctly, the sentence read completely, then the word defined, not necessarily verbatim in dictionary language, but meaningfully in your own language. All this should be done before looking at the definition on the back.

8. After you have defined the word to the best of your ability, turn the card over to check on the accuracy of the definition.

9. If you are not satisfied with your definition, place a dot on the front of the card in the upper right-hand corner. The next time you go through your cards, a dot will remind you that you missed on a previous try. When a card has three or more dots, it is time to give that word some special attention.

10. After the small stack of cards has been mastered, return the cards to a file and pick up additional ones for mastering.

11. The words that have been mastered should be reviewed from time to time.

With the mastering of the precise meaning of each frontier word, there will be more than a corresponding advance in your reading, writing, speaking, and thinking.

8

IMPROVE YOUR GENERAL READING SKILLS

WALTER PAUK

NANCY V. WOOD

It is difficult to answer the seemingly simple question, "How can I improve my *reading?*" There are many different purposes in reading, and many different techniques that can be used, and all are included in the single word, *reading.*

It has been said that one can tell what is highly valued in a culture by the number of words used to describe a single object. The desert Bedouin, for example, has thirty-six separate and distinct words to describe the *camel:* it may be young, old, male, female, for riding, military use, pack-carrying, and so forth. There is no question as to the life-and-death importance of the word *snow* to the Eskimo, who has forty to fifty separate and distinct words for it. In the Philippines, where rice is an important food, ninety-two varieties of rice are specified. In our culture, we find many words for horses and cattle. We have words like *filly, foal, colt, mare, stallion,* and *gelding.* For *cattle,* we have *cow, calf, bull, bullock* and *heifer.* But for reading, we have only one word, despite the fact that there are as many varieties of reading as of camels, horses, cattle, snow, or rice.

Consider, for example, the many different purposes for which we read—and this short list is far from complete.

1. *Leisure reading.* To relax for an hour or refresh our minds we read popular magazines, novels (both easy and hard), biographies, popular histories, and so on.
2. *Reading to keep up-to-date.* Newspapers and news magazines fill us in on local, national, and international events and issues.
3. *Reading for professional information.* Professional and trade journals and a variety of special magazines give us background information for our particular interests and occupations.

99

4. *Studying.* We need to read textbooks, how-to books, repair manuals, and memoranda in some detail. They supply specific information we need in order to make decisions.

The manner in which we read depends on our purpose. For relaxation, we may skim a news magazine and spend most of the time looking at the pictures. Or, if we are a chess enthusiast, we may study the details of a game reported in the same magazine. Here are some of the techniques of reading.

Skimming	Close, slow reading
Scanning	Note-taking
Skipping	Memorizing

When a variety of reading techniques is combined with a variety of reading materials, hundreds of combinations are possible. No wonder it is ordinarily so difficult to answer the question, "How can I improve my *reading?*" The right combination of reading material and reading technique depends primarily on your purpose. However, when this question is asked by a student, it is usually safe to assume that he means, "How can I *speed* up my reading so I can finish my homework in half the time with high comprehension and almost complete retention?" There is no easy answer to that question, despite the numerous brochures, newspapers, magazines, and television episodes that extol the marvels of speed reading. Many students, as well as the general public, are convinced that speed reading is a technique readily acquirable and universally applicable to any page of print. Unfortunately, speed reading is virtually useless to anyone who desires to learn from the printed page.

If you desire high comprehension and almost complete retention, then you must use systematic study techniques. There is no other way to master your studies. This entire book is devoted to making mastery learning a reality through use of efficient study skills. And this chapter focuses on specific skills you can use in reading. Before examining them, however, we must take a little time to explain the drastic limitations inherent in the concept of speed reading and its companion "technique," that of eliminating vocalization.

We emphasize these negative aspects for two reasons: first, for academic improvement through speed reading, and we don't want you to spend your time, money, and energy on this dead end. Second, by "clearing the decks" of an "easy way" to reading and studying, the stage is set for presenting study systems that can do the job.

SOME FACTS ABOUT SPEED READING

Newspapers have carried several sensational stories about high school students reading at astronomical speeds. One student, as the story put it, was "clocked" at the rate of 40,000 words per minute. Another student was timed at 50,000 words per minute. A peculiar characteristic of all such stories is that they add the statement, "with nearly 100 percent comprehension."

How fast is 40,000 words per minute? By dividing 300 (the number of words on an average page) into 40,000, we find that to attain a reading rate of 40,000 per minute, a person would have to read 133 pages per minute! The reader (or more accurately, the page turner) would have less than one-half of a second to spend on a page. Some students find it difficult to *turn* 133 pages within a minute, let alone see any words on those pages; some students who are fast page-turners might visually snatch a word or two from each page as it flutters by. This would hardly lead to "almost 100 percent comprehension." With such an assortment of quickly snatched words, however, the student would be hard put to reconstruct the ideas contained in the 133 pages.

The basic premise of speed-reading advocates is this: The eye is able to see a vast number of words in one fixation. Some say the eye can see phrases at a glance; others say entire lines; still others say paragraphs at a time; and a zealous few say an entire page at a glance. But let us look at the facts.

First, eye movement photography clearly shows that the average college student makes about four eye fixations per second. Second, it is a fact that the eyes can see plainly *only* when they pause during this momentary fixation. Third, eye movement photography shows that the eye sees an average of only 1.1 words during each fixation. Eye movement photography records seldom discover any person, trained or untrained, who has a usable span of recognition of over 2.5 words.

Using these facts arithmetically, we find that only a most unusual person can see 10 words per second (2.5 words per fixation x 4 fixations per second). So, in sixty seconds it is arithmetically possible for the eye to take in 600 words. And this calculation does not include the time needed to move the eyes from one group of words to another, time to return the eyes to the beginning of each line, and time to turn pages.

The Peep-Sight Experiment

Most students learn more about how the eye works (at least, the outward manifestations) through one easy experiment than through listening to a lecture on eye-movements. Here is the experiment and how it works.

Punch a hole through the big, black dot in the center of Figure 8-1; then place the "back" of the page to your eye, facing the printed experiment toward your partner, who will read it silently. As your partner reads, count the number of eye fixations (stops) that he makes per line. You will notice that the eye moves across each line in a series of pauses and fast movements—like a typewriter. After your partner has finished reading, let him observe your eyes as you read.

Instructions to the reader.   When reading the material, actually slow down your rate so that your partner will be able to count, as well as carefully observe, the eye movements.

Calculations.   You can make a rough calculation of the number of words perceived by the eye by dividing the number of eye pauses into the total number of words on a line. For example, if the first line is comprised of eleven words and the reader pauses five times, he is taking in roughly two words per fixation.

Figure 8-1 The Peep-Sight Experiment*.

A knowledge of words, what they are and how they function, is the first and last essential of all liberal education. As Carlyle says, "If we but think of it, all that a University or final highest school can do for us is still but what the first school began doing — teach us to *read*." When a student has been trained to make the words of any page of general writing yield their full meaning, he has in his possession the primary instrument of all higher education.

●

In these days when the nation is asking that its schools produce good citizens first and specialists second, there is a marked need for a rich and wide "universal" training of the mind. This book on reading is designed to forward the process by which the whole mind, intellectual and emotional, becomes a more accurate instrument for the reception and transmission of thoughts and sensations. If our system of education does not so train the minds of its students, if it does not teach them to recognize differences, to distinguish shades of meaning, to feel as by intuition not only the hypocrisy of the demagogue and the flattery of the bootlicker but also the depth of a statesman like Lincoln and the insight of a poet like Shakespeare, it fails of its purpose.

---

*See page 101 for directions.

From E.A. Tenney and R.C. Wardle, *Intelligent Reading* (New York: F.S. Crofts & Co., 1943), preface.

Try it!

The main purpose of the experiment is to give you first-hand evidence of natural eye movement. Don't try to manipulate your eyes in some unnatural manner, such as trying to see an entire line in one fixation. By accepting the natural way in which eyes look at words, you can improve your reading by building on reality instead of on fiction.

The basic premise of speed-reading advocates—that the eye can take in a vast number of words at one fixation—is rejected by other evidence as well.

In the *American Journal of Optometry*, Richard Feinberg reported that when a reader focuses on a word, "only four to five letters immediately around the fixation point are seen with 100 percent acuity" (sharpness). The letters of words half an inch from the point of fixation are seen with only 40 percent acuity, and those at one inch from the point of fixation are seen with only 26 percent acuity. If the reader has less than normal vision, the fall-off in acuity is even more pronounced.

How Much Can the Mind See?

Although our emphasis has been on the question, "How many words can the eye see in one fixation?" a more basic question is, "How does the mind process the words that are imprinted on the retina of the eye?"

If the eye takes in three words at a single fixation, does the mind impose a meaning upon the entire three words instantly and simultaneously, or must the mind consider each word in sequence, one at a time, to get at the meaning of each word? If the mind must take from the retina of the eye only one word at a time, however swiftly, wouldn't it be easier for the eye to deliver to the mind one word at a time in the first place?

The Limitation of the Mind

Research done at Massachusetts Institute of Technology, using M.I.T. undergraduates, gives scientific evidence that the mind can attend to only one word at a time. In one part of the study, as reported in *Scientific American,*

> . . . the letters of two different six-letter words were presented simultaneously in pairs for brief intervals of time. If the words were *canvas* and *dollar,* for example, *c* and *d* would appear in the first frame, *a* and *o* in the second frame and so on to the end of the words.[1]

You can see how this test was presented by imagining that you yourself were shown the following frames one at a time.

When the M.I.T. students were asked to identify either one of the two words, they scored correctly on 57 percent of the trials; but when they were asked to identify both words, the score was only 0.2 percent (one correct report in 420 trials). The researchers concluded that "even the skilled reader has considerable difficulty forming a perception of more than one word at a time."[2]

A reader often has the impression that he is seeing more than one word at a fixation because the eye is moving rapidly from left to right, taking in words in rapid sequence. It is almost like watching a movie. Although each film frame is a still picture, we subjectively see motion and action when they are projected at a rate of twenty-two frames per second. Similarly, words projected on the brain at the rate of seven or eight words per second give us the impression of living, moving ideas. Nevertheless, we are still "viewing" only one word at a time.

Speed Reading and Remembering

A final objection to speed reading is that it does not give the mind time to consolidate new information. Even if the eye were able to take in several thousand words a minute (impossible) and the brain were able to comprehend the meaning of them all (impossible), the mind still would not have time to consolidate the meaning before it was assaulted by the next batch of several thousand words. As we saw in the chapter on building a strong memory, the brain requires a certain period of time in which to convert a temporary idea into a permanent one.

[1]Paul A. Kolers, "Experiments in Reading," *Scientific American* 227:1 (July 1972): 84-91. Copyright © 1972, Scientific American, Inc. All rights reserved.
[2]*Ibid.*

SOME FACTS ABOUT VOCALIZATION

For many years it has been thought that vocalizing while reading was a bad habit and that it should be eliminated. There are four types of vocalizers: the person who *whispers* each word audibly, the one who pronounces each word with *lip* movements, the one who moves only his *vocal chords,* and the one who *thinks* the sound of each word. Those who try to eliminate vocalization claim that vocalizing slows down one's reading speed. This claim is probably true. However, the assumption that vocalization can and should be eliminated is highly questionable, because there is no research to support it. On the contrary, there is strong evidence that vocalization of one kind or another is an essential part of all reading.

A Practical Experiment

It is often difficult to convince people that sub-vocalization (silent pronunciation) takes place in all readers to some extent. Now silent pronunciation is not the syllable-by-syllable pronunciation of oral reading; rather, when sub-vocalization takes place, the sound of the word is heard by the "inner ear" instantly and whole.

The following excerpt, using the English alphabet, is written phonetically. For those who claim that they read with their eyes, not with their voices, this excerpt will be challenging. Most people find that they cannot "sound out" the words with their eyes; but when they pronounce the words either aloud or silently, they know the word and understand it. Watch yourself carefully; it is easy to pronounce the word with the voice mechanism so subtly that you may think you have read the word only with your eyes.

■   An Interesting Letter

dir mis bowyer: .just to sho yu what i meen, this iz ritten in stabilized inglish orthography.

.i am konvinst that our idiotik orthografy iz the kulprit in our "kriminal" ejukashun, with regorrd tu reeding. .even the beginer notisez that "a" and "A" orr not the same letter—and luzez konfidens in eny techer or parent hu trize tu tel him thay orr the same. .then he gets sulen and diskurajd—quiting skule at the furst opurtunity.

.oltho our alfabet iz insufishent for truly fonetik spelling, it iz quite sufishent for a majur impruvment—bi mirly stabilizing the yuse ov the letterz we du hav. .the fakt that eche ov the voulz haz tu basik sounds (long and short) iznt purtikeulurly konfeuzing. .the konfeuzhun storrts when thay orr aloud tu tresspass upon wunanutherz teritory. .the spelling "w-i-n-d" never kozes eny truble in spite ov its tu pronunsiashunz, and it mite be kunsiderd fonetik ethur way! .the final silent "e" jenurally indikates a long voul in the last silabl, and a duble konsonant jenurally indikates a preseding short voul.

.eny sujestshun i mite ofer for aproching the "pourz-that-be" tu make them realize the tru siriusness ov the sitchuashun wood be baste on the fakt that our dikshuneryz du not diktate our orthografy; thay mirly rekord that which iz in komun yuse. .in short, eny chanje in spelling kumz thru "komun yusaje" bi the laymen—or yusaje ov the more kulchural 50%, i shood say. .and the very fakt that the dikshuneryz rekord this aprovd pronunsiashun and spelling opurates tu make it, tu sum extent, the kreator ov our yusaje, rather than thru ofishal dekree from the "hi-ups." .thus the best we kan hope for iz ofishal akseptans ov the chanjez inishiated bi the laymun (inkluding studentz).[3] ■

What Does Research Say?

Robert A. Hall, Jr. an internationally famous linguist, has this to say about vocalization, or inner speech:

■ It is commonly thought that we can read and write in complete silence, without any speech taking place. True, many people learn to suppress the movements of their organs of speech when they read, so that no sound comes forth; but nevertheless, inside the brain, the impulses for speech are still being sent forth through the nerves, and only the actualization of these impulses is being inhibited on the muscular level, as has been shown by numerous experiments. No act of reading takes place without a certain amount of subvocalization, as this kind of "silent speech" is called, and we normally subvocalize, when we write, also. Many slow readers retain the habit of reading out loud, or at least partially moving their lips as they read; fast readers learn to skip from one key point to another, and to guess at what must lie in between. The good rapid reader knows the subject-matter well enough to guess intelligently; the poor reader does not know how to choose the high spots or guess what lies between them. As the rate of reading increases, the actual muscular movements of pronunciation are reduced; but, just as soon as the going gets difficult, the rate of reading slows down and the muscular movements of pronunciation increase again, even with skilled rapid readers.

From these considerations, it is evident that the activities of speaking and reading cannot be separated. . . . Curiously enough, literary scholars are especially under the delusion that it is possible to study "written language" in isolation, without regard to the language as it is spoken; this is because they do not realize the extent to which, as we have just pointed out, all reading and writing necessarily involve an act of speech on the part of both writer and reader.[4] ■

[3]Reprinted by permission from Leo G. Davis, "An Interesting Letter," *Spelling Progress Bulletin,* 1 (June 1961): 2.
[4]Robert A. Hall Jr., *New Ways to Learn a Foreign Language* (New York: Bantam Books, Inc., 1966), pp. 28-9.

Åke Edfeldt, of the University of Stockholm Institute of Reading Research, has studied vocalization with a team of medical doctors who used electrodes to detect movement in the lips, tongues, and vocal cords of volunteer readers. After exhaustive medical tests, Edfeldt concluded:

> On the basis of the present experimental results, earlier theories concerning silent speech in reading may be judged. These theories often appear to have been constructed afterwards, in order to justify some already adopted form of remedial reading. In opposition to most of these theories, we wish to claim that silent speech occurs in the reading of all persons.
>
> In any case, it seems quite clear that all kinds of training aimed at removing silent speech should be discarded.[5]

A Final Word

Decades ago, E. L. Thorndike said that "reading is thinking." And psychologists agree that thinking is silent speech. So if reading is thinking, and thinking is silent speech, then reading must also be silent speech. It seems that if we spend our time and energy trying to knock out vocalization, we are in fact trying to knock out comprehension. Vocalization cannot and should not be eliminated, because it is the main part of the reading process.

HOW TO IMPROVE YOUR READING

As we have seen, improvement in reading cannot come through any mechanical technique of turning pages faster, or of moving the eyes in some artificial pattern. There is no magic in such concoctions.

Most of the methods for improvement put forth in this section require hard work, but the rewards are great. A few of the ways require only the willingness to try a new way of using old knowledge; and here, too, the rewards are great.

The Intonation Way

Don't try to suppress vocalization. It is part of the reading-comprehending process. Use it to help you read faster and with a high degree of understanding.

The most efficient use of vocalization is through the process of *intonation,* which is the rise and fall of the voice in pronouncing a sentence. In other words, reading with intonation means reading with expression. The importance of intonation is that it provides a natural means for bundling up individual words into meaningful mental "bites."

When you use this system, your eyes move rapidly and no sound is emitted from your vocal chords, but your mind swings along each line with an intonational rhythm that is heard by the "inner ear."

[5] Åke W. Edfeldt, *Silent Speed and Silent Reading* (Chicago: The University of Chicago Press, 1960), p. 154. Copyright © 1960 by University of Chicago Press and reprinted with permission.

The passage in Figure 8-2 has been divided into thought units through intonation. The units or clusters of words are shown by the extra spaces and slash-marks separating them. Different readers may group these same words into different clusters, depending on their individual intonation. Read the passage silently, letting the eyes move rapidly over the lines and permitting the "inner voice" to cluster the words through intonation. When you read with intonation, you will probably notice how rapidly your eyes move and how easy it is to comprehend the meaning.

To make silent intonation a regular habit, try reading aloud. In the privacy of your room, spend ten or fifteen minutes reading aloud a chapter from a novel. Read with exaggerated expression, as if you were reading a part in a dramatic play. Such practice establishes in the mind your own patterns of speech, so that you will "hear" them more readily when you read silently.

The Vocabulary Way

There is probably no surer or sounder way to make a deep and permanent improvement in one's reading ability than by building a strong, precise vocabulary. In a precise vocabulary, every word is learned as a concept: You know its Latin and Greek ancestry, its principal definition as well as several secondary ones, its synonyms and the subtle differences among them, and its antonyms. Then, when your eyes fall upon a word that you know thoroughly, this vast store of knowledge will flash before you, illuminating the sentence, the paragraph, and the idea which the author is trying to convey. If you have not yet read Chapter 7 on building a precise vocabulary, this would be a good time to do so.

The Background Way

A tremendous improvement in your reading skills comes through reading good books. Here's why: First, you will be practicing the art of reading. Second, and more important, you will be storing a stock of concepts, ideas, events, and names that will lend meaning to your later reading. This kind of information is useful surprisingly often.

For example, the following statement would be rich with meaning to a person who already knew the full story of Scylla and Charybdis:

> In dealing with management and labor, the arbitrator must be as wary as passing between the Scylla and Charybdis.

A few words of explanation: In Greek mythology we find that Scylla, a beautiful maiden, was loved by a sea-god, Glaucus. Circe, an enchantress, became jealous and changed Scylla into a dangerous monster that she rooted to a rock in the Messina Straits, a narrow neck of water separating Sicily from Italy. Opposite Scylla was the whirlpool of Charybdis, where the water was so turbulent that the "furious waves mounting up touched the very sky." This narrow neck of water was a terrifying passage for mariners. It could be safely made only if the captain steered a perfect course; unfortunately, to avoid getting too close to Charybdis, the ship

Figure 8-2   Reading by Word Clusters: the Intonation Way.

Athens and Sparta / were both Greek cities / and their people / spoke a common language. / In every other respect / they were different. / Athens rose high from the plain. / It was a city / exposed to the fresh breezes / from the sea, / willing to look / at the world / with the eyes / of a happy child. / Sparta, / on the other hand, / was built / at the bottom / of a deep valley, / and used the surrounding mountains / as a barrier / against foreign thought. / Athens / was a city of busy trade. / Sparta / was an armed camp. /*

From *The Story of Mankind* by Henry B. van Loon and Gerard W. van Loon. Reprinted by permission of Liveright. Copyright © 1972 by Henry B. van Loon and Gerard W. van Loon.

would usually sail within Scylla's grasp. Odysseus steered too close to Scylla, and in a frightful ordeal lost six of his crew to the monster.

Now to interpret our original statement: the arbitrator must be perfectly impartial. If he leans slightly toward labor, he will be accused by management as being unfairly pro-labor, and if he leans slightly in the other direction, he will be accused of being pro-management. In other words, the arbitrator is in between the devil (Scylla) and the deep blue sea (Charybdis). Although it takes some time to describe these two words, a person who already knows the full story would hardly pause in his reading, for this store of information would be ready to spring to his conscious mind when triggered by the words Scylla and Charybdis.

Building a background.   Begin your extra reading today. Do not wait for the "someday-when-I-have-more-time." You'll never have as much extra time as you have now. Look how Herbert Morrison found time. His formal education stopped at elementary school. By educating himself through reading books, he rose to the leadership of the British Labor Party, and was once deputy prime minister of England. His description of his education follows.

> The thrill of learning seized me—one of the greatest joys I had ever known. I struggled for time and a place to read. I rose in the morning an hour earlier than usual. After dressing in my heatless room above the grocery store, I wrapped myself in a blanket and read as much as I could before the grocer's wife called me to breakfast. My room was too cold to read in at night, so I went to a coffeehouse a few blocks away. There I settled myself with a book at a corner table, ordered a cup of cocoa for a halfpenny and nursed it through the late evenings. That way I read Ruskin, Matthew Arnold and Prince Kropotkin's *Fields, Factories and Workshops.*
>
> Later, when I became a telephone operator in a brewery, I read Herbert Spencer's *First Principles of Psychology* and Charles Darwin's *Origin of Species* while riding to and from work on the bus or train.[6]

[6]Reprinted with permission from the March, 1956 *Reader's Digest,* Copyright © 1956 by the Reader's Digest Association, Inc.

Never too late. One often hears students in their late teens or very early twenties say, "I guess I should have started reading more when I was young. It's too late now." This seems ironic when one recalls that Grandma Moses took up painting at seventy-nine. Remember the popular saying, "Today is the first day of the rest of your life." You *can* start now to do what you want to do.

Yes! But what shall I read?   First, read the *great* books; for it is in these books that the wisdom of the ages is passed on to posterity. In these books you will have a chance to "talk" with princes, kings, philosophers, travelers, playwrights, scientists, artists, and novelists. Time and life are too short for anything else. You will need some guidance, however. Then, within the framework of such guidance, begin with the books and subject matter that interest you. Don't worry about narrow interests. Once you begin reading, your interests, like the ripples caused by a dropped pebble, will naturally widen.

Here are some books that will guide you in the selection of books:

The Wonderful World of Books, edited by Alfred Stefferud (Mentor).

Books That Changed the World, by Robert B. Downs (Mentor).

A Guide to Basic Books, by Booksellers Catalog Service, Inc., (American Booksellers Association).

The Lifetime Reading Plan, by Clifton Fadiman (Avon).

Good Reading, edited by J. Sherwood Weber (Mentor).

Much Loved Books, by James O'Donnell Bennett (Premier).

Highlights of Modern Literature (Mentor).

The College and Adult Reading List of Books in Literature and Fine Arts, prepared by the Committee on College and Adult Reading List, National Council of Teachers of English (a Washington Square Press Book).

Reading for Success in College, a Student's Guide to Recommended Books for College Background Reading and a Practical Handbook for Developing College Study Skills, by Walter Pauk (Academia Press, P.O. Box 125, Oshkosh, Wisconsin 54901).

These not only tell you about books but also suggest titles, lists, and plans. Explore the possibilities, decide on your special interests, map out a course of action, and start reading. You will be pleasantly surprised at the results from even fifteen minutes a day.

Gibbon's way: great recall. The great English historian, Edward Gibbon (1737-1794), author of the famous book *Decline and Fall of the Roman Empire,* made constant use of the "great recall" technique. This is simply an organized and rather intense use of one's general background.

Before starting to read a new book, or before starting to write on any subject, Gibbon would spend hours alone in his study, or take a long walk alone to recall everything that he knew about the subject. As he pondered some major idea, he was continually surprised how many other ideas and fragments of ideas he would dredge up.

Gibbon's system was highly successful because he had some natural learning principles on his side.

1. His old ideas were brought to the forefront of his mind, ready for use.
2. His old ideas could act as magnetic centers for new ideas and new information.
3. This type of great recall promotes concentration.

The Paragraph Way[7]

Reading improvement means improvement of comprehension. There is no other way to make progress, and the place to start is with the paragraph.

The first step in mastering a paragraph is to understand its component parts. All expository paragraphs are made up of just three parts: main ideas, supporting material, and transitional words. Your job is to know the difference.

You may well remember that when you were learning to write compositions, the teacher would continually remind you that good writers build each paragraph around one main idea. The reason: it is easier for writers to organize and control their thoughts by taking up one idea at a time, supporting it with details, then going on to develop another idea in another paragraph. Knowing how writers write paragraphs should help you to read paragraphs: always try to locate main ideas.

To locate and isolate a main idea, it is helpful to know that most writers state the main idea, or at least provide a focus for the paragraph, in the *topic sentence*. The topic sentence most frequently is located at or near the beginning of the paragraph. Once stated, the writer's immediate job is to support the main idea by providing statistics, data, examples, comparisons, contrasts, analogies, and so forth.

In reading textbooks, your main job in each paragraph is to distinguish the main idea from its supporting material. If you should happen to fasten upon some interesting or exciting example and mistake it for the main idea, you will then misunderstand the author's point. One way to find your mistake is to focus your attention on the portion which you believe is the main idea, then try to relate everything else in the paragraph to it. If you find some *general* item that just doesn't support your chosen "main idea," then switch and try relating everything to that general item. If everything relates, then you have found the main idea.

One good way to keep alert is to read the entire paragraph, then go back to locate the main idea. In your own textbook, underline only the main idea, or write a brief summary in your own words in the margins of the page. This procedure will force you to make a choice. Also, the underlining or summary will preserve your efforts and understanding for later use when you are reviewing. When reviewing for an exam, all you need to do is follow the author's development of the chapter by skipping from one underlining or summary to another. A warning: do not underline so much that nothing stands out.

There are other types of paragraphs. Sometimes an idea is so big that the writer needs five or more paragraphs to develop it. In such cases, the usual procedure is to

[7]Adapted from an unpublished article by Nancy V. Wood, "Main Ideas."

place the main idea in one paragraph with a few additional sentences indicating that the following paragraphs will contain the supporting materials.

In addition to main idea paragraphs and supporting material paragraphs, there are introductory, transitional, and summary paragraphs. The introductory paragraphs contain no main ideas, but set the stage by outlining what is to come. The transitional paragraphs often mark a division, or connect two divisions. In them, the author may state that he has completed one cluster of ideas and is now moving on to another cluster. Summary paragraphs, of course, contain a restatement of all the main ideas.

The Organizational Pattern Way[8]

We have just discussed the importance of being able to distinguish the main ideas within paragraphs. But suppose an assigned chapter contains fifty paragraphs. Are you going to memorize fifty separate main ideas for tomorrow's class? Some students would try, but they would rarely succeed. There is a better way.

The human mind seeks order in everything and feels satisfied only when it can place new information in some sort of order. For example, if we are given a grocery list of twenty random items, we naturally begin grouping the items under such categories as meats, vegetables, dairy products, and breads to facilitate remembering. We even take a further step. If we know the layout of the store, we place the categories in the order that we would find them on the route we take as we push the market-cart up and down aisles.

In writing a chapter in which he wishes to present fifty ideas, the author would organize them in a manner roughly similar to the way we reorganized the grocery list. This organization makes it easier for the author to write the material, and for the reader to comprehend and remember it.

The organization of every chapter and every book is as much a part of its author's thinking as the facts and ideas he has to convey. It requires careful and conscious planning; and a study of the structure can further your understanding of any work.

The organization of a piece of writing is a highly individual matter, and no pattern is ever exactly repeated. But certain elements of organization can be identified in all coherent presentations. If you develop sensitivity to these in your reading, you should know where you have been, where you are at the moment, and where you are going. The purpose of this section is to help you see the pattern of organization in whatever you read.

Five elements of organization.   You know that every effective piece of writing has a beginning, a middle, and an end. In addition, it has a direction or goal, and it has numerous signposts to guide you along the way. This may sound too simple, but it is the heart of the problem both of grasping the facts and ideas present by others and of organizing your own. Let's examine in detail the elements of good organization.

1. *The introduction* may be found in any and all of several places: in the

[8]In this section I have drawn substantively on an unpublished article by Nancy V. Wood, "Organization."

preface to the book, in the first chapter, and in the initial paragraphs of each chapter. Often it is tempting to skip prefatory or introductory material, but this is usually a mistake. The introduction or the preface is there to perform one or more of three functions.

First, the author may try to inspire or motivate his readers by pointing out the importance or usefulness of the subject. Such introductions may be read rapidly since they contain very few ideas.

Second, the author may set forth the pattern of his organization for the entire book. An introduction of this sort should be read carefully, since the author will often outline all his main ideas for you. Then you will know what is coming and you can read to see how the author explains his ideas.

Third, an author may even show how his approach differs from that of other writers on the same subject. One author of a textbook on economics said something like this:

> I am not going to take the traditional approach of citing authorities to cover both sides of a question; rather, I am going to put forth my own critical and positive views without inhibition.

Any student who skipped reading this preface would be in for a difficult time, because he would probably find the ideas in that book difficult to relate to anything that he had previously studied in economics.

2. *The problem (or argument or objective)* is often stated in the preface as well as at the beginning of most chapters. It may be stated in a sentence or a paragraph. For example, the revised edition of a textbook in geology contains these sentences in its preface:

> Throughout the revised treatment the attempt is made to give the student an appreciation of Earth-features as the results of processes that are still active. Practical and philosophical aspects of geology in relation to mankind are given emphasis.[9]

Although it occupies very little space, it is of utmost importance. It provides the focus, and if you miss it you may founder aimlessly to the end. When you find the problem, argument, or objective, mark it or make a note of it, and keep it firmly in mind as you read on.

3. *The body* of the chapter and book usually amount to nine-tenths of the whole. It includes the point-by-point presentation of data or of steps in a process by which the author attempts to amplify his problem, argument, or objective. Here he gives his information or tries to support his point of view. Once you have the problem, argument, or objective clearly in mind, your main job in reading is to see *how* and with *what* the author develops and supports it. You will need to relate his topics, as he takes them up, grouping facts and data in a meaningful order so that you can more readily remember them.

4. *Transitions,* or guideposts, are invaluable clues to organization. They show the relationship among ideas and they indicate that the author is passing from one

[9]Chester R. Longwell et al., *Outlines of Geology,* 2nd. ed. (New York: John Wiley & Sons, 1941).

idea to another. Transitions may be elaborate: "Having discussed five causes for the flooding of our farm land, I would now like to turn to a consideration of ways to avoid such catastrophies in the future." Or transitions may be very simple, only a phrase: "in contrast to," "at the other extreme," "on the other hand," "What was the result? Just this . . . ." Frequently, an author uses an elaborate transition to take you from one main section to another section of equal importance. Shorter transitions are used to lead you from a main idea to a subordinate idea, or to show the relationship between two ideas in the same paragraph. A reader who becomes adept at spotting transitions will always know at what point the author stops talking about one idea and moves on to another.

Another technique employed by authors to clarify their organization is the use of headings and sub-headings to introduce the various main sections of a chapter. These headings are separated from the paragraphs of material and are in boldface or italic type. They are used extensively in textbooks. It is often tempting to ignore there headings when you read, but this is a mistake. A good reader will stop for a moment when he encounters a boldface heading and fix the idea or topic it suggests clearly in mind. Then he will read the following material to see how the author treats the new topic.

5. *The summary or conclusion* is used by the author to pull together and restate the important points already presented. Summary material gives you an opportunity to check your understanding of what you have read. We usually think of summaries as final statements at the end of a chapter or book. This is not the only place you might find a summary, however. Often an author uses an internal summary to restate the main points made in one small section of a chapter. Whenever you encounter summary material, whether it occurs within the chapter or at the end, you should note how much material is being summarized and how significant it is.

You will be amazed how much easier it is to follow a reading assignment or a lecture once you have in mind the general principles of organization and gain skill in following organization as you read. With practice, too, you will learn to see when a writer is successful or unsuccessful in organizing his materials, and you will be able to evaluate the validity of his conclusions from the way he presents his information or supports his problem, argument, or objective. You will also learn how to relate what you read to a meaningful pattern of your own.

Kinds of organization.   Beyond these general elements of coherent organization, there are certain kinds of organizational arrangements that are largely shaped by the nature of the material itself. Biography, history, and narrative, for example, fall readily into a *chronological* (time-related) pattern. Description of a house, machine, or geographical area is likely to assume a *spatial* (space-related) pattern. But most expository presentations—and this includes the greater part of what you will read for your assignments and will hear in lectures—are *topical,* that is, arranged according to logical divisions of the thought, rather than by order of occurrence in time or space.

Once you detect *chronological or spatial arrangement,* the pattern is usually easy to follow. Most stories, biographies, and historical accounts proceed chronological-ly, moving steadily from past to present, though occasionally a narrative will begin in the middle or even at the end and then go back to the beginning. When this happens there are usually clues, but the reader who has never encountered this kind of arrangement may be confused the first few times he meets it. On the other hand, nearly everyone is familiar with the so-called "flashback" technique, in which the main line of the story is occasionally interrupted by scenes that describe earlier events. Straight chronological order is also used in expository writing that explains a process—for example, how to pitch a tent, make a pair of shoes, or write a research paper. In such writing, the problem is not so much to find the pattern as to master the steps in the procedure.

Spatial arrangement usually offers even fewer complications. A geography of the United States may move from New England to the Middle Atlantic States to the Southeast, and so on; it will almost never skip from Maine to California and back to Massachusetts. But within such a large spatial pattern, there may be a number of topical headings that are not always immediately apparent.

Topical arrangement is a broad term that may cover a variety of patterns. Thus under each of the spatial divisions in a geography book, there may be such subjects as agriculture, industry, climate, topography, and population. If these are taken up in one-two-three order, without indication of any particular relationships among them, we have the simplest of all topical schemes, one that sets up topical headings or categories merely for the sake of presenting one thing at a time in clear and orderly fashion.

A more complex kind of topical arrangement—and one that is far more common—makes use of relationships among topics, particularly *cause and effect* relationships. Thus a geographer may argue that climate and topography influence agriculture, and that these in turn influence population. He may therefore begin his discussion of New England by describing the harsh winters, the thin and rocky soil, and then point out that for these reasons this is a poor agricultural region. He may then describe New England's seaports, fisheries, and abundance of water power, and show how these and other factors have affected commercial and industrial development. In both parts of the discussion he is using a topical arrangement which leads from cause to effect—and these relationships become as much a part of his total meaning as the facts of climate, rainfall, and production.

Many topical arrangements are even more complex. An economist discussing the great crash of 1929 would almost certainly divide his subject into three main parts: events leading up to the crash (causes); the catastrophe itself; and its aftermath (results). But he would not necessarily have to discuss them in this order. For dramatic effect he might begin with a description of those black days in October 1929 when ruined investors were throwing themselves from the windows of Wall Street office buildings, and move from that to a description of the plummeting stock market which caused their despair and suicide. Following the event itself, he might then go back to enumerate and analyze the causes of the crash—inflated stock values, excessive installment buying, and so on. Finally, he might discuss the long, slow recovery during the years of the great depression in the 1930's, the far-reaching results of the central event.

In following any topical organization, you should be alert to relationships, particularly causes and results. The clues to these are often suggested in introductory material in books and articles, and in the first minutes of lectures—so frequently lost in the flurry of opening your notebook and finding the place. Further clues to organization of topics can be found in transitions.

If you understand the basic types of organization, you can do a better job in your own written work—themes, research papers, answers to examination questions, and so on. The use of an appropriate pattern not only helps you put your thoughts in an order that is understandable to the reader, but it helps you say more nearly what you want to say.

The mind works best when it works logically. Orderly thinking can become habitual; and when it does, your reading, writing, and listening become much more productive.

The Pivotal Words Way

No words are so helpful while reading as the prepositions and conjunctions that guide your mind along the pathways of the author's ideas. A word like *furthermore* says, "Keep going!" *However* says, "Easy!" Master these words and phrases and you will almost immediately become a better reader, for they will whisper directions in your inner ear.

Additive words. These say, "Here's more of the same coming up. It's just as important as what we have already said."

also	further	moreover
and	furthermore	too
besides	in addition	

Equivalent words. They say, "It does what I have just said, but it does this too."

as well as	at the same time	similarly
equally important	likewise	

Amplification words. The author is saying, "I want to be sure that you understand my idea; so here's a specific instance."

for example (e.g.)	specifically	as
for instance	such as	like

Alternative words. These point up, "Sometimes there is a choice; other times there isn't."

either/or	other than
neither/nor	otherwise

Repetitive words. They say, "I said it once, but I'm going to say it again in case you missed it the first time."

again	in other words
to repeat	that is (i.e.)

Contrast and change words. "So far I've given you only one side of the story; now let's take a look at the other side."

but	on the contrary	still
conversely	on the other hand	though
despite	instead of	yet
however	rather than	regardless
nevertheless	even though	whereas
in spite of	notwithstanding	

Cause and effect words. "All this has happened; now I'll tell you why."

accordingly	since	then
because	so	thus
consequently	hence	therefore
for this reason		

Qualifying words. These say, "Here is what we can expect. These are the conditions we are working under."

if	although	unless
providing	whenever	

Concession words. They say, "Okay! We agree on this much."

accepting the data	granted that	of course

Emphasizing words. They say, "Wake up and take notice!"

above all	more important	indeed

Order words. The author is saying, "You keep your mind on reading; I'll keep the numbers straight."

finally	second	then
first	next	last

Time words. "Let's keep the record straight on who said what and especially when."

afterwards	meanwhile	now
before	subsequently	presently
formerly	ultimately	previously
later		

Summarizing words. These say, "We've said many things so far. Let's stop here and pull them together."

for these reasons	in brief
in conclusion	to sum up

THE SKIMMING WAY

Here is a learning-by-doing technique that can improve your reading and study skills overnight. You practice it as you use it. Skimming has various uses, but its greatest use is in mastering textbook assignments, so we will begin there.

Skimming the Textbook Chapter

Skimming can be looked upon as the "grease" that makes subsequent reading and studying more efficient. A good scholar would no more begin reading a chapter without first skimming it than an automotive engineer would run a car without first greasing it. The grease does not supply the power, but without it the gasoline would not be of much use. Yet student after student turns on the ignition key and tries to speed over the lines of print without first lubricating the mechanism of reading. Inefficiency and "burning out" are the results.

In the first chapter of this book we introduced Linda, a sophomore who wanted to become an elementary school teacher. Although she had trouble with her studies in some ways, she had developed the technique of skimming almost to a fine art. Here is her account.

■ I first spend two or three minutes trying to get the full meaning out of the title of the chapter. I even wonder briefly why the author picked such a title. Then I shove off by saying to myself, "Let's see what he has to say about this subject."

Next, I read the first couple of paragraphs in the regular way. If I don't do this, it's like coming into the middle of a conversation: I can't make head or tail of it.

Then I let the printer guide me. My eyes dart to the big-type headings and subheadings. I read them because I know that they are like the small headlines for newspaper items. They are little summaries. I then read a sentence or two underneath these headings. My eyes float over the rest of the material looking for other islands of information. They might be marked by clues such as italicized words, underlined words, and changes in the type.

When I first started to skim, I used to skip all the illustrations, charts, and diagrams. But after getting burned on exams, I found I could learn a lot very easily just by reading the captions and noticing what the lines on the diagrams and graphs meant. At least for me, illustrations stick in my mind better than words do; so during an exam, I take advantage of this. I close my eyes and see the illustration on the blackboard of my mind.

I'm always careful to read the last paragraph or last section marked "summary." That's where the author gathers together all the main ideas of the chapter.

Finally, I pause for a few minutes to bring all these pieces and fragments together before I begin reading and taking notes on the chapter. Sometimes to bring things together, I go back to the beginning of the chapter and leaf through the pages without reading, just looking at what I have already looked at.

There are a few other things that skimming does for me. First, I no longer put off studying. Skimming is easy, so I don't mind getting started. Second, once I get into the chapter, I find that most of the chapters contain some interesting information, and so I become rather interested. Third, because I am interested in the material, I concentrate better. And fourth, the topics that I touched on in skimming somehow make good topic-headings under which I cluster my notes. I asked a professor about this once, and the professor said that these topic headings I had in mind acted as "advance organizers" that provided anchorage for the new material. The professor also said something about "magnetic centers." He said that these topic headings are centers around which will cluster other like ideas, supporting material, and details. I don't know much about these explanations, but I do know this: whatever I'm doing it works! ■

The Harvard Experiment

As an experiment, Dr. William Perry, director of a reading course at Harvard, presented 1500 freshmen with a complete chapter from a history book to read. He told them to read and study the chapter in any way they thought best to enable them to answer brief questions and write a short essay.

Twenty-two minutes later he stopped them, and to find out the methods of study they had used, he gave a multiple-choice test on the details. The entire class scored high. Then he asked them to write a short statement on what the chapter was all about. Only fifteen of "1500 of the finest freshmen readers in the country" were able to do so. These were the only ones who had "the moral courage" to pull themselves out of the details of the chapter to first skim through the pages and read the headings and sub-headings, and to read the last paragraph clearly marked "Summary." In this particular chapter, the summary was unusually clear and well-organized. Half a minute's study of this summary paragraph would have given the reader a clear overview of the entire chapter.

Dr. Perry's demonstration of "obedient purposelessness" shows the "enormous amount of wasted effort" in freshman study, especially when one considers that "a student sits with his books for nearly a thousand hours each year." Most freshmen "open the book and read from word to word," disregarding the purpose of the assignment. Dr. Perry says that an effort must be made "to shake students loose from this conscientious but meaningless approach." He urges students to use their judgment as to what to read or skip, and to "talk to themselves" while reading, constantly asking, "Is this the point I'm looking for?"

Skimming: A Lot of Other Uses

Some people avoid skimming because they think that skimming is reading at a superficial level, and that "anything worth reading is worth reading well." Such people fail to see that skimming may be used as a preparation for thorough reading, not as a substitute for it. For example, through skimming, the student can eliminate books or portions of books not worth reading, thus saving time for a thorough reading of material he really needs to learn.

The wise use of skimming to locate important concepts also helps the student grasp the author's ideas more quickly and with a clearer view of the overall organization.

Skimming is a versatile technique since it can be used to accomplish a variety of tasks, but the speed of skimming must be adjusted to the reader's purpose. The following kinds of skimming each require a different speed and focus while you read.

1. *Browsing.* A professor of literature may place on an open shelf in the library about fifty books for unassigned, secondary reading. He may urge you "to open them, explore, and read bits here and there."

2. *The research paper.* After writing down numerous titles of books and articles gleaned from the card catalogue and from the *Reader's Guide to Periodical Literature,* the student is faced with the problem of boiling down the references to a manageable number. Books can often be eliminated from your list by skimming the preface, the table of contents, the index, and some of the summarizing paragraphs or sections.

3. *Textbooks.* Skimming the textbook as a whole before the term really gets under way, and skimming each chapter as it is assigned can set the stage for more rapid and thorough reading.

4. *Novels.* Understandably, many people say that the reader should not read the last chapter of a novel first to find out how the story ends. Nevertheless, there are several practical uses of skimming a novel, especially if you are reading it for a course rather than for relaxation. If the assignment permits a choice of novels, you might skim up to the middle of the book to find out whether it interests you. Or, once you have chosen a novel, you may skim through for the story, plot, setting, characterizations, and conclusion. You may even profit from a second and third skimming: once for criticism and evaluation, and once for meditation and speculation.

5. *Newspapers.* The news items of a newspaper are organized for easy skimming: the title of the news item is the conclusion, and the first paragraph is the summary. Each succeeding paragraph contains information in descending order of importance. A reader who wants to finish the Sunday edition of *The New York Times* can read the headline and the first paragraph of each article, then skim the balance of the paragraphs, reading more thoroughly only those that interest him.

Skimming techniques help students overcome the over-cautious approach to the printed word. We find that readers often reflect their job traits: chemists, engineers, and accountants tend to read every word of a newspaper as if it were a formula or the fine print of a contract. Using intensive reading to cope with relatively simple, straightforward material is like mooring your rowboat with a line strong enough to hold a battleship. Skimming will add versatility to your reading.

NONVERBAL MATERIAL: THE ON-THE-JOB WAY

Sizable portions of science and social science books are devoted to tables, graphs, diagrams, and pictures that convey a great deal of information. They are often as important as the written word, yet many students give them no more than a passing glance.

The very best way to learn to master nonverbal materials is through an intensive study of every table, graph, diagram, and picture that you encounter in your assigned reading. This may sound like the hardest way to do it, but actually you will be killing a covey of birds with one stone. You will be learning a skill that will be useful to you now and in many future assignments, and as you use it, you'll become more and more proficient. Furthermore you'll be learning important material, and not be wasting time on separate workbook "practice material." Finally, you will be highly motivated because you'll be learning material that you had to learn anyway.

Tables

Tables present a large amount of factual information, usually statistics, in a compact, orderly arrangement that makes complex relationships immediately clear. For example, a table on the expectation of life and mortality at specified ages can show in a three-inch square just how life expectancy varies with age, race, sex, and occupation. The column headings list one set of "variables," and the side headings (stubs), another. The relationship between any two of these is shown at the intersection of a vertical and horizontal column.

Graphs

Graphs, like tables, show relationships between two sets of variables. A line or curve graph also shows continuity; when the individual plotted points are connected, you can see and evaluate them in the context of past, present, and projected future.

Diagrams

In some science textbooks—zoology, for example—diagrams are used on almost every page. A labeled diagram of an insect or of the internal structure of a frog helps you visualize and understand the complex relationships of the parts. The student who studies by reproducing labeled diagrams from memory is the student who will know his subject.

Pictures

Pictures in a textbook are there because they have a job of teaching to do. They can help you visualize places, people, objects, situations; they can convey mood and tone. Don't merely glance at a picture; study it in relation to the text. If there is a caption, read it carefully. Try to see why the picture is used and how it is intended to deepen your understanding of the subject. A picture of a Greek temple can tell you a good deal about the mind of the ancient Greeks as expressed in their architecture. A photograph of a rock formation can clarify a geological principle that would be difficult to describe in words alone.

READING THE CLASSICS

Some books should be read almost word by word. Some should even be read aloud, to capture the flavor and nuance of every phrase. These books are the classics, books that have become known and loved over the years for their incomparable grace and wisdom.

The King James version of the Bible is a classic. *The Pickwick Papers,* by Charles Dickens, is a classic. So are many of the poems by T. S. Eliot. *Jonathan Livingston Seagull,* a recent best-seller by Richard Bach, is well on its way to becoming a classic.

Such books deserve to be read with great care and attention. To swallow them whole because of the pressure of too many other assignments is an injustice, both to yourself and to a great book. One of my teachers assigned a different play by Shakespeare to be read each night for five weeks. Result: mental indigestion. At the other extreme was a man who limited himself to reading only one of Plutarch's *Lives* each year. He wanted to make the experience last as long as possible. So make time for reading the classics in an unhurried way. Be receptive to the author's mood and "tone of voice."

However, a slow reading pace does not mean that your mind should be sluggish. In fact, to get the most out of any book, your mind should be alert and questioning. When you read a classic, ask yourself questions like these.

What mood is the author trying to establish?
What are his key ideas?
What is his attitude toward his subject, and toward his readers?
How does the author organize his ideas?
How does he handle the language? What kinds of words does he use?
Does the author accomplish what he sets out to do?

To understand and appreciate a book, there must be active inquiry, as well as a receptive frame of mind. Then the book becomes a means of communication between you and the author.

IV

THE
ACADEMIC
SKILLS

9

THE CLASSROOM LECTURE: TAKE GOOD NOTES

What goes on in the classroom is just as important as what goes on in a textbook, and sometimes even more so. Yet many students don't see it that way. Students who would never skip an assigned textbook chapter often view classroom work as fair game for skipping. It appears to be standard practice to skip classes to study for examinations, to get another hour's sleep or to take the full number of allowable "cuts." Even more serious than these practices is the skipping that goes on inside the classroom: skipping the opportunity to take good notes, skipping most of the discussions by letting the mind freely "float" on a boundless sea of mingled thoughts. It may be that the informality of some of the questions, discussions, and lectures creates a take-it-or-leave-it climate. Although most students "take it," far too many "leave it."

WHY TAKE NOTES?

The objective of taking notes in class is to capture on paper the teacher's ideas in the order in which he delivers them so that you can take them back to your room to study, and hopefully to master. We have to take notes, or we will forget the important ideas! If we have notes, we can read them and study them to recapture the ideas. You will recall that in our chapter, "Forgetting: The Relentless Foe," Ebbinghaus demonstrated that after twenty minutes, 47 percent of nonsense material learned was forgotten.

In a study in which meaningful material was used, Spitzer found that a group of students retained only 21 percent after fourteen days.

The Leon-Clyde episode demonstrated the devastating effect of forgetting when material is given in lecture form. On the day following the lecture, though both men marvelled at the force and clarity of the speaker, and the wisdom of "the four points," neither of the men could recall the subject matter of the lecture or the contents of any of the four points.

We usually fail to see the relationship between our textbooks and our lecture notes. A textbook chapter is read, underlined, and noted when first assigned. Later, before examinations, it is reread and restudied. Yet more than a few students think that because they listen to and understand a lecture, no further time needs to be devoted to that lecture.

The lecture notes, however, should be looked upon as a *hand-written book,* and should be studied just as one studies a book set in type. After all, the instructor will examine you on the ideas in his course, regardless of the source.

THE CORNELL SYSTEM FOR TAKING NOTES

Over the years a special system of notetaking has been developed at Cornell University. It can be applied to almost all lecture situations. What makes the Cornell system different? Obviously, it is a *means* to an end—to master the ideas put forth in a lecture. It avoids the common error of being so complicated and formal that hardly anyone can use it. Its key-note is simple efficiency. Every step is designed to save time and effort. There is no retyping or rewriting in this system. Furthermore, each step prepares the way for taking the next natural and logical step in the learning process. In other words, it is a do-it-right-in-the-first-place system.

The First Step: Preparing the System

Use a large, loose-leaf notebook. The large size provides ample room for developing meaningful notes, recording examples, and drawing diagrams. The loose-leaf feature enables you to insert mimeographed "hand-outs" and assignment sheets in topical or chronological order.

Another suggestion is to take notes on one side of the page only. Later, while studying, it is a great help to spread out the pages to see the pattern of a lecture.

The key to the system is to draw a vertical line about two and one-half (2½) inches from the left edge of each sheet. This is the recall column. Classroom notes will be recorded in the space to the right of the line. Later, key words and phrases will be written to the left of the line (see Figure 9-1, page 129).

Before each new lecture, take a few minutes to look over the notes on yesterday's lecture so that you can connect them with the lecture you are about to hear. Otherwise, you are likely to have a compartmentalized view of each day's lecture. This condition might be depicted by a series of unconnected links:

On the other hand, a brief review just before class will help form a strong chain of association, helping you see the development of the lectures as a continued series:

The Second Step: During the Lecture

During the lecture itself, follow these simple directions.

1. Record your notes in simple paragraph form. Your object should be to make your notes complete and clear enough so that they will have meaning for you weeks and months later.
2. It is not necessary to make elaborate outlines, using Roman numerals, capital letters, Arabic numerals, and small letters, etc., with various indentations. This traditional form may give the appearance of thoroughness and understanding, rather than actually achieving them. Besides, it is sometimes hard to remember which number or letter comes next.
3. Strive to capture general ideas rather than illustrative details. In this way, you will be able to follow the train of the argument or development of an idea. You can get names and dates from the textbook.
4. Skip lines to show the end of one idea and the start of another. Indicate sub-ideas and supporting details with numbers or letters under the major idea.
5. Using abbreviations will give you extra time to listen and to write. Avoid, however, using too many abbreviations or ones you might have trouble deciphering weeks or months later. (See list on pages 137-38 for ideas.)
6. Write legibly. You can if you discipline yourself. Later when you review, legible handwriting will let you concentrate on ideas and facts rather than on figuring out your scribblings. Doing your notes right the first time also saves time in rewriting or typing them. Copying or typing notes is *not* a form of review; it is a mechanical process that wastes your time.

Third Step: After the Lecture

Since forgetting is constantly taking its toll, it would be wise to consolidate your notes during your first free time after class, or during the evening at the latest. First, read through your notes, make any scribbles more legible, fill in spaces purposely left blank, and emerge with an overview of the lecture. Then underline or box in the words containing the main ideas.

Now, you are ready to use the recall column on the left side of the page. In this column jot in key words and key phrases that will stand as cues for the ideas and facts on the right. In making these jottings, you will have reread all the lecturer's ideas, rethought them in your own words, and reflected on them as you tried to think of a brief summarizing phrase or a key word. In doing so you will have organized and structured the lecture both in your notebook, and more important, in your mind.

Now cover up the right side of the sheet, exposing only the jottings in the recall column. Using the jottings as cues or "flags" to help you recall, RECITE aloud the facts and ideas of the lecture as fully as you can, in your own words and with as much appreciation of the meaning as you can. Then uncover the notes and verify what you have said. This procedure of reciting is the most powerful learning technique known to psychologists.

Dr. Jerome Bruner of Harvard said, after surveying the experimental studies of thousands of researchers, that the most fundamental thing that can be said about the human memory is that detail must be organized through reflection under meaningful categories, or it is rapidly forgotten. Therefore, take the sheets for a day's lecture out of the binder and overlap them so that only the recall columns are exposed. They key words and phrases in the recall columns are actually your categories—your organizational framework. Glance up and down these columns, notice the sequence of categories, see how they hang together to make an integrated whole. By acquiring a mental picture of the whole, you are far more likely to remember the material.

With these splendidly organized notes readily available, you should review them from time to time to keep your retention at a high level. Think, too, what a headstart you will have for the reviewing that must be done before for the final exam.

The Cornell System Format

This section of this chapter illustrates and describes how notes should be taken on various types of lectures, all within the format of the Cornell system. We are not suggesting that there is one ideal kind of note-taking for each specific course. The kind of notes you take will depend partly on the subject matter, partly on the way your teacher customarily does his thinking, and partly even on the particular lecture on a particular day.

Figure 9-1 shows the basic format for using the five R's of note-taking. The five R's include many of the principles we have already covered.

1. *Record.* During the lecture, record in the main column as many meaningful facts and ideas as you can. Write legibly.
2. *Reduce.* As soon after the lecture as possible, summarize (reduce) these ideas and facts concisely in the recall column. Summarizing clarifies meanings and relationships, reinforces continuity, and strengthens memory. Also, it is a way of preparing for examinations gradually and well ahead of time.
3. *Recite.* Now cover the main column. Using only your jottings in the recall column as cues, state the facts and ideas of the lecture as fully as you can, not mechanically, but in your own words and with as much appreciation of the meaning as you can. Then, uncovering the notes, verify what you have said. This procedure helps transfer the facts and ideas to your long-term memory.
4. *Reflect.* A reflective student separates his own opinions and musings from his notes. Such musings help him make relationships among them. A reflective student may write his ideas, opinions, and experiences on cards or in a separate section of his notebook. He labels and indexes them, puts them into structures, outlines, summaries, and categories. He files them and rearranges

Figure 9-1   The Cornell System Format.

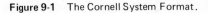

←————2½"————→	←———————————————6"———————————————→
Reduce ideas and facts to concise jottings and summaries as cues for *Reciting, Reviewing,* and *Reflecting.*	*Record* the lecture as fully and as meaningfully as possible.

them from time to time. It is most important that the essential ideas be placed in categories and reviewed from time to time. In this way a student's own best thoughts can be kept fresh and ready for use in many different contexts.

5. *Review.*   If you will spend ten minutes every week or so in a quick review of your notes, you will retain most of what you have learned, and you will be able to use your knowledge more and more effectively.

The type of notes you take depends on the nature of the material presented in the lecture.

In Figure 9-2, the material consists of definitions and explanations of words; consequently, most of the notes are short. Long explanations were not needed.

At first glance, it may appear that the notes follow a formal outline but this is not really so. The lecturer announced a main topic, animism, then went on to explain its unique features. The numbering and the lettering were used to keep items separate, not to indicate any relationship among them. If these items had been recorded in sentences and paragraphs, they would have been too tightly packed.

In the recall column, in most instances, only one word was written to stand for the entire fact. This key word will make it easy to recall the full fact later. When the lecture column is blocked out for reciting, glance quickly only at the main topic in the recall column for your cue; then look away and recite aloud as many of the complete facts as you can remember. In other words, do not stare at the jottings in the recall column, because they would tell you too much. You would not be getting the full benefit of the recall technique.

You may wonder, then, why so many key words were jotted there in the first place. The answer is twofold: first, the key words that you chose have a good chance of sticking in your mind; and second, when you review this lecture later in the semester, you can do so more quickly.

Figure 9-3 shows the use of sentences for notes on ideas and concepts. It also shows how assignments, and diagrams, and bibliographic items can be worked into a page of notes.

The material in Figure 9-4 fell naturally into a topic-and-idea format. The lecturer mentioned a topic, then expanded on it. Again the student made no

Figure 9-2 Lecture Notes in the Cornell System: short phrases for definitions and terms.

October 10, (Mon.) – Soc. 102 – Prof. Oxford

A. *Animism*

Stick has mind-power.

Power – mana

1. Object has supernatural power.
2. Belief object has mind – a power.
3. Animism associated with Polynesia.
4. Power called mana (not limited to objects)
   a. Objects accumulate mana.
      Ex. Good canoe has more mana than poor one.
   b. Objects can lose mana.

Can gain or lose mana

   c. People collect objects with lots of mana.
   d. Good person's objects collect mana.
   e. People, animals, plants have mana, too.
      Ex. Expert canoe builder has mana – imparts mana to canoe.

Good people have lots of mana

   f. Chief has lots of mana – too dangerous to get too close to chief – mana around head.

Too much mana = Tabu.

5. Tabu
   a. Objects with powerful mana are tabu.

Use Tabu to regulate economy

   b. Chief can manipulate mana – If certain animal becoming scarce, can place tabu on animal for a while.

Cause & Effect (mixture) (rain)

B. *Magic*

1. Science of primitive man – cause & effect.
2. Make mixture (cause); Then it rains (effect).
   a. Don't know why it works, but when mixture made, rain comes.

Sympathetic = clay model

3. Two kinds magic.
   a. *Sympathetic* – make model or form of person from clay, etc., then stick pins into object to hurt symbolized person.

Contagious = fingernail clippings

   b. *Contagious* magic
      (1) Need to possess an article belonging to another person.
      (2) Ex. Fingernail clippings. By doing harm to these objects, feel that harm can be thus transmitted.

Good or evil uses.

   c. All magic not necessarily evil – can be used for both good and evil.

Figure 9-3   Lecture Notes in the Cornell System: sentences for ideas and concepts.

Key Terms:
 apocalypse
 millennium
 regenerate
 cataclysmic
 	
 Def. of
 Apocalypse
 	
 Origin of idea
 of apocalypse
 	
 Idea of
 apocalypse in
 theories of
 history:
 	
 2 greek ideas:
 1. ——
 2. ——
 	
 Hebrew view —
 	
 2 peculiarities
 of Hebrew view:
 	
 (Biblio.)
 	
 Modern idea —
 man taking
 over.
	Romantic Masterworks – Abrams 9/30/74
	 Topic: Background for Reading Apocalyptic Literature
	 [Assignment:]
	 Read <u>Genesis</u> and <u>Revelations</u> before next class meeting.
	 I. Def. of apocalypse: a vision of a new world —
	 the last days in which world is regenerate and (in New
	 Testament) all time stops and we're back in infinity.
	 II. Idea of apocalypse a Hebrew invention. Greeks
	 had nothing like it.
	 III. Various views of hist. & how apocalyptic idea
	 figures in them.
	     A. First Greek view: the "cycle pattern" —
	     "everything repeats itself;" "there's nothing
	     new under the sun." Goes on w/o end:

Figure 9-4   Lecture Notes in the Cornell System: topics and supporting ideas.

1. Composition indiv.→ groups generalization	Economics 105 - Professor Terry - Oct. 27, 1974 (wed.) ① **Some Basic Laws & Principles** 1. Fallacy of Composition 　a. What seems to be true or good for individuals is not always good for society. 　b. Dangerous to generalize from indiv. cases.
2. Diminishing 　Returns - -point where 　extra inputs... -Malthus pop - land - food -Improved -methods -technology	2. Law of Diminishing Returns 　a. Refers to amount of extra output we get when we add additional inputs; but, after a point, the extra inputs yield decreasing amounts of extra output. 　b. Malthus' views depended on this law. Just so much land, but population could increase more rapidly than food supplies. 　c. Improved methods of production have offset the law of dim. ret. in many instances, eg. Malthus. 　d. Industry - improved technology overcomes dim. ret. 3. Money 　a. Medium of exchange; measuring rod of values 　b. Barter = no guarantee that desires of two parties will coincide. 　c. Commodities - hard to det. equivalent values. 　d. Paper money = convenient; social invention, value easily recognized.

attempt to follow a formal outline. The numbering and the lettering are there just to show separations of topics, not to show relationships among them.

The notes in Figure 9-5 are written in paragraph form. No extra time or effort was used to write grammatically perfect sentences; rather, the writing is telegraphic in style. Notice, however, that the sentences are in sufficient detail to permit instant and easy rereading and reviewing. It is a mistake to have one or two words standing for an idea. Later, too much time will be wasted trying to recall the meaning that the words were to convey.

Notice, too, that the writing is in a form of modified printing. This kind of writing, which is easy to learn, is highly recommended for several reasons: first, it is fast; second, the words are usually more legible than in cursive writing; and third, the words can be made more legible by reforming some of the individual letters later on.

Some abbreviations were used. Caution: Only use abbreviations that are very familiar to you, and don't use too many of them.

Figure 9-5   Lecture Notes in the Cornell System: topics and paragraphs.

1. Unity
  – well-rounded
  – knowledge
  – body
  – activities
	① World Lit. 106 – Prof. Warner – Nov. 6, 1972 (MON.)
	    Greek Race
	1. Unity = Well-Rounded
	  Early Greeks vigorous. Goal was to be well-rounded: unity of knowledge & activity. No separate specializations as law, literature, philosophy, etc. Believed one man should master all things equally well; not only knowledge, but be an athlete, soldier, and statesman, too.

2. Competition
  – loved
  – Olympics
  – Delphi
	2. Competition
	  Loved competition: oratory, athletics, etc. Athletic competition best known to us; games held at Mt. Olympus & Delphi.

3. Religion
  – polytheism
  – gods = human qualities
  – cities founded
	3. Religion
	  Strongly religious. Early religion based on nature = polytheism means many gods. Greek gods had human images to make them real. Gods had power, but weaknesses, too. Every city was est. by some god. Goddess Athena founded Athens.

4. Death
  – "black death"
  – loved life
	4. Death
	  Not looked at as "eternal bliss." Called it "black death." They loved life because they lived fully & in the midst of it. The Greek citizen practically lived in the market place.

SOME QUESTIONS ABOUT NOTE-TAKING

Does note-taking interfere with listening?

No! The widely-held assumption that note-taking interferes with listening is contrary to research findings. For example, a meticulously controlled study by Paul McClendon demonstrated that the students who listened without taking notes and the students who took copious notes scored equally high on a test given directly after a fifty-minute lecture.

Are listening and comprehension aided more by taking notes on the main ideas only than by taking full, detailed notes?

No! Again McClendon's study showed conclusively that comprehension, as tested by an examination at the end of the fifty-minute lecture, was equal for two note-taking groups. There was *no* difference between students who took many notes and those who took only a few.

How about long-range remembering? Is "just listening" superior to note-taking?

No! When McClendon tested the two groups five weeks later, there was *no* difference between groups that "just listened" and those that took notes. Neither was there any difference because of the type of notes taken; a group that took "only main ideas" and a group that took "main ideas and details" both scored uniformly low.

At this point it should be emphasized that all notes were collected and retained by McClendon at the end of the lecture; therefore, no student had an opportunity to take them home to study or review. As we learned earlier in this chapter, the purpose of note-taking is to record the lecturer's ideas for *later* intensive study. That's when learning and retention take place.

How *much* more remembering is achieved when review is permitted?

In Sones' experiment, a group that reviewed immediately after a lecture recalled one and a half times more than a group that had no review. The groups were tested six weeks after the lecture.

In another study, a group which did not review showed an average retention of only 20 percent after two weeks.

What can we learn from research?

There are three important findings in the studies described above. First, note-taking of any kind does not interfere with listening and comprehension. Second, when a student studies his lecture notes using the recitation method, he will remember one and a half times more after six weeks than a student who did not review. Third, when a student has no notes, or does not study his notes, he will have *forgotten* approximately 80 percent of the lecture by the end of two weeks.

From these findings we can logically conclude that the student who takes copious notes, then studies them using the recitation method not only directly after the lecture, but also several additional times before an examination, would stand a good chance of remembering between 90 and 100 percent of the material.

Are main ideas enough?

No! Main ideas and general statements are not very valuable without the sub-ideas, details, and examples that provide the underpinnings. The point to remember is: come away from the lecture with enough information to form a full-bodied concept.

In taking notes, should notes be in your own words?

Not necessarily! Remember, the purpose is to record the lecturer's ideas for later study, so capture the ideas in any way that is best for you. Don't waste valuable time trying to find fuzzy synonyms for the lecturer's precise words.

Use your own words later, when you have had a chance to understand more fully the lecturer's ideas.

Should you reflect on the ideas during a lecture?

No! If you stop to reflect on idea number one, the chances are great that when your mind finds its way back to the on-going lecture, you will hear the lecturer say, "And idea number four is . . ." Reflection is valuable but must be done later. Your job in the classroom is to capture the ideas on which to reflect outside of class. It's a matter of priority.

Should you make a note on the instructor's headings?

Yes! To have well-organized notes, you need to listen attentively to detect the instructor's main headings and sub-headings. You can then list under these headings the ideas, facts, examples, and details.

If you cannot detect such headings, take notes anyway. After the lecture, it is up to you to impose some organization upon what appears to be disorganization. Do this by clustering. The thinking that you do in trying to organize the material will pay off handsomely with deeper understanding and longer remembering.

Does pre-reading a textbook chapter help note-taking?

Yes! Often an instructor's classroom lectures will follow the topics in the order in which they appear in the textbook. By pre-reading your textbook chapters, you will be sufficiently familiar with the material in the lecture so that you can anticipate points and easily follow the development of the topic.

How do you cope with a lecturer who talks much too fast?

Use a two-page system. On the left-hand page record only the main ideas in a bold, non-formal way. Make sure that you grasp the key words. Immediately after the lecture, as well as during lulls in the lecture itself, record as many pertinent details as you can on the right-hand page. Record the details opposite the main ideas which they support. In effect, you will have a fairly full lecture in brief form on the left, which will be easy to study for a review, and a full page of supporting details on the right.

Should you type your lecture notes?

Definitely not! Time is one ingredient that college students never have enough of. One sure way to *waste* time is to do the same job twice. The mind cannot concentrate on two activities simultaneously, that is, typing and studying. Typing is a hard task requiring one's full concentration; so is studying. So do it right the first time. Write legibly!

Should you take your lecture notes in shorthand?

No! Before you can study the ideas and facts, the shorthand notes *must* be transcribed. Transcribing and typing take a lot of energy and time with little or *no* learning taking place during the process. You are not in the classroom to record the lecturer's every word; rather, you are there to capture his ideas. Besides, after taking notes in longhand, you can study immediately. Shorthand notes are no good until transcribed.

How about using tape recorders or cassettes?

Don't use tape recorders or cassettes. This practice sounds like a good idea, but it isn't. When the lecture is on tape, you cannot review the lecture in five or ten minutes as other students can; you have to replay the entire tape. If you take notes later by replaying the lecture, you have wasted valuable time; you could have done the note-taking in class in the first place. Besides, if you have only tapes, review will take as much time as the original series of lectures, and you have done no work of your own in organizing and really learning the ideas.

THE USE OF ABBREVIATIONS AND SYMBOLS

To help you take notes more rapidly, the following list of general ideas for abbreviations and symbols is provided. One warning; you must use abbreviations judiciously. It is wise to introduce into your note-taking system only a few of the abbreviations at a time. The over-use of abbreviations may leave you with a set of notes that is difficult to read. The criterion of good note-taking is that you can read and reread your notes with no hesitation and with clear comprehension. Converting the words into "hieroglyphics" is not the objective of taking notes.

General Rules for Abbreviations

Do not try to perfect a definite system of "shorthand." Here we have simply brought together the various ideas we have picked up over the years. You may select one or any combination of these ideas to try out in your own note-taking. Naturally, only those ideas that fit your needs should be used.

1. Symbols. Symbols are especially helpful to students in engineering and mathematics.

   $\neq$ = does not equal
   $\underline{f}$ = frequency

2. Create a family of symbols.

   ○   = organism
   ⊙   = individual
   ⑤   = individuals

3. Leave out the periods in standard abbreviations.

   cf   = confer (Latin, compare)
   eg   = exempli gratia (Latin, for example)
   dept   = department
   NYC   = New York City

4. Use only the first syllable of a word.

   pol   = politics
   dem   = democracy
   lib   = liberal
   cap   = capitalism

5. Use the entire first syllable and only the first letter of the second syllable.

   subj   = subject
   cons   = conservative
   tot   = totalitarianism
   ind   = individual

6. Eliminate final letters. Use just enough of the beginning of a word to form easily recognizable unit.

   assoc   = associate, associated
   ach   = achievement
   biol   = biological
   info   = information
   intro   = introduction
   chem   = chemistry
   conc   = concentration
   max   = maximum
   rep   = repetition

7. Omit vowels from the middle of words, and retain only enough consonants to provide a recognizable skeleton of the word.

   bkgd   = background
   ppd   = prepared
   prblm   = problem
   estmt   = estimate
   gvt   = government

8. Use an apostrophe.

    gov't   = government

    am't   = amount

    cont'd = continued

    educat'l = educational

9. Form the plural of the symbol word or abbreviated word by adding "s."

    □s   = areas

    chaps = chapters

    co-ops = cooperatives

    fs   = frequencies

    /s   = ratios

10. Use "g" to represent "ing" endings.

    decrg   = decreasing

    ckg   = checking

    estg   = establishing

    exptg   = experimenting

11. Use a dot to represent rate. A dot placed over a symbol or a word indicates the word "rate."

    $\updownarrow$ = vibration rate

    $\dot{f}$ = frequency rate

12. Short words should generally be spelled out. Symbols, signs, or abbreviations for short words will make the notes too dense with "shorthand."

    in   but

    at   for

    to   key

13. Leave out unimportant verbs.

    went   came   be

14. Leave out "a" and "the."

15. If a term, phrase, or name is initially written out in full during the lecture, initials can substituted whenever the term, phrase, or name is used again.

    Initial writing: . . . and the effect of the Modern Massachusetts party

                             will be felt . . .

    Subsequently: *MMP*

16. Use symbols for commonly recurring connective or transitional words.

    &   = and

    w/   = with

    w/o   = without

    vs   = against

    ∴   = therefore

Speed-Notes for Engineers and Technicians

In addition to the general rules we have just suggested, there are many symbols and abbreviations that are widely used in technical fields. They will probably cut your writing time in half almost immediately. Some of the basic symbols are shown in Figure 9-6. Common technical abbreviations are given in Figure 9-7.

Figure 9-6 Examples of Technical Symbols.

+	plus, positive, and	↕	vibration, motion
—	minus, negative	log	common logarithm
×	algebraic x, or multiplied by	ln	natural logarithm
÷	divided by	ϵ	base of natural logarithms
≠	does not equal	π	pi
≈	equals approximately, approximates	∠	angle
>	greater than, greatly, increased, increasing	⊥	perpendicular to
<	less than, reduced, decreasing	‖	parallel to
~	sine curve, cosine curve	$a°$	a degrees (angle)
→	approaches as a limit, approaches	a'	a minutes (angle)
≧	greater than or equal to	a''	a seconds (angle)
≦	less than or equal to	∫	integral, integral of, integration
≡	identical to	f	frequency
∝	varies directly as	f_n	natural frequency
∴	therefore	cps	cycles per second
$(\ )^{1/2}$	square root	m	mass
$(\ )^n$	nth root	Φ	phase
vs	versus, against	F	force
⏚	ground	/	ratio, the ratio of
↔	varied, variation	⊤⊤	base, support, mount, foundation
❏	area	(	curve, curvilinear

Figure 9-7 Typical Technical Abbreviations.

anlys	analysis	pltg	plotting
ampltd	amplitude	reman	remain
asmg	assuming	rsnc	resonance
cald	called	rltnshp	relationship
cnst	constant	smpl	simple
dmpg	damping	smpfd	simplified
dmnsls	dimensionless	stfns	stiffness
dfln	deflection	systm	system
dfnd	defined	sgnft	significant
dstrbg	disturbing	ths	this
eftvns	effectiveness	trnsmsblty	transmissibility
frdm	freedom	thrtly	theoretically
frcg	forcing	valu	value
gvs	gives	wth	with
hrmc	harmonic	whn	when
isltr	isolator	xprsd	expressed
isltn	isolation		

Reprinted by permission from G. H. Logan, "Speed Notes for Engineers," *Product Engineering*, September 30, 1963. Copyright © 1963 by Morgan-Grampian, Inc.

Other symbols and abbreviations, for many different technical and nontechnical fields, are often found in special sections in unabridged dictionaries. Look them up the next time you are in the library.

10

MASTER
YOUR
TEXTBOOK

How do you cope with your textbook assignments? Are they harder to face every day? Does each day's assigned chapter become more difficult to study than the previous one? If you stop to think about the situation, it would seem that with all the practice you get, you'd become better and better at studying your textbook. If this is not the case, you probably need a system or a process that can be used over and over again, in chapter after chapter, and in book after book.

On the other hand, if you have a system, and you are still having a lot of trouble, maybe your grip is all wrong. You know that the first time you pick up a tennis racket you are likely to hold it incorrectly. When this happens, your natural grip causes unnecessary strain and weakens your stroke. Even with practice, you don't improve. So it is with a study system. A wrong one causes strain and weakens your efforts.

I agree with you that most textbook reading systems are too long, too complicated, and take too much time. Furthermore, a system that is just right for your roommate may not be just right for you. You can tell when a system is the right one for you, because then your work goes along surely and easily and you get better at it day by day.

In this chapter, I'm going to present a novel approach for mastering a textbook. It has worked extremely well with hundreds of Cornell freshmen. It is a do-it-yourself study skills kit.

To intelligently pick out the units (the building blocks) with which to construct your own system for mastering textbooks, you need to know, first of all, what these units are all about. Mainly, we will explore *how* these units are used and *what* they are supposed to contribute toward learning mastery. Each unit will be presented in the sequence in which it is ordinarily used. Then it will be up to you to put together your own homemade, personalized system.

I. PRIOR THINKING

Some psychologists recommend that before you begin reading a chapter, you should spend a few minutes just thinking about its title and its position in the table of contents. Doing so will limber up your mental processes and help you view the chapter in relation to the rest of the book.

As mentioned previously, Edward Gibbon, the great English historian always used this technique. Before beginning to read or write, he would take a long, solitary walk, or lock himself in his study to bring to mind everything he already knew on a subject. In addition to generating interest in the subject, he was also simultaneously setting the stage for a strong memory by associating many other ideas with his subject.

II. READING THE PREFACE

Although it takes time, this step is nevertheless strongly advocated by some reading experts. Many students say "Why read the preface? It is never assigned." Be that as it may, a preface can be well worth the time spent reading it.

The preface provides almost the only chance for the author to be a living, breathing person, rather than a faceless writer of a cold textbook. Consequently, many take this opportunity to tell the reader, in plain words,

1. What the subject is, and what it is not.
2. How this book is different from others and why it is necessary.
3. Why he is competent to deal with the subject.
4. The organizational pattern he plans to follow.

Following are some very brief excerpts taken directly from prefaces to illustrate some of the points enumerated above. Notice how, in only a very few lines, you can pick up a vast amount of information which can be used to develop strategies in reading a specific book. For example, a strategy based on the author's organizational pattern will help you to read more swiftly and surely. You can pick out the author's main points very easily because you have "inside" information about his interests and goals.

What the subject is:

> This little book aims to give a certain perspective on the subject of language rather than to assemble facts about it.[1]

What it is not:

> It [the book] has little to say of the ultimate psychological basis of speech and gives only enough of the actual descriptive or historical facts of particular languages to illustrate principles.[2]

[1]Edward Sapir, *Language* (New York: Harcourt, Brace, Jovanovich, 1921), p. v.
[2]*Ibid.*

How different, and why necessary:

> Many histories of philosophy exist, and it has not been my purpose merely to add one to their number. My purpose is to exhibit philosophy as an integral part of social and political life; not as the isolated speculations of remarkable individuals.[3]

Why competent:

> It is obviously impossible to know as much about every philosopher as can be known about him by a man whose field is less wide; I have no doubt that every single philosopher whom I have mentioned, with the exception of Leibniz, is better known to many men than to me. If, however, this were considered a sufficient reason for respectful silence, it would follow that no man should undertake to treat of more than some narrow strip of history.[4]

Organizational plan:

> This book is organized, therefore, neither along chronological lines nor the less obvious logical line of proceeding from simple narration to varying emphases. The arrangement is, if anything, psychological.[5]

These examples are from prefaces that are somewhat difficult to understand. Others are much easier. But easy or hard, the preface is sure to give you valuable information that will make the rest of the book easier for you.

III. SURVEYING THE CHAPTER

This step goes under various names. Some writers use the word *overview*, others use *preview*, but they both mean the same as *survey*.

Although this step is advocated by almost all reading and study skills experts, most students strongly resist it. They feel that surveying a chapter is a waste of time. Instead, they want to dig directly into the first paragraph of the assigned chapter to get on with the job. In view of this strong student resistance, let us consider just what the advantages of this step can be.

The Survey Step in Action

In this step you are urged to read the chapter through fairly fast merely to find out what it is all about. As you read the paragraph and section headings try hard to determine what *ideas* are being explained, what *problems* are being raised, and what *questions* are being posed. With your mind actively holding an idea, problem,

[3]Bertrand Russell, *A History of Western Philosophy*, p. x. Reprinted by permission of Simon and Schuster, Inc., New York and George Allen Unwin, Ltd., London. Copyright © 1945 by Bertrand Russell.
[4]*Ibid.*
[5]From William M. Sale, Jr., James Hall, and Martin Steinmann, Jr., eds., *Short Stories: Tradition and Direction* (Norfolk, Conn.: New Directions, 1949), p. xii. Copyright 1949 by New Directions Publishing Corporation. Reprinted by permission of Martin Steinmann, Jr.

or question, read the first and last sentences in each paragraph and section because they are generally the topic and summarizing sentences. These sentences will go a long way toward providing you with general answers. Read slowly and completely the summary paragraph or section at the end of the chapter.

Of course, this type of spot-reading cannot give you all the information in a chapter. Surveying can provide only the general outlines of main ideas, problems, and questions. Its most important function is to provide you with *vision*. Once you have viewed the broad canvas, you will be able to see more clearly how the individual ideas fit to make up the complete picture.

If you skip this step to save time, you may burrow and grub through one paragraph after another, unearthing one compartmentalized fact and idea after another, but never learning how these facts and ideas relate to each other. You have "tunnel vision," like a mole. So take the time to look around first.

Surveying Provides Familiar Landmarks

Besides showing relationships, surveying provides a special kind of familiar landmark that psychologists call *advance organizers*. These are topics or categories established in your mind before you begin your serious reading. Then, when you do begin reading, you are able to cluster ideas, facts, and details around these mentally held categories.

G. Katona tested this principle in one experiment with two groups of students. One group was given a selection in which a general principle of physics or economics was stated. Then examples supported this main idea. The other group was given the same selection without any statement of the general principle. These students read only the examples and had to reason out the general idea by themselves. When the students in the first group were tested, they not only remembered the specific content better than the second group, but they were able to apply the general principle to other cases as well. When tested, the students in the second group failed to see the relationship between the principle and the examples that described and illustrated it. The advance organizer made all the difference between the two groups.

Surveying: Conqueror of Inertia

Some writers advocate surveying a chapter because it helps to overcome inertia, that is, students often find it difficult to get started on the task of opening their textbooks to begin reading. If you find yourself using all sorts of delay tactics to avoid studying, a quick survey of a chapter doesn't seem as demanding as serious reading. It is a good way to ease yourself into studying.

IV. ASKING QUESTIONS

Asking questions while reading is a practice that dates back to the ancient Greeks. It has a dual function: first, to keep you mentally alert; and second, to force you to read for specific answers, rather than for general, undifferentiated impressions.

One well-known technique is to ask specific questions. When beginning to read a chapter, *turn the topical and sub-topical headings into questions.* For example, the main heading, "Basic Aspects of Memory," could be instantly turned into a question: "What are the basic aspects of memory?" The sub-topical headings of "The Memory Trace," "Rate of Forgetting," and "Types of Remembering," could be turned into the following questions:

> What is the memory trace?
> What is the rate of forgetting?
> What are the types of remembering?

After turning a heading into a question, the reader then reads the section to answer the question formulated. This technique helps preclude the aimless or purposeless reading of just words.

Some experts warn, however, that if you hold onto a specific question too single-mindedly, you run the risk of missing new and unexpected ideas and facts put forth by the author. In other words, by concentrating on a question totally, you narrow your perception.

Some readers therefore prefer to ask general questions that will elicit specific facts and ideas. Other readers enjoy conversing with the author through the use of the general question-and-answer technique. In either case, an active searching attitude is created, thus making reading an active, rather than a passive activity. Some general questions that may be asked are these:

> What does this paragraph tell me?
> What is the main point in this section?
> What is the really important idea?
> How does this paragraph fit in with this chapter?
> What questions might I be asked about this paragraph?
> What are the important supporting details?
> Does this example make the main point clear?
> How?
> Can I think of other examples?

Some practical readers not only ask, "What is the author saying?," but also, "How can I use this information?"

V. READING THE CHAPTER

The objective of all the previous steps is to prepare you to sit down and seriously read through the chapter. In other words, you were just warming up for the main event. Now you must enter the author's realm to try to comprehend all his ideas.

The Paragraph-by-Paragraph Method

Since most authors present their ideas paragraph by paragraph (usually one main idea to a paragraph), readers usually achieve great success when they read to achieve paragraph-by-paragraph comprehension.

After overviewing a chapter, return to the first paragraph and read it thoroughly enough to answer only one question: What did the author say in this paragraph? If you are unable to answer this persistent question, you must be realistic enough to *read* and *reread* the paragraph until you can answer the question. Until you can answer the question, you have not gained a functional understanding of the paragraph.

This is the most crucial step in the entire process of studying a textbook. You must not forge ahead to succeeding paragraphs before comprehending the preceding ones. The practice of moving one's eyes over the lines of print without truly understanding the author's ideas is all too common. This practice is a carry-over from reading easy novels in which the action is vividly portrayed and the reader doesn't have to make much of an effort to enjoy the book. In a textbook, you have to read for the ideas and concepts behind the words, not merely for a good story. To keep from falling into this error, here are some further suggestions.

Try viewing each paragraph as though you were going to have to teach the material to someone else: What is it in this paragraph that I need to know to *describe* or *tell* others what I have read? With this in mind, pause at the end of a paragraph, or at the end of a series of paragraphs that go together, and in your *own* words describe the author's main idea together with the supporting details. When you have *described,* you have *understood.*

Sometimes reading mainly for the topic sentence is a good technique. In the following paragraph, note (1) the opening sentence, which states the subject of the paragraph, (2) the examples that support the topic sentence, and (3) the final sentence, which rounds off the paragraph by referring back to the topic sentence.

■ **Harlem, physically at least, has changed very little in my parents' lifetime or in mine.** Now as then the buildings are old and in desperate need of repair, the streets are crowded and dirty, there are too many human beings per square block. Rents are 10 to 58 percent higher than anywhere else in the city; food, expensive everywhere, is more expensive here and of an inferior quality; and now that the war is over and money is dwindling, clothes are carefully shopped for and seldom bought. Negroes, traditionally the last to be hired and the first to be fired, are finding jobs harder to get, and, while prices are rising implacably, wages are going down. All over Harlem now there is felt the same bitter expectancy with which, in my childhood, we awaited winter: it is coming and it will be hard; there is nothing anyone can do about it.[6] ■

Don't inch along sentence by sentence, trying to understand every single point. When you can describe the author's main idea and its supporting details in your

[6]James Baldwin, *Notes of a Native Son* (Boston: Beacon Press, 1955), p. 57.

own words, go on to the next unit: the paragraph, a series of paragraphs, or the section. Do not get lost in details!

Sentence-by-Sentence

There is an exception: sometimes it is necessary to read sentence–by–sentence. President Corson of Cornell, formerly Dean of the College of Engineering, said that engineers and other students in science and mathematics must often "crack" the meaning of an idea or concept one sentence at a time. If comprehension does not occur even at this snail's pace, then ask the instructor for assistance. But, before you do, ask yourself this question, "What is it that I don't understand?" President Corson laughingly said, "Once the student clarifies what it is that he doesn't understand, he will have understood."

In reading a sentence, make full use of organizational clues. If a sentence or paragraph begins "On the one hand," watch for the inevitable "On the other hand," which introduces the other side of the argument. Innocent little everyday words like "as," "since," "because," and "although" are as important in relating parts of a sentence as a plus, minus, or square root sign is in a math problem. Ignoring or misreading them can get you in serious trouble.

In following an author's development of his thought, keep his aim in mind. If you lose the thread, turn back to his introduction or his statement of his thesis, or look ahead to his conclusion, to get a better idea of where you are.

If you get bogged down in a really difficult sentence or paragraph, try reading the material without any modifying phrases. Find the simple subject of the sentence, the verb, and the simple object, to avoid getting lost in a maze of language. When the framework shows through clearly, so that you can grasp the main idea, then go back and read the material with all its "trimmings" to get the full sense.

Making Notes

Once you have described a paragraph or a series of paragraphs, it will be an economy of time and effort to capitalize on your hard-earned understanding by recording it in any one or a combination of the following ways: (1) underlining, (2) notes in the margins or the text, and (3) notes in your notebook. These techniques are so important that we have described them fully in the next chapter, "Textbooks: Marking and Note-taking."

However, I want to emphasize now that being *selective* in taking notes is crucial to the whole system of mastering your textbook. It is usually the unsure student who takes too many notes. Because he doesn't know how to discriminate between the essential and the nonessential, he takes notes on everything. Remember, if you cannot pick out the essential ideas with the open book in front of you, you won't be able to do so without the book tomorrow in class or two weeks from now in an examination. You can train yourself to discriminate by starting this minute to select courageously what *you* believe is important. With practice you'll become better and better at it.

VI. RECITATION OF IDEAS

Reciting to combat forgetting is the most powerful technique known to psychologists. It is sad that every year thousands of students either fail or suffer low grades, not because they lack ability but because they either do not know or do not use the technique of reciting. Without reciting, massive forgetting takes place. How discouraging it must be to lose so much learning in so little time.

Reciting is done by simply covering up the printed page of your textbook, exposing only the cues in the margin, or if you are using the notes in the notebook, by exposing only the jottings in the left margin. Then say aloud the full ideas in your own words. In reciting, avoid mental mumbling; express the ideas in complete sentences and paragraphs, inserting proper words of transition. Also, when enumerating ideas or facts, say "first," "second," and so forth.

For the truly conscientious student, writing out your answers as if you were writing an examination, in addition to reciting them, would cement the ideas even more strongly in your long-term memory. If you recite while writing, you will be learning through several channels: ears, eyes, and muscles.

It is a fact that the mere act of reciting can help us remember about 80 percent of what we learn. Psychologists explain it in this way: To transfer a memory trace from the short-term memory to the long-term memory, the idea must be held in the mind for a short time. When we recite our minds are thinking and holding an idea long enough to consolidate the neural trace in our brain. Without this conscious holding of an idea in our mind, the trace fades. Reciting does the trick!

VII. REVIEWING THE MATERIAL

Reviewing includes two different and separate activities, both very essential.

The first kind of review means *pulling together the separate facts and ideas into a unified whole.* To make this point clear, let us briefly review the major steps taken thus far.

1. Prior thinking
2. Reading the preface
3. Surveying the chapter
4. Asking questions
5. Reading the chapter and taking notes
6. Reciting ideas

In our work so far we have gone from a very general view of the material to a close-up look at the specific details and facts in a chapter. Now we need to stand back and again view the material as a unified whole—a much richer, more detailed view than when we started.

Working with the separate ideas of a chapter is like working with a jigsaw puzzle. Usually we see the picture on the box; it gives us a general idea of what the puzzle is all about. Then we work on each piece separately, and we see it only in its immediate surrounding context, which itself is merely a larger fragment. When we finally finish the jigsaw puzzle, we don't just walk away and leave it. No! We look at it for a few moments to appreciate the completed picture.

So it is with a textbook chapter. We *ought* to end up with a mental construct of the whole chapter. It is much easier to retain one complete picture than a multitude of separate and seemingly unrelated ideas.

The second meaning of *review* is the traditional one of restudying the material after a passage of time. True reviewing is not just "looking over" lecture and reading notes. It is an active process of trying to remember, without prompting, what has already been learned. From time to time, go back over a section of your textbook or your reading notes, practice reciting as much as you can, then look again at books or notes to see where you were right, where you made mistakes, and what you left out. Continue reciting and verifying until you master the material.

To vary the process, put yourself in the instructor's place. What would you ask if you were giving a test? Write out three or four questions that you believe cover the main issues; then answer them. You will be surprised how often these same questions come up in quizzes and exams. This is not out-guessing the instructor —this is studying to learn.

VIII.   REFLECTION

Professor Alfred North Whitehead, philosopher and mathematician, spoke about the knowledge that grows out of throwing ideas "into fresh combination." He was referring to speculation, projecting one's thoughts beyond familiar experience, considering new knowledge and ideas in the light of old, and the old in light of the new.

Reflections should not be left vague. Pursue them until ideas take definite shape. If you need more information, an encyclopedia or a standard book on the subject will often give you what you need to bring fuzzy ideas into focus.

Besides gaining creative new ideas by putting old ideas into fresh combinations, students who reflect have another, more mundane advantage. They gain a permanent grasp of principles because ideas they have reflected upon have time to consolidate and enter the long-term memory.

Reflection is a skill you can take with you wherever you go and make use of in spare moments. You can reflect while walking from one building to another, standing in line, waiting for a friend, or riding a bus. Men who have made great discoveries have reported that some of their best insights came in unlikely places and at odd times.

The subconscious plays an important role in creative thinking and discovery. We have all had an exciting idea or even the solution to a problem suddenly flash upon us when we're not consciously thinking about it. The subconscious continues to work on concepts introduced deep enough into the mind through reflection.

Reflection means investigating the implications of ideas, following up insights, asking questions, noting reservations. Most of all, reflective thinking adds quality and creative excitement to our intellectual lives.

HOW TO USE A STUDY SYSTEM

You have just finished reading about a great many study skills, techniques, and principles. I do not recommend that you try to use all of them. In fact, you should not use any of them mechanically and serially. The purpose of the chapter has been to introduce the various possibilities and to fortify each possibility with a rationale. It is up to you to select only the techniques you think you need and can benefit from. Beware of an overload!

Don't be like the overburdened knight in armor. At first, the armor of a knight consisted of a shield, then a helmet to protect the head. Next came the coat of mail to protect the heart and chest. After that, there were no bounds except the imagination of the lord and his blacksmith. They concocted and made all sorts of special armor to eliminate any Achilles' heel. By the time the knight was fully armored, he was as protected and heavy as a hippopotamus, and as slow as a snail. Worst of all, he couldn't do the job (fighting) that he was originally supposed to do. Likewise, don't let the weight of technique keep you from doing your main job, studying.

When you have finished a textbook chapter, there is just *one* thing that you must be able to do: Without looking at the printed pages, you must be able to *explain* to your instructor, orally or on paper, the ideas and supporting details contained in that chapter. But explaining the contents of a chapter is not very easy. It is the end result of a lot of necessary work. Explaining is like the visible one-eighth of an iceberg. The invisible seven-eighths of the iceberg is like the hours and hours of work you invested in making the explanation possible.

OTHER TEXTBOOK SYSTEMS

The following systems for studying textbooks may give you some ideas on how other authors have combined and sequenced the various study steps. They are added here as a kind of postscript to the chapter, because you may want to select or modify one of them for your own use. You could even reconstruct one to fit your own personality and academic needs.

The 3 R's for Academic Survival

Here is a lean and wiry system containing all the essential techniques for mastering textbook assignments. This is an "exam passer."

R 1.   *Read.*   Read the chapter paragraph by paragraph. Read and reread until you can answer the question: "What did the author say in this paragraph?"

R 2.   *Record.*   Once you are able to *describe* what is in the paragraph, you will want to retain that learning by *underlining, making notes in the margin,* or *making notes in your notebook.* Above all, be courageously selective.

R 3.   *Recite.*   Cover up your notes or printed page and *recite* aloud. Remember! If you can't say it now, you won't be able to say it tomorrow in class, nor write it next on an exam. So, while you still have a chance, try and try again until you can say it right.

The OK5R Method of Studying a Textbook

Figure 10-1 outlines the OK5R method, a complete system that includes both exam-passing techniques and knowledge-provoking techniques. Most of them have already been presented in this chapter, but with slightly different emphasis. You will be surprised to see how easily and quickly you can master your textbook chapter using this system.

The SQ3R Method of Studying a Textbook

This is probably the first (1941) truly systematic method devised for studying a textbook. It gained popularity not only because of its sound academic principles, but also because its name makes it easy to remember. This method is the product of a well-known psychologist from Ohio State University, Francis P. Robinson. Almost all textbook systems by other authors were either partially taken from this work or inspired by it.

SURVEY	1.	Glance over the headings in the chapter to see the few big points that will be developed. Also read the final summary paragraph if the chapter has one. This survey should not take more than a minute and will show the three to six core ideas around which the discussion will cluster. This orientation will help you organize the ideas as you read them later.
QUESTION	2.	Now begin to work. Turn the first heading into a question. This will arouse your curiosity and thereby increase comprehension. It will bring to mind information already known, thus helping you understand that section more quickly. The question also will make important points stand out at the same time that explanatory detail is recognized as such. Turning a heading into a question can be done at the instant of reading the heading, but it demands a conscious effort on your part.
READ	3.	Read to answer that question, i.e., to the end of the first headed section. This is not a passive plodding along each line, but an active search for the answer.

[7]Francis P. Robinson, *Effective Study*, 4th ed. (New York: Harper and Row, Publishers, 1970), pp. 32-33. Copyright © 1970 by Francis P. Robinson. Reprinted by permission of Harper and Row, Publishers.

Figure 10-1   A Systematic Approach to Mastering Your Textbook Chapter.

BEFORE

O   *OVERVIEW.* Sample the chapter to find out what it is all about. Glance at the headings and subheadings to determine what ideas are being explained, what problems raised, and what questions posed. Get the big picture. Don't burrow into paragraphs. Avoid "tunnel vision!" Headings and subheadings will be future categories (advance organizers). Overview to overcome inertia and gain momentum for studying.

DURING

K   *KEY IDEAS.* All textbook writing is made up of just three literary elements: *main ideas, supporting material,* and *transitions.* Your main job is to separate the main idea from the mass of supporting material.

R1   *READ.* Read only a paragraph or short section; then stop to ask: What is the main idea? How do the supporting materials support it? Which transitional words point to the main idea, and organize the supporting material? Finally: What is it in this paragraph that I need to know to describe or tell others what I have read?

R2   *RECORD.* Record your comprehension! Make marginal notes and underline only key words and phrases. Better still, summarize main ideas and supporting materials in your notebook. Avoid summarizing sentence by sentence, for it's a sure sign you are missing the essential points. Chew on ideas, not words.

AFTER

R3   *RECITE.* To counteract forgetting, *recite!* Cover your textbook or notebook page, exposing only the jottings in the margins. Then using your own words, recite aloud the ideas and supporting material. After reciting, check for accuracy. Read, record, recite in this way, paragraph by paragraph, until you complete the chapter.

R4   *REVIEW.* After reciting, take a fresh look at your notes to fit them into a complete picture. It is easier to remember one complete jigsaw picture than a multitude of separate, seemingly unrelated jigsaw pieces. So it is with individual ideas and the total picture they present. Also, notwithstanding reciting, some forgetting will occur, so intersperse an occasional review to keep retention at a high level.

R5   *REFLECT.* Now, mentally manipulate these ideas, turn them over, speculate on them, compare one with the other, notice where they agree and differ. Organize and reorganize them into larger categories, or compress them into smaller units. Finally, free these ideas from the chapter and the book by weaving them into your existing knowledge, blending the new with the old.

RECITE   4.   Having read the first section, look away from the book and try briefly to recite the answer to your question. Use your own words and cite an example. If you can do this you know what is in the book; if you cannot, glance over the section again. An excellent way to do this reciting from memory is to jot down brief cue phrases in outline form on a sheet of paper.

Now repeat steps 2, 3, and 4 with each successive headed section: that is, turn the next heading into a question, read to answer that question, and recite the answer by jotting down cue phrases in your outline. Read in this way until the entire lesson is completed.

REVIEW   5.   When the lesson has been read through in this way, look over your notes to get a bird's-eye view of the points and their relationship and check your memory of the content by reciting the major subpoints under each heading. This checking of memory can be done by covering up the notes and trying to recall the main points. Then expose each major point and try to recall the subpoints listed under it.

These five steps of the SQ3R method—survey, question, read, recite, and review —should result in faster reading, and fixing of the important points in the memory. You will find one other worthwhile outcome: Quiz questions will seem familiar because the headings turned into questions are usually the points emphasized in quizzes. By predicting actual quiz questions and looking up the answers beforehand, you know that you are effectively studying what is considered important in the course.

11

TEXTBOOKS: MARKING AND NOTE-TAKING

When we talk about reading a novel, we picture ourselves relaxed in a comfortable chair. But when it comes to reading a textbook, we have an entirely different picture. Now we are sitting alertly at a desk with a businesslike pencil, pen or magic marker poised menacingly over the page. It seems that reading and marking are almost synonymous.

MARKING A TEXTBOOK

Why Mark a Textbook?

Marking a textbook helps us understand it better, both now and in the future. For the present, the activity of selecting and marking forces us to seek out the essential ideas. For the future, judicious marking blazes a direct trail through the pages so that weeks later we can recapture the ideas in half the time.

Since marking the textbook is so important, we should be careful to *do it right the first time,* judiciously and systematically. The following sections present guidelines for judicious marking, and symbols to facilitate systematic marking.

Guidelines for Marking a Textbook

1. Finish reading before marking.   Never mark until you have finished reading a full paragraph or a headed section. This procedure will preclude your grabbing at everything that looks important at first glance. During the act of reading, it is difficult to determine whether the author is stating a new idea or merely the same idea in different words. You will be able to spot these duplications by looking back *after* having finished the paragraph or section.

2. Be extremely selective.   This is probably the most important rule of all. Many other sub-rules follow from this main one. First, two *don'ts:* one, don't blaze too many trails, since they will be hard to follow, especially in your review·work. Two, don't overload your memory. Yet don't be so brief that you will find it difficult to reconstruct the meaning of a page when you review it later.

3. Your own words.   The jottings in the margins should be in your own words. Since your own words represent your own thinking, they will later be powerful associational cues to the ideas on the page.

4. Be swift.   You don't have all day for marking. Read, go back for a mini-overview, and make your markings. Then attack the next portion of the chapter.

5. Be neat.   Neatness takes conscious effort, not time. Later when you review, the neat marks will encourage you and save you time, since the ideas will be easily and clearly perceived.

Be Systematic! Use Symbols

Have you ever seen a scholar's well-worn copy of a favorite book? A book he cherishes usually bears his mark—notes that have deep significance for him, underlinings, papers slipped between pages, cross references, and an array of favorite symbols.

A well-marked book becomes very much your own. You may underline words and phrases which are the essence of the main ideas. Some people use a double underline for main ideas and a single underline for important supporting ideas. Beware of underlining too much, however. When three or more consecutive lines of text seem very important, use a vertical bracket at the outer margin instead of underlining. An asterisk may be used to stress particularly important ideas. Some people box or circle key terms, or words of enumeration and transition. Many symbols are listed in Figure 11-1. If some of them appeal to you, work them into daily use a few at a time.

You may also wish to make concise summary notes in the margins. These should be brief yet full enough to serve later as cues for review. Numbers written above words or in margins opposite underlined portions show series of ideas, arguments, steps or facts. A question mark beside lines you do not understand serves as a healthy reminder to clear up the point with another student or with your instructor. When you disagree with the author, you can write "disagree" in the margin or develop a symbol of your own to express the same idea.

Record insights—the kind that pop into your mind while you read—in the top or bottom margins, or on small sheets of paper inserted between pages. Rereading

Figure 11-1   Suggestions for Marking Textbooks.

EXPLANATION AND DESCRIPTION	SYMBOLS, MARKINGS, AND NOTATIONS
1. Double lines under words or phrases signify the main ideas.	<u>Radiation can produce mutations</u> . . .
2. Single lines under words or phrases signify supporting material.	<u>comes from cosmic rays</u> . . .
3. Small circled numbers above the initial word of an underlined group of words indicate a series of arguments, facts, ideas, either main or supporting.	Conditions change . . . ①<u>rocks rise</u> . . . ②<u>some sink</u> . . . ③<u>the sea dashes</u> . . . ④<u>strong winds</u> . . .
4. Rather than underlining a group of three or more important lines, you may use a vertical bracket in the outer margin.	had known . . . who gave . . . the time . . . of time . . .
5. One asterisk in the margin indicates ideas of special importance; two, ideas of unusual importance; and three, ideas of outstanding importance: reserved for principles and high-level generalizations.	＊ When a <u>nuclear blast</u> is . . . ＊＊People <u>quite close</u> to the . . . ＊＊＊ The main <u>cause of mutations</u> . . .
6. Circle key words and terms.	The ⬭genes⬭ are the . . .
7. Box in the words of enumeration and transition.	⬜fourth,⬜ the lack of supplies . . . ⬜furthermore,⬜ the shortage . . .
8. A question mark in the margin, opposite lines you do not understand, is an excellent reminder to ask the instructor for clarification.	? The latest . . . cold period . . . about 1,000,000 . . . Even today . . .
9. If you disagree with a statement, indicate that in the margin.	Disagree Life became . . . on land only . . . 340 million years . . .
10. Use the top and bottom margins of a page to record any ideas of your own that are prompted by what you have read.	*Why not use carbon dating?* *Check on reference of fossils found in Tennessee stone quarry.*
11. On sheets of paper that are smaller than the pages of the book, write longer thoughts or summaries, then insert them between the pages.	*Fossils* *Plants = 500,000,000 years old* *Insects = 250,000,000 " "* *Bees = 150,000,000 " "* *True fish = 350,000,000 " "* *Amphibians = 300,000,000 " "* *Reptiles = 300,000,000 " "* *Birds = 150,000,000 " "*
12. Even though you have underlined the important ideas and supporting materials, still jot brief summaries in the side margins.	*adapt –* *fossil –* *layer –*

these notes during review sessions may help you recapture other associations previously made, thus deepening your understanding.

Caution!

A word of warning is in order. Textbook marking can be a useful aid to study and review, but it must be done with thought and care. Otherwise it becomes mere busy-work—just another dodge to avoid genuine recall, reflection, and review. Drawing underlines and boxes, inserting symbols and question marks can give you a false sense of accomplishment if you are not thinking deeply about what you read. Besides, if you over-mark your book, you defeat the purpose of quick identification of important points, and when you come to reread, you will find yourself deciphering a code instead of reviewing ideas. Figure 11-2 shows a page that has been sadly overmarked.

A final point is that the "you" that marks the book will not be quite the same "you" that reviews it. You grow in knowledge; many of things that seemed so important to underscore, box, circle, star, question, comment on, or disagree with in October or November will be accepted and commonplace by January or June, and your earlier marks may only hamper your later rereading. Use the help that marking your text can give you, by all means; just don't go overboard.

Sample Pages

On the following pages are samples of appropriately well-marked textbook pages. You can learn something about good marking by reading the comments about each sample, but you will learn even more by studying the samples themselves.

Figure 11-3 shows how a brief marginal note can expand a title into a summary that will be invaluable for review. It gives the dates of the Crusades, since dates are important, and ties them to a date that is instantly meaningful—1492. The cryptic "13C" is an abbreviation for "thirteenth century." Notice also the summary notes in the margin and the circle representing concepts and geographical locations to be looked up. The underlining is used sparingly and effectively, so that review will be easy. However, keep in mind that sparse and effective underlining can be done only if you have completely understood the material in the first place. Only then will the underlined words bring back to mind the full idea.

Figure 11-4 shows how material can be organized by numbering key concepts. If they are already numbered for you in the text, fine. If not, impose your own organization. Add your own numbers, and letters, too, if they are needed for subtopics. In any case, carry the numbers and letters over to your marginal notes, so that later you can recall the entire "package." In this instance, only the bare key words were placed in the margin, primarily for the purpose of using them as cues for reciting. Too much information in the margin will make your reciting too easy. After reciting, you can make a fast check for accuracy by referring to the page itself.

Figure 11-2   Too Much Marking. A well-meaning, over-conscientious student can defeat his own purpose by doing so much marking. In trying to emphasize too much, it emphasizes nothing. And it makes reviewing a real chore.

Handwritten margin notes:

I. Color vision in people.
  A. Can't explain how we see color
  B. All shades matched through mixing primary colors
  C. No proof all people see color in same way — assume they do — can't assume with animals

Disagree? what kind of proof is needed that all people experience color in same way? If all people call something red, isn't that proof?

II. Color vision in animals.
  A. Can animals see light of a given color?
    1. Chickens
    2. honeybees

B. Can animals distinguish color?
  1. bees can distinguish colors

  2. other animals which can

Color Vision in Animals

Color vision is extremely puzzling to the physiologist; we have no satisfactory theory of color vision, nor can we explain how we see color. For example, we cannot explain why we see white light if we mix spectrally pure red (656 mμ) and blue-green (492 mμ), or why the sensation of spectral green can be perfectly matched by a mixture of yellow and blue. We do know, however, that all shades of color can be matched by appropriate mixtures of three so-called primary colors: red, yellow, and blue. A deviating color vision, known as color blindness, is associated with reduced acuity for shades of green or red (or both). It is quite common in man, occurring in about 8 per cent of all males and 0.6 per cent of females.

From our own experience, each of us knows that he sees colors and that these colors have names, and by inference we assume (although we have no proof) that when somebody says "red" he has the same experience we have. Such inference, however, is completely unjustified when it comes to animals of a different species, with whom we cannot talk; but even so, we can discover some facts about color vision in animals. We really want the answers to two questions: first, whether an animal can see light of a given color at all and, secondly, whether different colors are perceived differently so that they can be distinguished.

Some simple tests can often answer our first question. If a chicken is fed in a darkroom that has rice grains scattered on the floor and the grains are illuminated with spectral colors, the animals will pick up all the grains in red, yellow, and green light, but not the ones in blue light, although these are clearly visible to us. Evidently the chicken eye is not able to perceive blue as light. In a similar fashion we can show that honeybees are insensitive to red, and, by using red light, we can observe their life in the "darkness" inside the hive without disturbing them. On the other hand, bees are sensitive to ultraviolet, which we do not see.

Our second question—can animals distinguish colors? —has been answered by training experiments. If, for example, bees are trained to feed from a dish of sugar solution placed on a yellow disk, they will rapidly learn to seek food on a yellow background. If the full dish is now placed on a blue background and an empty dish on the yellow, the bees will continue seeking food on the yellow background. With a careful application of this and other training experiments, we are able to show that bees can distinguish colors (although we do not know what they see). In similar ways, it has been shown that at least some teleost fishes can discriminate colors, but elasmobranchs cannot. Turtles, lizards, and birds have color vision, but most mammals, except man and monkeys, are unable to discriminate color.

Text from *Animal Physiology* by Knut Schmidt-Nielsen, pp. 89-90. Copyright © 1960 by Prentice-Hall, Inc., Englewood Cliffs, New Jersey. Reprinted by permission of the publisher.

Figure 11-3   Simple Marking of a Textbook Page.

The Crusades

From the time when they occurred to the present, the crusades have commanded public attention and called forth innumerable chronicles, histories long and short, and even poems. Their place in the historiographical tradition of Europe is thus assured, and the very word crusade has become familiar in our vocabulary. But if <u>historians,</u> mediaeval and modern, have <u>agreed</u> that the crusades were <u>interesting and important,</u> they have <u>differed</u> widely in explaining their <u>origins</u> and interpreting their <u>significance.</u> Indeed, it might be questioned whether they belong in a discussion of the mediaeval church. They were, however, <u>launched originally by the papacy;</u> and the <u>church's role,</u> though it diminished, was <u>never negligible.</u> In this brief account it will be possible only to summarize the more generally accepted conclusions.

<u>First,</u> it is clear that the <u>eight large expeditions</u> from <u>1096</u> to the <u>later</u> years of the <u>thirteenth</u> century, as well as the many less important ventures, were <u>occasioned by</u> the political and military <u>successes of Islam.</u> In particular, they were a response to a comparatively new menace presented in the second half of the eleventh century by the Seljuk Turks. The (Seljuks) had overrun the Bagdad (caliphate) and as a consequence of a resounding victory over a Byzantine army at <u>Manzikert in 1071</u> opened the way to the conquest of Asia Minor. <u>Byzantium</u> had faced Islam across the straits before, but never had it <u>lost the entire hinterland of (Asia Minor.)</u>

<u>Second,</u> the crusades were <u>made possible</u> by the religious, political, and economic <u>energy</u> so characteristic <u>of the eleventh century.</u> The (Cluny) reform reached a climax in the second half of the century, and it was not difficult for an ecclesiastically militant church to direct its forces to the military defense of Christendom and the recovery of the Holy City, Jerusalem. <u>Politically and economically,</u> eleventh-century Europe was entering one of those <u>periods of expansion</u> which have characterized its civilization down to modern times.

Handwritten margin notes:
- 1096– to late 13C – and 200 yrs. before Columbus
- Causes
  1. Seljuks
- Manzikert
- 2. 11C energy; Cluny; expansion

Reprinted from Marshall W. Baldwin, *The Mediaeval Church*. Copyright 1953 by Cornell University. Used by permission of Cornell University Press.

Figure 11-5 shows a page from a novel, Herman Melville's *Moby Dick*. It is seldom necessary to mark a novel in the same way as an expository textbook, but striking and significant clues to character, event, or interpretation may be specially marked, as shown on the sample page. It is a good idea to list marked pages on the flyleaf for easy reference, ideally with a cue, which in this case might be: "page 51, Ahab's scar—a symbol?"

Figure 11-4   Marking a Textbook: Numbers and Letters.

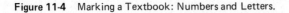

Memory

Psychologists have identified at least three different methods of ①measuring remembering. The evidence for retention may be from Ⓐrecall tasks, in which the subject must demonstrate memory without the aid of significant stimuli, Ⓑrecognition tasks, in which the subject is required to demonstrate familiarity with stimuli which are present, and Ⓒrelearning tasks, in which the subject is expected to show savings of time or effort in relearning previously acquired skills.

There is some evidence that ideas, stories, scenes, and even isolated facts which are remembered undergo predictable ②changes with the passage of time.

In Ⓐsimplification parts of the original story or drawing did not appear in the reproduction. In Ⓑelaboration certain details are emphasized, presumably at the expense of those which are omitted. In Ⓒconventionalization unfamiliar features are invariably changed in the direction of increased familiarity.

Handwritten margin notes:
1. Measuring remembering
   (a) recall
   (b) recognition
   (c) relearning
2. Change w/time
   (a) simplification
   (b) elaboration
   (c) conventionalization

Adapted from Munn, Fernald and Fernald, *Introduction to Psychology* Copyright © 1969. Boston: Houghton Mifflin Co., pp. 272-73. Reprinted by permission.

TAKING NOTES ON TEXTBOOKS

Students prefer note-taking to textbook marking for various reasons. Some students claim that note-taking helps them to be more active, systematic, and thorough readers. Note-taking forces them to concentrate, and so they actually move through their chapters faster. Other students find that note-taking keeps them awake. The activity of writing out a one-sentence summary for each paragraph breaks up the solid reading of a chapter. A great many other students find the main benefit a psychological one: it is a great comfort in reviewing to go back to several sheets per chapter, rather than to the twenty to thirty pages per chapter in the textbook itself.

Guidelines for Taking Notes on Textbooks

1. Use the Cornell format.   Rule your paper with a 2½-inch margin on the left, leaving a six-inch area on the right in which to make notes. This is the ideal format for recording, reciting, and reviewing. Figures 11-6 and 11-7 illustrate this format.

2. Finish reading before taking notes.   Never write a note until you have finished reading a full paragraph or a headed section. This procedure will preclude your grabbing at everything that looks important at first glance.

Figure 11-5   Marking a Novel.

---

behind us. It was one of those less <u>lowering</u>, but still grey and gloomy enough mornings of the transition, when with a fair wind the ship was rushing through the water with a <u>vindictive</u> sort of leaping and <u>melancholy</u> rapidity, that as I mounted to the deck at the call of the forenoon watch, so soon as I levelled my glance towards the taffrail, foreboding shivers ran over me. Reality outran <u>apprehension;</u> Captain <u>Ahab</u> stood upon his quarter-deck.

tone

There seemed no sign of common bodily illness about him, nor of the recovery from any. He looked like a man cut away from the stake, when the fire has overrunningly wasted all the limbs without consuming them, or taking away one particle from their compacted aged robustness. His whole high, broad form, seemed made of solid bronze, and shaped in an unalterable mould, like Cellini's cast Perseus. Threading its way out from among his grey hairs, and continuing right down one side of his tawny scorched face and neck, till it disappeared in his clothing, you saw a slender <u>rod-like mark,</u> <u>lividly whitish.</u> It resembled that perpendicular seam sometimes made in the straight, lofty trunk of a great tree, when the upper lightning tearingly darts down it, and without wrenching a single twig, peels and grooves out the bark from top to bottom, ere running off into the soil, leaving the <u>tree still greenly alive, but branded.</u> Whether that mark was born with him, or whether it was the scar left by some desperate wound, no one could certainly say. By some tacit consent, throughout the voyage little or no allusion was made to it, especially by the mates. But once Tashtego's senior, an old Gay-Head Indian among the crew, superstitiously asserted that not till he was full forty years old did Ahab become that way branded, and then it came upon him, not in the fury of any mortal fray, but in an elemental strife at sea. Yet, this wild hint seemed inferentially negatived, by what a grey <u>Manxman insinuated,</u> an old sepulchral man, who, having never before sailed out of Nantucket, had never ere this laid eye upon wild Ahab. Nevertheless, the old sea-traditions, the immemorial credulities, popularly invested this old Manxman with preternatural powers of discernment. So that no white sailor seriously contradicted him when he said that if ever Captain Ahab should be tranquilly laid out—which might hardly come to pass, so he muttered—then, whoever should do that last office for the dead, would find a <u>birth-mark on him from crown to sole.</u>

Scar - Symbol

---

3. Be extremely selective. Pick out the essentials and write them concisely. This rule is probably the most difficult of all, because to be selective, you must read critically enough to separate the wheat from the chaff. Once you have selected the wheat, you'll be able to summarize a paragraph in one sentence. Here is a way to check yourself: when you begin to write a summary that is longer than the paragraph itself, you may be sure you haven't separated the wheat (the main ideas) from the chaff (the supporting material). So reread the paragraph to get to the core of the author's idea. With practice you'll quickly catch on.

4. Use your own words.   After finishing the paragraph or section, ask: What is the author's main point? Recite it; then quickly write it in the words you just spoke. If you hold your finger on the line of text and begin copying, you will be mechanically transferring the words from the textbook to your notebook, by-passing your mind. It is a waste of time and energy.

5. Write full sentences.   Don't make notes in traditional outline form. Rather, write full sentences expressing full thoughts. This is the way you will have to do it during the exam. Also, when you review and restudy, you will be able to perceive the idea instantly. You'll be glad, too, if your notes are neatly written.

6. Be swift.   You don't have all day and night for note-taking. So keep alert and press for efficiency: read, go back for a mini-overview, recite the author's idea, and write it. Then attack the next portion of the chapter.

Sample Notes

Figure 11-6 shows the kind of notes you might use for material that requires an orderly listing of facts, principles, or rules. Though at first glance the notes in this sample may appear to be a formal outline, this is not the case at all. The facts under the general rules for contour lines form a simple list, and the sentences are almost complete.

Figure 11-7 shows notes on material that deals more with ideas and their relationships than with facts. Here you will be reading for concepts and theories that are likely to span many paragraphs. The skimming you do in your overview will give you an idea of what the main concepts are and how extensively they are treated. Your task then is to summarize and condense many paragraphs into one or two, as shown in the sample.

With other material, you may want to condense each paragraph to a sentence or two. Such condensing prepares you to reverse the procedure when it comes to writing an answer during an exam; that is, you expand each topic sentence to a paragraph.

This type of note-taking is meant to save time in the long run. By going through the textbook chapter in this thorough manner, you will not have to reread the chapter again. The notes will enable you to review the chapter in a matter of ten to fifteen minutes, whereas without the notes you would probably have to spend about as much time to recapture the ideas as you spent during the original (first) reading. This may mean an hour or two.

Slow readers often find that note-taking forces them to concentrate better; consequently they finish a chapter faster than before. Rapid readers slow down a bit, but they learn to read with a new thoroughness.

Figure 11-6   The Cornell Format Used for Material Emphasizing Facts.

Key Words   Notes on Chapter

Contour Lines	General Rules for contour lines.
1. steep slope	1. Steep slope – lines close together.
2. gentle slope	2. Gentle slope – lines are spread.
3. cross	3. Lines never cross.
4. streams	4. Lines crossing streams – bend upstream.

Figure 11-7   Reading Notes on Material Emphasizing Ideas and Relationships.
Type: Summary and Condensation.

Key Words   Notes on Chapter

Song of Roland	Song of Roland (medieval epic)
defeat French valor magic horn no love story knighthood	One of the noblest poems in Europe. Celebrating a defeat, the French fought with such supreme valor that the defeat was vindicated. Roland had a magic horn which Charlemagne could hear. Poem is wonderfully concentrated on a single incident. Virtually no love story. A rugged, primitive poem. The finest ideals of knighthood have been crystallized in it.

Drawing Diagrams in Your Notebook

A word about taking notes on maps, charts, diagrams, and tables is in order. Such materials are not window-dressing; they are an important part of the text and convey information that either supplements or explains it. A map of a military campaign, a chart showing how the average dollar is spent, a diagram illustrating how distances are measured by triangulation, a table giving figures on increase in population—all these should be studied and if important enough, sketched in your notebook. These nonverbal notes, just like your verbal notes, should be studied by the process of recall. In biology, for example, one sure way of memorizing the structure of the amoeba is to sketch it, labeling its parts and properties, until you can easily reproduce it so that it looks something like Figure 11-8. After sketching and seeing the diagram repeatedly, you will be able to visualize it whenever you wish.

COLLATERAL MATERIAL: READING AND NOTE-TAKING

In most undergraduate courses the assignments and the lectures revolve around a single textbook. In such cases, the students are responsible for almost everything in that textbook, both main ideas and supporting details.

When the instructor makes a reading assignment in an outside book, he does not expect you to master the collateral material in the same way that you master your one and only textbook. It is not an additional textbook. Why then, you may wonder, should the teacher assign all that extra work. Here are some of the reasons.

1. The book may amplify the topics already read in your textbook or taken up in the classroom lectures.
2. The book may go into greater *detail;* for example, it may contain long excerpts from original documents or sources.
3. The author of the collateral book may hold another *point of view* or a different *philosophy.* The instructor wants to expose you to a different treatment of the subject.
4. In a science course, the instructor may want you to read about the education, training, and professional life of some outstanding scientists.
5. In history, the reading of one individual's diary might be assigned to provide a glimpse into the daily life of the times.

And there are many other reasons, of course.

How to Cope with the Assignment

The assignment has been made, and you must cope with it. But how? In addition to this collateral reading, you have all your regular assignments to do; consequently, you cannot spend an inordinate amount of time. But still, you must extract something definite from your reading. How can one go about this assignment efficiently? Here are some suggestions.

First, try to figure out why the book was assigned. You might ask the instructor. If you find out, then you can skim the book looking for pertinent material, disregarding all the rest.

Second, read the preface. As you already know, the preface provides the reader with a great deal of "inside" information. Since your instructor assigned the book for some purpose not served by your regular textbook, it may well be that the preface will contain the information on how this book is different.

Third, study the table of contents. Notice especially the titles of chapters, to see whether they are like the ones in your textbook or whether some are different. If the chapters with similar titles contain the same information as the chapter in your regular textbook, then read the chapters not included in your textbook. Do this with the topics covered in your classroom lectures, too. Try to find a connection.

Fourth, if you have not found an "angle" so far, then read the summarizing paragraphs at the end of each chapter. Make brief notes on each chapter from the information thus gained. With these notes spread out before you, try hard to see the

Figure 11-8 Diagramming as a Study Aid. This sketch shows the short reflex arc from a sense organ to a reacting organ.

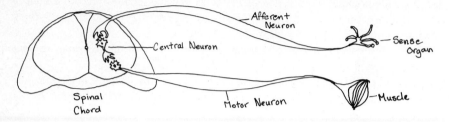

overall pattern. And from the overall pattern, come up with the author's central thesis, principle, problem, solution, or whatever.

Fifth, don't leave the book with only a vague notion of what it is all about; or, with nothing except, "Well, I read it." You must come up with something so definite that you can talk about it the next day, or write about it two weeks hence. Do not waste time on details, but be ready, however, to answer general questions: What was the author's central approach? How was it different from that of your textbook? How was it the same? What was his thesis? Look for central issues around which everything is organized.

Sixth, have the courage to think big. If you lack courage, you'll waste time on minor details that you won't remember anyway. Select the big issues and concentrate on them.

Taking Notes on Collateral Material

When a highly condensed summary of a book or long selection is required, you need a special approach. Here the organizational pattern of introduction —thesis—body—conclusion sequence is useful in forcing you to understand clearly the material and the way the author develops and supports it. Furthermore, a summary of this kind can be highly condensed; you may be able to capture the main ideas of a collateral book in only a page or two of notes. Figure 11-9 is an example.

NOW THAT YOU HAVE NOTES, REMEMBER THEM

When you have read and comprehended the assignment and summarized the central points, you are ready to practice the active recall that will convert facts and concepts into knowledge you can retain and use. Read over your notes to be sure they say what you mean and are clear enough to mean the same thing weeks and even months later. Write summarizing notes and recall cues in the left-hand column. Now study one section of your notes at a time; cover the section with a piece of paper and from the cues try to recall the section, reciting aloud or even writing it out; then look again at your notes to see what errors you made or what

Figure 11-9   Reading Notes in the Form of a Highly Condensed Summary: Organizational Pattern System

I. Introduction

Experiment in living close to nature.

Thoreau voluntarily withdrew from a civilization which he felt was getting too complicated. He spent 2 yrs., 2 mos., and 2 days living at Walden Pond to regain the simplicity of life which comes when one lives close to the soil.

II. Thesis

Each man should pause to decide just how he should spend his life. Is he paying too dearly for unessentials?

In a complex civilization, the fast flowing current of unessentials stemming from custom, tradition, advertising, etc., somehow sweeps a man away from the genuine goals in life.

Only by temporarily cutting oneself off from civilization, could man realize that his life need not be so complex. By getting back to nature to rethink the basic issues of life, man could chart his course, and attempt to steer his life in accordance with these standards (not the expediencies set up by the pressures of complex civilization).

III. Body

Thoreau did not wish to hold up progress or civilization; rather, he wished that man would be more contemplative and selective in his actions.

Man should awaken and become aware of real life.

Live simply & you will live more fully.

Thoreau chronicled his experiences at Walden Pond. He wanted to become familiar with nature.
  a. He built his own hut.
  b. Average cost of living a week was 27 cents.
  c. He observed nature: trees, birds, animals, etc.

He believed that every man ought to measure up to the best he could do. What the best is, depends upon the individual. To have a standard to measure up does not mean that all must have the same, but every man should measure up to a standard in the best way he is able to.

IV. Summary

Urged people to reject unessentials, and get back to fundamentals.

Thoreau wanted to demonstrate that many so-called necessities were not necessary at all. He wanted man to observe, appreciate, and evaluate what was important in life. Once man had set his sights upon the good life, he should follow it without compromising.

you forgot; then repeat the process until you can successfully reproduce the material. This is the same process recommended for effective study of lecture notes.

There is no better way to prepare for an examination than by training yourself so thoroughly in the technique of active recall that you can reproduce your notes without looking at them.

12

HOW TO
STUDY
FOR EXAMS

The day or two just before the final exam is far more valuable (perhaps five times more valuable) than any equivalent time during the regular semester. Time is more valuable now because of the vast amount of high-quality work that can only be done now. To do well on the exam, you must use *this* time for organizing and consolidating the facts and ideas gained throughout the course.

If you use this time on tasks that could have been done previously, you are subtracting from the grade that you could have attained. In other words, when the time arrives for studying for the final exam, all your textbook reading should have been done and *ready* for direct study; all your classroom notes should be in perfect order for immediate study; all your term papers should have been written and handed in; your entire mind should be free to concentrate on *organizing* and *consolidating* your material.

BE PREPARED

You might ask, "But how can I arrive at this perfect state?" The reply is, "It's easy, if you *do it right the first time.*" To show you how, let's go back to the beginning of the semester.

Classroom Notes

The classroom notes on every lecture must be taken, using the Cornell format, and reviewed that same day. The key words and phrases must be decided upon and written in the 2½-inch column. On occasion, you must spend five to ten minutes in reviewing each lecture. Then, at the end of the semester, you will have a notebook full of well-organized, slightly-reviewed notes that are ready to be studied immediately.

The Textbook

The textbook assignments must be kept up to date. Selective underlinings, thoughtful marginal notes, and meaningful notebook notes are the great conservers of time. Such chapters may be reviewed in ten to fifteen minutes, but unmarked or over-marked chapters take almost as much time to read as when they were originally read. You must remember that from the first note in the classroom and the first underlining in the textbook, you are getting ready for the final examination.

On the other hand, if you did not prepare in this manner, then you might fall into the extreme position depicted in the lower portion of Figure 12-1. We are assuming that neither the classroom notes nor the textbook chapters have been recited or reviewed throughout the semester; another assumption is that each of your five courses consisted of forty classroom lectures and about twenty textbook chapters. A quick calculation shows that you probably attended 200 classroom lectures and were assigned 100 textbook chapters to read.

Forgetting and remembering.   On the Ebbinghaus graph shown in Figure 12-1, the L's and T's are for one course only. Imagine superimposing and intermingling 160 classroom lectures and 80 textbook chapters from four additional courses on this same graph! Such a mountain of conglomerate material is enough to boggle even the best of minds.

Even with only one course represented, this graph shows how failure is inevitable when a student does not do his daily work with an eye toward the future. It is nearly impossible for a person to take this mass of material from around the 20 percent line and lift it mentally to the 80 percent line in only two days. This is why cramming day and night turns out to be primarily a terrible punishment to mind, body, and spirit. In most cases, the task is so hopelessly immense that students give up, or they may go through the motions of studying to claim, later on, that they somehow tried.

If a student keeps his work up to date, recites both his textbook reading notes and his classroom notes, and intersperses several short review periods, experiments show that he can remember about 80 percent of what he learned.

If all the 200 classroom lectures, and all the 100 textbook chapters were within the 80 percent cluster, the student could take a final exam immediately and do a fairly good job. But given an opportunity to organize and consolidate, the student could do a superior job, because his base is already so close to the 100 percent mastery mark.

ORGANIZING AND CONSOLIDATING

With notes and books in order and overall retention around 80 percent, you are now ready to get on with the job of organizing and consolidating your material so that you can carry it mentally into the examination room.

Figure 12-1   Retention Curve Lectures and Textbook Superimposed

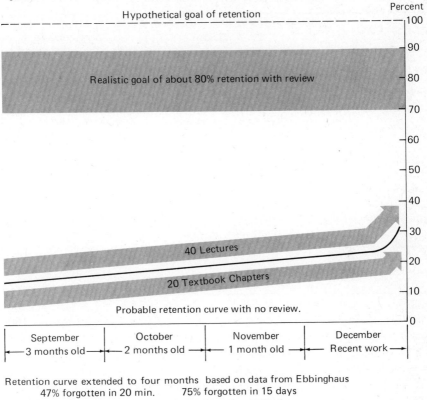

Retention curve extended to four months based on data from Ebbinghaus
47% forgotten in 20 min.   75% forgotten in 15 days
62% forgotten in 1 day   78% forgotten in 31 days

Once there, your performance will depend largely on how well you have organized the material in the course. The basic goal is to organize the many ideas and facts into separate categories or blocks.

Once you have memorized blocks of material, your problem is only to retrieve them from your memory. One proven way to have such blocks available during an examination is to tie tags onto them. These tags are cues; that is, whenever you create a block of information, always say to yourself, "This block of information is exactly what I'd need if I were asked about the effect of wind speed on temperature." So, if in an examination an essay-type question is asked about "wind speed and temperature," then the question itself supplies the cue that you need for prompt retrieval. The tags help you associate the material with external cues.

The Summary Sheet System

To organize and consolidate your notes into easily remembered categories and blocks, the *Summary Sheet* system is advocated. By clustering the important ideas and facts in blocks of material under categories, your classroom lecture notes

Figure 12-2   Summary Sheet of Classroom Lecture Notes.

	Sociology 103 – Dr. Lind	
	19th CENTURY	20th CENTURY
Head of family	1. Patriarchal. Father head of family.	1. Now, individualistic & democratic
Stable- non extended fam.-	2. Family stable.	2. Family less stable.
	3. Many children and relatives under one roof = extended family	3. Smaller in size. Only two generations (parents & children)
non- mobile -	4. Non-mobile, Rarely moved. "Old family homestead"	4. Mobility increased & residence changes often
women & work	5. Women: housework and children	5. Women: work outside & care for children after hours
sex—	6. Puritanical on sex matters.	6. Increasingly liberal
family types—	7. Family types in community alike	7. Greater variability in family type
family functions	8. Family had many functions: political, religious, economic	8. Now: function- procreation and socialization

should be reduced to ten pages, and your textbook underlinings or notes should also be reduced to about ten pages. In your mind, of course, you will hold a vast background of knowledge and information on both subjects, but the summary sheets will hold all the cues, helping you use the recitation technique.

Once the summary sheets have been made, the voluminous classroom notes and the thick textbook may be safely pushed aside, permitting you to concentrate on mastering a manageable amount of notes.

Figure 12-2 represents more than ten pages of notes taken during two classroom lectures. The lecturer elaborated on each of the sixteen points in a straight sequence. The categories, with points set up opposite each other, show the value of organizing and consolidating. The notes lend themselves to answering any question dealing with a comparison of family characteristics. The end result is a block of valuable information that can be readily retrieved during an examination.

Notice, too, that the notations made in the column of key words are brief, so that they hint at but do not supply a full-blown answer.

The textbook sample summarized in Figure 12-3 fell into natural categories of "proprietorship," "partnership," and "corporation." The author did not, however, list his material under the captions of *advantages* and *disadvantages*. That information was scattered throughout his explanations and descriptions. But during this organization and consolidation stage, when you are actively striving to put the facts and ideas into categories and into block form, your chances of discovering such relationships are greatly increased. The notations in the key word column, too, were easy to write once the main body of notes was properly categorized and blocked.

Figure 12-3 Summary Sheet for Textbook Chapter.

Economics 102 - Professor Maxwell

I. Single
   Adv:
   1. freehand
   2. profits-his
   Disadv:
   1. liable
   2. "venture capital"

I. Single proprietorship

ADVANTAGES
1. Can do what desires
2. All profit goes to owner

DISADVANTAGES
1. All losses hurt owner (unlimited liability)
2. Commercial banks ordinarily will not provide "venture capital"

II. Partner—
    Adv:
    1. Common pool
    2. "vertical integration"
    3. "horizontal   "
    Disadv:
    1. death & change
    2. liable

II. Partnership

ADVANTAGES
1. Pool wealth, profits, losses
2. "Vertical integration" = gain control of resources, become own wholesaler
3. "Horizontal integration" = buy out competitors; add products; improve products

DISADVANTAGES
1. Each time a member dies or leaves, a new partnership needs to be formed
2. Unlimited liability, even if own a small share

III. Corporation
     Adv:
     1. legally formed
     2. stock-capital
     3. limited liability
     4. perpetual—
        board
     Adv. to society:
     1. production-eff.
     2. continuation
     3. creates capital
     4. pays taxes

III. Corporation

ADVANTAGES
1. Easy to form (legal permission needed)
2. Issue stock to raise capital; banker underwrites stock issue and sells to public.
3. Limited liability – Corp., distinct from its owners, can sue and be sued.
4. "Perpetual succession", or existence. Board of directors.

ADVANTAGES TO SOCIETY
1. Technical efficiency - production of goods & services
2. Pool business risks - Continuation of production
3. Creates further capital for expansion or finance new.
4. It is taxed

Summary Sheet System: A Variation

In all cases, a summary sheet is advocated. There are, however, some subjects that can be handled more easily by a summary sheet that omits the 2½-inch space on the left. The key words used for reciting are still vital, but in this system the *categories*, *titles*, and *subtitles* act as the key words. (See Figure 12-4.)

To use this kind of summary sheet for recitation, place a blank sheet of paper over it. Then draw the blank sheet down to expose the first heading, and recite.

After reciting, expose the notes under the heading to check for accuracy. After checking, draw the blank sheet down to expose the next heading, and so on to the bottom of the sheet.

After reaching the bottom always take a few minutes to cast your eyes over the page just completed to see the relationships and continuity among the various categories. Thus you end with a mental view of the whole.

Figure 12-5 can be reviewed in the same way. The only difference between this sample and that shown in Figure 12-4 is that this one summarizes the material in paragraph form. The main topics are still easy to identify and use as key words. Whether you use a semi-outline form or a paragraph form depends partly on the material, partly on your personal preference.

CRAMMING

"Should a student cram?" is a question often heard. The answer is, "Yes! Definitely, if he does not know his material." Cramming, sometimes an unfortunate necessity, must be done according to a system if it is to do any good. The following case illustrates the do's and don't's of the system.

Extreme Case of Non-Preparation

Suppose that a student has taken notes on almost every lecture, but has not recited or reviewed his notes since they were taken. Also, he has skimmed through each assigned textbook chapter, underlined the chapters indiscriminately, but has not taken any separate notes.

With the passage of time and with no reviews of the material, his retention, according to the Ebbinghaus study, is probably at the 10 percent level. Two days before the examination, he will be starting almost from scratch.

If all five courses are in this state of non-preparation, then he has an almost impossible task before him. If he foolishly tries the superman stunt of studying day and night to learn every idea, fact, and detail in all the material, he will learn almost nothing. The mind simply is not built to take such chunks of undigested material in such a short time. Trying to digest all the material would be just as impossible as digesting 100 banquet-sized dinners (textbook chapters) and close to 200 guest-sized luncheons (classroom lectures), all within a few days. Even a week would not be enough time.

The Selectivity System

If your only chance to pass a course depends on cramming, the one word to remember is *selectivity*. You must avoid falling into the trap of trying to learn too much. It will be extremely difficult to resist the temptation of picking up important-appearing bits of information along the way. Picking up information takes merely 15 percent of your time and effort, but remembering takes 85 percent.

Figure 12-4   Summary Sheet in Semi-Outline Form. The separate column of key words has been omitted because the key words are on the outline.

<u>The Hopi</u>

A. <u>Speech</u>
   1. Uto-Aztecan family (Ute, Paiute, Shoshone)

B. <u>Subsistence – Economic Life</u>
   1. Skillful farmers — growing maize (mainstay), beans, squash,
   2. Main fields not irrigated — small gardens irrigated. Cotton.
   3. Domestic animals not important.
     a. turkeys — for feathers.
     b. sheep — for wool.
   4. Wild flora — onions, potatoes, tobacco — yucca for soap.
   5. Hunting
     a. rabbit

C. <u>Settlement & Houses</u>
   1. Proximity of water
   2. Desire for security — mesa residence.
   3. Clay, Sandstone, mud — terraced effect — hole in top
                                    reached by ladder.
   4. Only women own houses.
     a. matrilocal residence — brings together matrilineal kin
     b. kinship groups are strong.

D. <u>Crafts</u>
   1. Basketry (not too good).
   2. Loom work — wool has become the principal textile material.
   3. Pottery (coiled) painted.

E. <u>Division of Labor</u>
   1. Men
     a. most of farming.
     b. spin, weave, tan skins, make clothing for selves & wives.
     c. housebuilding: both sexes work.
   2. Women
     a. make pottery.
     b. tend gardens.

F. <u>Trade</u>
   1. Other Pueblo
   2. Paiute, Apache, Navaho.

G. <u>Society — Lineage & Clan</u>
   1. Typical matrilocal residence. —— Underlie the clan system.
   2. Houses owned by women. —— " " " " " "
   3. All-important ceremonials associated with "maternal" lineage.
   4. Clans are exogamous.
   5. Clans have totemic names, but do not believe descended from
                                          totem.

H. <u>Family & Clan</u>
   1. Boy accompanies father to cornfields; learns from him.

I. <u>Government</u>
   1. Chief — head of Flute ceremony.
   2. Power vested in hierarchical council of headmen.
   3. Town chief must learn long ceremonial chants.

Figure 12-5   Summary Sheet Using a Main-Topic and Paragraph Format.

Greek Race

Unity, well-rounded

The early Greeks were a vigorous people who constantly strove to achieve a well-rounded life — a unity of human knowledge. The Greeks did not have a departmental view. They believed that one man should know all things in one lifetime. The well-rounded Greek, in addition to being well versed in the arts, had to be an athlete, soldier, and statesman.

Competition

The Greeks loved competition. For example, they got together for athletic games each year. The athletic competitions best known to us were the games held at Mount Olympus and at Delphi.

Human-Image

A strong religious force permeated their lives. The early Greek religion was an interpretation of nature — polytheism. The Greeks invested the gods with a human image in order to define these forces as tangible beings. These gods had greater power than humans, but they possessed human frailties. There was a close connection between government and religion. Every city was supposed to have been established by some god. For example, Athena was supposed to have founded Athens and the people were descended from her.

Each textbook chapter has to be skimmed and searched, and the main ideas and pertinent supporting materials must be ferreted out and written, in your own words, on a separate summary sheet ruled in the Cornell format. The watchword is selectivity. The same must be done with the notes taken on each classroom lecture.

When all the highlights have been thus skimmed off, push aside the books and notebooks, leaving in front of you only the ten sheets of notes taken on the textbook, and the ten sheets of notes taken from your classroom notes.

Now recite, recite, and recite. The notes you have selected will do you no good unless you embed them in your mind so that you can mentally carry them into the examination room. To make these notes your own, glance at the key words in the 2½-inch space, and recite these ideas, principles, and supporting details over and over again until you can confidently say, "Well, I'm sure that I know this much cold."

It is true that you have taken a chance by selecting only certain ideas, principles, facts and supporting materials, thus leaving many behind in both the textbook and classroom notes. My point, however, is that if you take too many ideas from these source materials, you would have almost nothing, because you cannot possibly memorize so much in such a short time. So, by judiciously selecting of the very top ideas and memorizing them, you definitely have a good chance of passing the examination. You may not remember very much after the exam, but the objective is to survive the battle so that you can come back next semester to continue the war.

Cramming Doesn't Replace Regular Study

Dr. Edward C. Tolman, after experimenting with rats over a long period of years, found that rats that learned to run a maze under the pressure of hunger took much longer to learn the maze than rats that learned under non-crisis conditions. Furthermore, the learning that did take place was of a narrow type; that is, after learning the "right" route, these rats panicked if one avenue were blocked off. They were not able to survey the field to notice alternative routes. On the other hand, when the rats were permitted to learn under non-crisis conditions, they later performed well in a crisis.

People react in similar ways. Under the pressure of an unannounced fire alarm, people in one experiment took two to three times as long to learn the escape route as they would under non-crisis conditions. It seems that the thinking mechanism is overstimulated and too jammed with unorganized thoughts, each of which counteracts the previous one, causing jerky, panicky reactions.

These same people, when given a fire drill in another building under non-crisis conditions learned the proper escape route quickly and well. After a few practice drills, these people could be counted on to act rationally under crisis conditions, not only finding the correct route promptly, but also finding an alternative route when necessary. This is the reason for fire drills in schools and especially on board ship.

This is a direct answer to the student who tries to learn under the pressure of cramming. During the crisis of the examination, on questions that require thinking beyond the facts or with different facts, the student will be panic-prone, and will often answer a question with wrong material, or will make many false, frantic starts, or will just "freeze." It seems that studying under intense pressure precludes later flexibility in thinking and acting.

By organized note-taking, regular recitation, and systematic review, you can be ready to study for the final examination. Then a few days spent with your final summary sheets will organize vast amounts of material in your mind, far more than you could ever learn by cramming. Moreover, you will be rested and confident.

In the next chapter, "How to Take Exams," we will explore the success factors involved in actually taking an examination.

13

HOW TO TAKE EXAMS

You have studied as well as you can for the examination. Ideally, you know at least 80 percent of the material in the course, and you have facts, ideas, and principles well under control.

However, to be sure of success, you need to be physically and emotionally ready, as well as intellectually prepared. And you need to know the best way to tackle different kinds of examination questions. This chapter discusses both aspects of success.

Physical and Emotional Readiness

There are two basic conditions for being exam-ready. First, you must have had enough rest. Second, you must feel confident, so that you can't be panicked. After all, a mind dulled by the lack of sleep and emotions out of control are hardly conducive to top performance in the examination room. The following are tips for good performance.

Plenty of sleep. The lack of sleep is the result of having carved out an impossible amount of work to do in the first place. As long as you have a self-created mountain of work before you, you will continue to rob yourself of sleep, decent meals, and all recreation, thus leaving both body and mind in poor shape. Even if you haven't prepared well, you should still get a good night's sleep before the exam.

Avoiding panic. By following the summary sheet system (see the preceding chapter), you will not overload yourself. Your task will be visible, and with every summary sheet that you master, the pile of work to be done will decrease. With such tangible evidence of progress, you will feel that you are in control of the situation; consequently, you will be able to go to bed on time, eat in a leisurely way, and take a few brisk walks. This rational behavior will keep the vicious circle of panic from ever getting started.

Your attitude toward exams.   Your attitude will definitely influence your success on an exam. If you take a negative attitude ("I'm sure I'll flunk"), or even a neutral one ("Let the chips fall where they may"), your efforts will be hampered from the start. To do well on an exam, you must think positively.

The night before the exam.   "A relaxing movie before the exam" is poor advice. Here's why: any activity that comes between the time that you learned a body of material and the time that you use it will cause forgetting. You worked too hard and too long to sacrifice some of your learning for a movie.

Sound advice is to finish the study session with a grand tour; that is, take your summary sheets and try to see how the individual topics and categories fit to make a total, meaningful picture. In other words, end up with a panoramic view of the whole. On that note, go to bed.

The morning of the exam.   Get up early enough so that there will be no need to rush. A few simple exercises and a shower may freshen you both physically and mentally. Take a last glance at your summary sheets. Then have a leisurely breakfast of good food, not a cup of coffee and a donut. You'll need protein at breakfast to keep you alert throughout the examination.

The exam room.   Arrive early to get a good seat. Sit where the light is good for you, where the proctor will not disturb you when he paces up and down, where you can see the blackboard, and in general, where there will be a minimum of distractions.

Do not sit near a friend if you can help it. Friends are distractions. Before the exam, any conversation with friends is likely to break the mental set you have developed for the exam. Then, during the exam, you are likely to break concentration if your eyes meet. If your friend leaves the room early, there is often a temptation to leave, too, so you can discuss the exam. Also, there is the danger of being accused of cheating.

Tenseness during the exam.   Some tenseness is good because it keeps you alert both mentally and physically. Too much tenseness, however, can touch off extreme nervousness, causing mental blocking. To forestall excessive tenseness, take these steps:
1. Take several slow, deep breaths, exhaling softly and, at the same time, letting your shoulders drop in a relaxed manner.
2. Place your hands limply in your lap.
3. Think briefly (very briefly!) about recreational and social events that will be your "reward" when examinations are over.

4. Occupy your mind positively, by recalling some of the key words on your summary sheets.

THE ESSAY EXAMINATION

An essay exam requires you not only to *recall* ideas and facts, but also to *organize* them into thoughtful, forceful sentences and paragraphs. To make full use of all the studying you have done, here are some suggestions to consider.

The Mechanics of an Essay Examination

Back of exam sheet. With a mind filled to capacity, it is good to unburden it by quickly jotting on the back of the exam sheet the ideas, facts, and details that you think you might forget. It is almost like putting down a summary of your summary sheets, before you even read the examination questions. Furthermore, it is a positive action involving you in the exam immediately. Do not, however, spend more than a minute or so making these notations.

Read the directions. Read the directions carefully. Notice especially whether you must answer all the questions, and whether there are any time limits. Frequently, you may be given a choice of questions.

Read all the questions. Before writing anything, read all the questions. If you have a choice among questions, select those for which you are best prepared. Also, by reading all the questions, you won't make the mistake of over-writing, that is, putting in information that could be better used in answering some other question.

Jot alongside each question. While reading each question, quickly note a few key words or phrases that immediately come to mind. With a few words alongside each question, your confidence should be at a high point.

Later, when you begin writing, use these jottings and those on the back of the exam sheet to organize your answer. A well-organized answer will yield not only a higher grade because your answer will be clear, but it will also save your valuable time because you won't be repeating yourself.

Calculate time. Though it has taken time to read each of these suggestions, in practice they use up very little time, especially in relation to the amount of time gained through efficient handling of each answer. Find out how much time is left after following these steps, then decide how much time to give to each question. Stick to your plan.

Start with the easiest question. There is nothing that inspires confidence and clear thinking more than getting off to a flying start with one question well answered. Conversely, there is nothing that will produce extreme tenseness, if not downright panic, more than passing the first ten minutes without anything written on the exam booklet. Don't stare at the question! Seize an easy one; number the answer correctly, and start writing.

Some important odds and ends

1. *Neatness.* A neat and legible paper does influence the grade.
2. *Use ink.* Pencil is not appropriate for a written exam.
3. *One side.* Write on one side of the sheet. When both sides are used, the writing usually shows through, giving the paper a messy look.
4. *Margins.* Leave a generous margin, especially on the left side. You will have a neater paper and provide space for the instructor's comments.
5. *Space.* Leave space between answers so that you can write an additional idea that may occur to you later. Such an idea may be blended into the answer by using an appropriate transitional phrase, such as, "An additional idea which pertains to this question is . . ."
6. *More about space.* When using an exam booklet, write only on the right-hand page, leaving the left-hand side blank. Then, if you need to change or add something, you can write it on the blank page and draw a neat arrow to the spot on the right side where you want it inserted.
7. *Time.* If you should run out of time, just outline your remaining points to show the instructor that you did, in fact, have the necessary material in mind. You will gain points.
8. *Time left.* If you have time left over, use it by going back over your answers to correct points of grammar or to insert clarifying words or phrases.

The Content of an Essay Answer

Your answer must demonstrate two things: first, that you understand the question with precision; and second, that you know the necessary facts and supporting materials. Your only way to demonstrate and convince your instructor that you "know your stuff" is through an organized answer. The following suggestions may help you "get organized."

1. *No introduction.* Above all, do *not* start your essay with an introductory paragraph, nor even with a high-sounding sentence such as "This is, indeed, a crucial question which demands a swift solution; therefore . . ."

A general approach like this forces you to scatter your ideas, whereas the instructor is looking for a sharp focus. He wants to know how you would answer the *question*. It follows, too, that without a sharp focus, you will do serious damage to the *unity* of your answer. The result could be an answer that contains all the necessary details, but in such fragmented form that they will not convince the instructor that you know what you are talking about.

2. *The direct answer.* The only solution: *The question should be answered directly and forcefully in the first sentence of the essay.* You then develop the essay from this single sentence. The key to the technique of a direct answer is in a

Figure 13-1   A Direct Answer.

Question: What do you think is the purpose of studying sociology?

Answer: I believe that the purpose of studying sociology is to make us aware and conscious that the people of the world are not one conglomerated mass; rather, that people fall into various groups, societies, and economic systems.

partial repeat of the question itself; that is, by using the question as the stem of your answer, you cannot help but come forth with a direct answer.

Notice how this principle works in the example in Figure 13-1. The question asks for the student's opinion; therefore, it is quite correct to start the sentence with "I believe." Notice that the first line in the answer includes some of the exact words that are used in the question. Such an approach keeps you honest; there can be no wiggling or off-focus answers. In other words, you commit yourself to a direct answer.

3. *Expand the first sentence.* Now all you need to do is to put down your ideas, facts, and details to support your first sentence. Notice how easy and natural this approach is. When everything you write pertains to the first sentence, you cannot help but achieve unity; that is, everything is not only pertinent, but it also hangs together.

In Figure 13-2, notice how directly the question is answered in the first sentence. The answer revolves around the "characteristic shapes" of dunes. All the other sentences in this short essay were on the right track as they amplified the main point: the shape. Note too that this question has two parts: one part asks for a yes–no answer, and the other asks you to "describe." Simple diagrams would have been appropriate to help describe the different shapes of the dunes.

4. *The extended essay.* For the extended essay (15 to 30 minutes), it is more important than ever that your direct answer comes first, but in the form of a full paragraph, rather than a sentence or two. Then your subsequent paragraphs will expand each of the sentences in the first paragraph. Again, the organization of the essay will develop easily and naturally. Since this essay is a longer one, the opening theme or proposition should be restated at the end to provide a conclusion.

In the opening sentence of Figure 13-3, the student places his answer in context. Then he immediately states his thesis sentence, "To help my students to improve their reading skills . . ." He next outlines the points he plans to cover and connects them with the rest of his answer by using a transitional sentence, "I shall discuss each of these methods briefly." Notice how the student makes his points stand out by lettering them: A, B, C, D. In making each point, he uses examples. These examples are supporting material, and definitely convey to the instructor the student's full grasp of the area under discussion. The final sentence in the answer repeats the points made in the thesis sentence. Notice the

Figure 13-2   A Paragraph-Length Essay.

Question: Are dunes recognizable after they have been covered with vegetation? Describe.

Yes, dunes can be recognized in the field after they have been covered by vegetation because dunes have characteristic shapes which cannot be entirely obscured or obliterated by vegetation. Dunes have a definite crest or summit, usually having a long windward slope and a much steeper leeward slope. They would be easier to recognize if they were barchans (crescent-shaped dunes). By studying the shape of the dunes it is often possible to determine the direction of the prevailing winds over a region; thus a person can ascertain the present direction of the prevailing winds to see whether the windward slope and the winds coincide.

transitional phrase "to sum up," which clearly labels this as a concluding statement.

5. *Don't save the best for last.*   Avoid the mistake of saving your best idea for a climax finish. If it is not included in your direct answer in the first few lines, your point may never become clear to the instructor. Also, your point may never be worked into the organizational pattern of your answer; then this precious concept you were saving for last might hang outside, conspicuously functionless.

6. *Use transitions.*   Transitions are often called "directional words"; they point to the turn in the road that the reader should take. When transitions lead the instructor from one idea to the next, he finds the paper clear, logical, and refreshing. To make better use of transitional words, study Table 13-1 on page 183.

TAKING OBJECTIVE TESTS

An objective question requires a short answer about a specific detail. "What year did Columbus discover America? Fill in the blank." "E. L. Thorndike is known as the father of psychoanalysis. True or false." These are objective questions. Their purpose is to let the teacher know how well you have mastered the supporting detail in a course.

Kinds of Objective Questions

Several different kinds of objective questions are commonly used. We have already mentioned two of them: The fill-in-the-blank or *completion* question, and the *true-false* question. Sometimes you must choose among several answers. Here is an example of such a *multiple-choice* question.

26.   A chemical end product of photosynthesis is

1.   Chlorophyll
2.   Formaldehyde
3.   ADP
4.   Glucose
5.   ATP

Figure 13-3   A Well-Organized Essay Answer.

Question: Name and briefly describe several specific methods that a classroom teacher may employ to aid her students in improving their reading skills. Consider this question in the context of the subject area in which you plan to teach.

A student's answer: I plan to teach high school English. To help my students improve their reading skills, I would teach them word analysis, how to read between the lines and interpret what they are reading, how to read with a purpose — and for different purposes — and how to better understand the structure of what they are reading. I shall discuss each of these methods briefly:

(A) Reading ability is greatly improved when the student has a grasp of most of the words with which he is dealing. To increase my students' working vocabulary I would teach them how to analyze words in context. We would learn prefixes, suffixes, and roots and would learn how to analyze these and put them together. Word analysis would also involve figuring out words from their contexts. By practicing these skills, the students should be better able to handle new words in their future reading.

(B) Interpretative reading or reading between the lines is another means of improving reading. To help students interpret what they read, I would have them read practice passages — especially of poetry — and have them answer such questions as "What was the author's attitude toward Silas Marner, as reflected in her description of him?" or "What did the poet think of the girl about whom he wrote, 'Your face is like a rose.'?"

(C) Reading with a purpose is basic to comprehension in any field. To get students used to reading with a purpose I would ask specific questions about the material, specifically about setting, character, etc. To get them used to reading for various purposes, I'd introduce various material — magazines, novels, poems, etc.

(D) I would try to improve students' reading skills by teaching them the structure of writings — the kinds of paragraphs, location of topic sentences, etc. Practice in writing would be beneficial.

To sum up, I would help my students improve their reading skills through word analysis, interpretive reading, reading with purpose, and analysis of the structure of writing.

In a course in which there are many new names and terms, you should anticipate questions of the type shown in Figure 13-4. Actually, you should study for such questions by listing in columns all new names and terms with their identifications. The column format permits you to use the recitation method: cover up the definitions, exposing the names and terms; then recite or, better still, write out the identifications. Do this over and over again until mastery is achieved. When the names and terms are mastered, a question like the one in Figure 13-4 will yield you many quick and easy points.

Notice the directness of the answers in Figure 13-4. Concentrate entirely on giving information. Grammatically complete sentences are not necessary, unless the teacher specifically asks for complete sentences. Even then, concentrate more on packing information into your answer than on graceful literary style.

Guidelines for Taking Objective Tests

Read the directions carefully.   More sorrow is caused by failure to follow directions than by any other single factor. Should the answers be expressed in complete sentences? Be sure to note that. Can two or more answers be marked on a

TABLE 13-1 TRANSITIONAL WORDS AND EXPRESSIONS

The experienced writer is continually aware of the importance of transitional words. He knows that they provide directional clues for the reader, that they show the relationship between sentences in a paragraph, to anticipate the writer's development ideas. For example, the word *furthermore* says, "Wait! I have still more to say on the subject." So the reader holds the previously read sentences in mind while he gathers the succeeding sentences promised by the transitional adverb, *furthermore*. The following list suggests other words and expressions that you might find valuable.

Transitional words and expressions	*Intention or relationship*
for example, in other words, that is	Amplification
accordingly, because, consequently, for this reason, hence, since, thus, therefore, if . . . then	Cause and effect
accepting the data, granted that, of course	Concession
in another sense, but, conversely, despite, however, nevertheless, on the contrary, on the other hand, still, though, yet	Contrast or change
similarly, moreover, also, too, in addition, likewise, next in importance	No change
add to this, besides, in addition to this, even more, to repeat, above all, indeed, more important	Emphasis
at the same time, likewise, similarly	Equal value
also, besides, furthermore, in addition, moreover, too	Increasing quantity
first, finally, last, next, second, then	Order
for these reasons, in brief, in conclusion, to sum up	Summary
then, since then, after this, thereafter, at last, at length, from now on, afterwards, before formerly, later, meanwhile, now, presently, previously, subsequently, ultimately	Time

multiple-choice question, or only one? Are you allowed to erase your first answer and substitute another?

Get a running start.   Time means points, so get started promptly. This does not mean, however, that you should plunge in heedlessly. Here is a sequence to follow: first read the directions carefully; second, skim the exam to become familiar with the types of questions asked; third, notice the various weights assigned to specific questions and sections; and fourth, quickly develop a time plan.

Don't get stuck.   If a question begins to take some thought, mark it, leave it, and come back to it later. You will get more points by adhering to your time plan than by puzzling out each difficult question.

A corollary to this suggestion is: Do the easy ones first. That is, move rapidly down the page and answer the questions you are sure you know. Be careful, however, to read *all* the choices given in a multiple-choice question. Test constructors often place a *correct,* but not necessarily the *best,* choice at the top of the list.

Figure 13-4   An Identification Question.

Directions:	Briefly identify each of the following within the spaces allotted.
Ziggurat	— A pyramidal structure that rose above the walls surrounding the castle or palace grounds. Found in Mesopotamia.
Law of frontality	— In sculpture, especially in Egypt, the figure had to be of such definite proportions that if a line were drawn down the exact center of the statue, it would equally dissect the figure.
Gizeh	— The city on the Nile, in Egypt, where the great pyramids, built by the rulers of the Ancient Kingdom, stand.
Megaron	— This building in Southern Greece was the model followed by later Hellenistic architects. In form, it had huge frontal columns, and a sloped roof.
Pylon	— A massive wall in which there is a portal by which entrance is gained to the Egyptian temples.

If you have boiled down the answer on a question to two choices but are not quite sure, place a distinctive mark in the test booklet indicating that you will return to it later. Before leaving the question, also place a tick mark beside the choice you favor. In this way, you will not have to go through your complete reasoning process all over again when you return to the question.

Time.   In making your original time plan, be sure to allow a few minutes for going back to reconsider questions you have marked for a second look. If after reconsidering these questions you still have time left, go back to the beginning of the exam to reread and reconsider each question. If you now believe you have a better answer, change the old one. Don't be superstitious about changing. Research studies show that students who change their original answers, after careful analysis, do increase their scores.

Guessing.   If there is no penalty for guessing, leave no questions unanswered, even though the directions may advise against "wild guessing." If in a cluster of five choices you can eliminate two choices as incorrect, then guess. If in a cluster of four choices you can eliminate one, then guess. But if you cannot eliminate any choices, skip the question entirely.

Trick questions.   You must assume that the instructor is sincere, unless proven otherwise. If you adopt a skeptical attitude, you will tend to read too much into the questions, and waste time in needless analysis and internal debate. Of course, there may be an occasional decoy set out to lure the unprepared student. But a well-prepared student will smile inwardly when he spots such decoys. As an overall approach, read each question carefully, but concentrate on the main point of the question, not on the details.

Standardized Tests

In the broad area of objective tests, there are two main kinds: teacher-constructed tests and standardized tests. Standardized tests are not made up by your teacher or the department but are available nationally and are usually characterized by separate answer sheets on which you write.

All the guidelines for objective tests that we have discussed so far are applicable to both teacher-constructed and standardized tests. However, the separate answer sheets for standardized tests are often machine-scored, and so a few additional guidelines are needed.

1. *Recording your answer.* Make a mark in the space provided with one firm stroke of the pencil, from top to bottom. Every fraction of a second saved will help you answer more questions.

2. *Stray marks.* Stray marks may be picked up by the machine as incorrect answers; so erase all stray marks.

3. *Position.* Fold back the test booklet so that the answer sheet is as close to the booklet as possible. If you are right-handed, place the answer sheet on the right so your arm will not cross over the reading portion of the booklet. You will be saving precious seconds of time.

4. *Changing answers.* Erase your previous answers cleanly; then record your new one.

5. *Check numbers.* Occasionally check to see that you are recording your answers in the space that corresponds to that number in the test booklet.

MONDAY-MORNING QUARTERBACKING

Your returned examination paper can be a valuable guide for learning. You may feel like never looking at it again, especially if you got a low grade, but take a few minutes to sit down and analyze your strengths and weaknesses. Besides showing you how to do better on future examinations, this analysis can be a good non-crisis time for engraving the information still more deeply in your permanent memory.

If your score is not as high as you would like, don't be despondent. Recognize your errors, analyze them, and learn how to correct them. Above all, study any comments made by the instructor, and if you have further questions, ask him. You may find that your trouble is not knowing how to take examinations more than not knowing the material.

The most impressive thing you can do in any course is to show steady progress. Few instructors give a term grade based on a cumulative average. The last examination in a course is usually far more important than the first. Consider, if you were a teacher, which of the following two students you would give the higher mark to. Student A starts with an 85, dips to 75, rises slightly to 80, and on his final exam staggers through with a 72. Student B fails his first test with a 60, pulls up to 75, then to 80, and is a class leader with a 90 on his final. A student's steady progress reflects credit on both himself and his instructor.

14

WRITING GOOD PAPERS: THE ART AND TECHNIQUE

JANE E. HARDY

Paper writing seems like a major obstacle to many students. A paper can loom over your head like a dark cloud that appears to get bigger the longer you postpone starting. But writing papers can be one of the most absorbing ways to learn about a subject in depth. Many students, once they've mastered the straightforward techniques I'll discuss in this chapter, find they'd rather write papers as a form of learning than take exams.

WRITING GOOD PAPERS IN COLLEGE

The techniques of writing a good paper are easy to follow. You should remember two important aspects that lead to success. First, start work early on the paper. Second, if you have a choice, choose a subject that you are interested in, or that you can develop an interest in.

Much of your work in college involves absorbing knowledge; when it comes to writing papers, you have the opportunity to put down on paper what you've learned about a subject, and perhaps your opinions and conclusions on the subject.

Writing is an important form of communication. To communicate well you must have something you really want to say. So if you have a choice of topics, choose one that intrigues you. If it isn't one that everyone else is writing on, all the better. If you're not sure about your choice of topic, do a little preliminary research to see what's involved in several topics before you make a final decision. Remember the caution about allowing yourself enough time? Here's where it comes into play. Take enough time to choose a topic carefully (see Chapter 15 for specific pointers).

Are you worried that your ideas are not important enough to express in a paper? Each individual has his or her own ideas to express. If you're willing to develop and support your opinion, it *will* be worth reading. How you interpret an idea is just as important as how anyone else interprets it, and perhaps your own ideas can shed new light on some part of a broad topic.

In addition, learning to write good papers can improve many of your skills. You'll especially tax your ability to think and organize, then commit to paper what you know.

Kinds of Papers

There are several kinds of papers you'll be asked to write, depending on the subject and the instructor's approach. Here are some of the most likely.

Themes. Usually fairly short, based on your own conclusions or drawn from your experience or from reading.

Reports. A factual discussion, usually in one of the sciences, of the results of a piece of research, with the format usually supplied to you by the instructor.

Critical essays. Your opinion on a book or other piece of writing, usually assigned in an English or other language course.

Research Papers. Of any specified length, usually at least four double-spaced typed pages, based on extensive research of written material on a subject. The topic may be left up to you, within fairly broad guidelines, or you may be given a particular assignment.

Most of the papers you will be assigned will be some kind of research paper. The other kinds of papers are handled a little differently, but the techniques for writing a research paper, once you've mastered them, will be useful in any paper you write.

The Assignment

Most papers are assigned well in advance of the date they're due. If the assignment is given at the beginning of the term, set up a schedule on your calendar that allows plenty of time for your research, time to write several drafts or versions—at least three—and time to make a final copy in plenty of time before the paper is due. *Don't* start the night before.

The length of an assignment is given in number of words or number of double-spaced pages required. Usually the instructor sets a length that is sufficient for covering the subject matter in appropriate detail. Try to stay within the limits, but don't use them as a hard and fast guide. The assigned length of the paper tells you how deeply you can get into the subject. A 500-word paper will focus on some specific aspect of a topic, while 2,000 words or ten pages gives you room to expand to a broader area of the topic. For example, you might use 500 words to discuss one presidential candidate's stand on the issue of price controls but ten or more pages to discuss his whole campaign and its implications.

Assignments may be very clearly written and well organized—so that you know precisely what you're expected to write on—or they may be phrased very obscurely. If you have any doubt about what your instructor expects you to cover in the paper, by all means make an appointment and discuss the paper with him. Be sure to find out the main points to cover, the approach he's looking for, and if you're not sure where to find research material, ask him for suggestions of books, periodicals and other sources.

DOING THE RESEARCH FOR YOUR PAPER

If you're writing a theme or a critical essay, you will be assigned the book or books to read. If you're writing a report, you will be reading about others' research or doing an experiment yourself and then writing the report. For these short papers, the assigned reading material will be quite specific. For a research paper, you need to do the kind of library research I'm going to discuss below. Another source of information, often overlooked, is interviews with experts on your topic who are on campus or who live in the community.

What Is a Research Paper?

Research papers are based on published (and occasionally unpublished) material that you use to support an argument or point of view, or perhaps to give several views on a specific subject. Your assignment will direct you to the right approach. Start your research on the subject early. Books may be in great demand when the deadline for a paper is approaching. If the assignment asks you to support one view and gives you a choice, don't decide definitely which one it's going to be until you've had a chance to do some preliminary research. Once you see what's available to support the different viewpoints, then you can decide which one you'll write on.

You'll Do Your Research in the Library

Most libraries give you a tour showing you where different kinds of books are found, and they may give you a booklet to use later. But if it's been some time since you've used the advice that booklet gives, here's how the information applies to doing research for your paper.

Libraries vary in resources, but the major sources you'll be concerned with are the *card catalog,* the *reference section,* and the *periodical section.* Find out where each of the sections is. Get a map or a friendly librarian to help you at first.

The *reference section* is the place where reference books are kept, everything from encyclopedias to telephone directories. More important for your research paper are the current indexes (lists) of articles in various periodicals (magazines).

These indexes are usually up to date. If the most recent ones are not on the shelves, the reference librarian can get them for you. If your assignment is on a subject that has appeared in the popular press in the last few years, you can easily find out what articles have been written about it, who wrote them, and in which publications they appeared.

After you find the articles that have been written on your topic, go to the card catalog to see if the library has copies of that magazine. If it does, does it have the particular issues that you need?

The publications will probably be physically located in the *periodical* section. There you will find magazines, newspapers, and other publications that come out periodically (weekly, monthly, etc.). Some libraries have microfilms of newspapers in a special location that is not part of the main periodical section. It is not hard to use microfilm readers (machines) and the librarian will help you.

The *card catalog* is your guide to the books, and all other materials in the library. It is usually, but not always, located near the entrance. If you don't see it, ask. If you don't know how to use it, ask or read about it. This one resource is the indispensable key for finding all that the library has to offer you.

In the card catalog, books are listed two ways, under the author's name and under the subject (sometimes under the title, too). They're cross-referenced, and you'll find some helpful duplication in subject, or similar areas. If you should draw a complete blank, a librarian may be able to suggest some other categories where you can look. (If you have the names of authors of books that deal with your subject, look them up first to see if they're available in the library.) Look up your specific topic in the card catalog, then go to a more general area to be sure you've found all that the library contains on the subject. For example, here are successive steps you could take to look up information on an American winemaker.

1. Look up his name in the card catalog.
2. Then look under American winemakers—information on your man may be included in a book about a number of people in the field.
3. Then look under wine.
4. Then look under grape growing—most winemakers grow their own grapes.

Recording Your Information

Now fill out the library cards to get the books, periodicals, and other sources you want to use. When you've located all that's available on your subject or that you think might be pertinent, set up an information gathering system that will be easy to work with. A good way is to use cards or slips of paper, 5 x 8 inches or 3 x 5 inches, one for each book or reference, to record the information you find. If there's more information than will fit on one card, you can use a second one.

Put information on a separate card for each book or reference (see Figure 14-1). If there's more than one reference in a book, use two cards, one for each piece of information you need. A slightly different format for note-taking is described in the

Figure 14-1   How to Set Up the Card. Add other paraphrased material or direct quotes from this source that you think you can use.

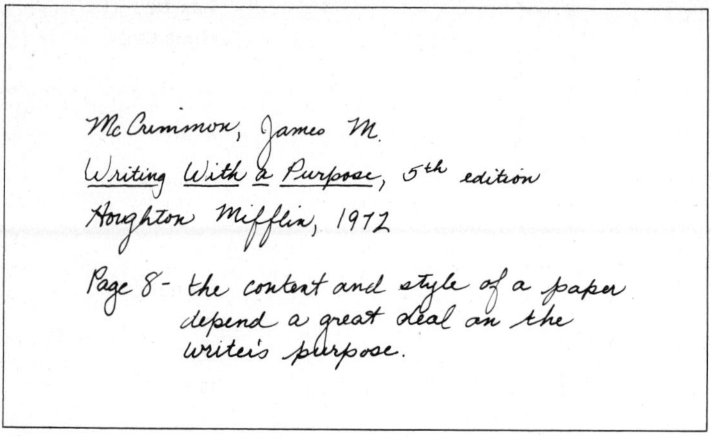

> McCrimmon, James M.
> Writing With a Purpose, 5th edition
> Houghton Mifflin, 1972
>
> Page 8 - the content and style of a paper
>   depend a great deal on the
>   writer's purpose.

next chapter. You may want to compare the two systems and then choose the one you like better. Whatever system you use, note-taking on cards will help you organize your paper in the order you decide will most effectively present your point of view. When you decide on the organization of the paper, you simply stack the cards in the order you'll use them and you can start writing.

Cards are also the basis of your bibliography. Each has all the information you need to put into the bibliography and you can arrange them in alphabetical order and simply type from them for the final version of the bibliography. (More about bibliographies later.)

Direct quotation.   When you quote exactly from a book or an article, use quotation marks on your card around the exact words copied from the reference. Then you'll know what is a direct quote and what you have put into your own words. Be sure that you have copied it exactly. Go back to the beginning and compare your quotation with the original. Be sure you spell things exactly as they are in the original. If you note what seems to be an error or misspelling—some spellings in English works are different from those we use—retain the exact spelling but use (sic) after the word. Here is an example:

> "They did research on the properties of chemical fertilisers (sic), and valuable research on animal nutrition."

Ellipsis.   If you leave out a section or even one word in the quoted material, you use an ellipsis (a series of three periods . . .) to indicate that you omitted something. If the omitted material comes at the end of the sentence, you add a period after the ellipsis. Usually what's omitted is left out because it doesn't relate to the point you're using the quote to support.

■ **Original quote:** "Now that we know what has been the causative factor in this area of disaster we can, without further concern, move on to eliminate that cause."

Quote with ellipsis: "Now that we know what has been the causative factor . . . we can . . . move on to eliminate that cause." ■

Paraphrasing.   When you want to use the essence of what an author says but do not want to quote the exact words, you may paraphrase. This method of using source material lets you condense the major thought. Even though you use mostly your own words the material must be attributed to its source. In other words, in your paper you must give the author credit for having supplied the idea.

For example, you might paraphrase the sentence quoted above by writing,

Now that the cause is known we can get rid of it.

Record all the pertinent information. If you find something you're not sure you'll need (remember that I suggested that you not decide exactly what approach your paper will defend or take until you've done the research), put it on a card anyway. It's easier to do this when you're in the library than to decide later that you need it. Then you may make a special trip to the library only to discover that the book isn't available because someone else is using it.

Be sure you have enough information. Too much is easier to work with than too little. If you haven't enough, you'll have to look up other references in the middle of writing your paper and this breaks your train of thought. Or you'll be tempted to pad skimpy information with words that mean little.

ORGANIZATION OF THE PAPER

Choose Your Basic Premise

Look over the information you've put on the cards from your research. Then ask yourself some hard questions. If there's a choice of viewpoint—for or against a question, for example—which view has the most evidence to support it? Or what should the basic theme or focus of your paper be? If you've done a good job of research, you should be able to decide now what you want to say in your paper, and you should have the evidence you need to support the view right at hand—on your cards.

Organizing Your Paper around the Basic Premise

Now comes a very important step. *Before* you start to write, organize your material. There are three important kinds of organization for a paper. Those you write will probably fall into one of these categories or some variation of one of them. The first kind of organization is a *time sequence*. This deals with material in the historical order in which it happened, with each succeeding event building upon the one that came before it. History papers obviously are in this category. So are papers that discuss how someone did something, leading to a final outcome. Sometimes only parts of a paper will fit this category, especially if you must give some historical background before you discuss a theory.

The next kind of organization is that of a *process*. This is a kind of time sequence, but it describes more closely papers that report an experiment, how it was done, and what resulted.

The third kind of organization is that of *development of an argument*. You state a premise, then set out to support it with logical examples that build to a conclusion. There may be more flexibility possible in this kind of organization than in the others.

The important thing is to decide what kind of organization is best for your basic premise. If you don't know how you want to proceed in your writing, the paper will probably appear haphazard and purposeless to the instructor.

Setting Up an Organization Chart

Now that you've decided what kind of organization fits the material you have, write down the points you want to cover in your paper. They can be in any order. Don't worry at this time whether the points are major ones or less important. Just write them down briefly in any order. Now go through and decide which are the major points under each appropriate main point (see Table 14-1). Here you may decide that some point isn't important to your argument at all. Maybe it's interesting, but it won't help support any of the major points. Set the card with this information aside. You should now have major points listed, with minor points under each major point. Now decide in which order you want to use the major points. Here's where your decision of time sequence, process, or development of an argument comes into play. Arrange the major points in the order that best fits what you've chosen, then organize the cards with the library information on them in the order of this organized outline. Number the cards in order from one to whatever, and you're ready to start writing.

WRITING THE RESEARCH PAPER

Where Do You Write?

You should be reasonably comfortable, away from distractions you can't control, like music or other people's conversation, when you begin to write. You should be free from bothersome tasks that may worry you while you're writing. Get the immediate demands out of the way. Feed the cat, do the dishes, read your assignment for class tomorrow, or study briefly for tomorrow's quiz. Or decide that you have time tomorrow for this sort of task and then put it out of your mind.

TABLE 14-1. HOW TO SET UP AN ORGANIZATION CHART

I. Introduction: Pertinent quote or striking statement if you use it.
    a. Your purpose.
    b. How you will accomplish it.
II. (Major Point 1) State this point concisely.
    a. Example of incident and supporting evidence.
    b. Another example.
III. (Major Point 2) State it as above.
    a. Support for major point 2.
IV. (Major Point 3) Again, state it clearly.
    a. Facts or quotes to support major point 3.
    b. More examples to support major point 3.
V. (Major Point 4) State the major point.
    a. Supporting evidence for major point 4.
    b. More examples.
    c. Other supporting evidence.
VI. Conclusion.

The light should be good, the chair reasonably comfortable. If you must type where the table is too high or your chair gives you a backache when you sit in it, find a better place to work. Usually you can modify your environment in some way to be more comfortable. It's hard to write if you're too hot or cold or hungry. Take care of these needs. But don't let these details eat up all your time. Most can be dealt with quickly—perhaps in half an hour. Have the materials you need ready.

Now How Do You Start?

You start by writing. If you're typing or writing in long-hand, just start. You can start with "Mary had a little lamb" if you wish. Once your hands are going through the physical motions of writing, your brain will follow, and then you can get into the meat of the paper. You already have most of it worked out—information, sources, organization. So now all you have to do is put it into sentences and paragraphs. Remember that you are planning to leave time for at least two if not three drafts, so what you write on this first one need not be perfect. You can always discard the first part if you don't like it, or rewrite it.

On the first draft copy, write as rapidly and spontaneously as possible. Recording your thoughts as they go through your mind will help ensure continuity. It is when you stop to ponder alternatives that gaps in continuity occur. Although this manner of writing often results in too much material, don't be concerned, because it is easier to cut than to add.

If your first sentence doesn't sound just as you would like it to, don't worry about it. No writer ever comes out with the perfect beginning sentence. What you read in books and magazines is always the result of revision and rewriting. So you shouldn't expect to succeed in this respect when others also have a hard time. *Just start writing.*

Writing the Main Body of the Paper

Now you're ready to start writing the body of the paper. First comes your introduction, one or two paragraphs to state your purpose and perhaps catch the reader's interest. For now, just write out a general sentence of introduction, stating simply what you want to do in the paper. This can and probably should be in very rough form right now. Forget it, and go into the main body of the paper. Take each card in order and write. Start with main point one, state what it is, then use the supporting evidence to show why this is so, or what happened. As you use a reference from the card, note the card number in your paper. You can put in the footnotes later, taking the exact information from the card. Following your organized and numbered cards, write the body of the paper.

Be sure to develop and support the important points. Students often state a main point, then go on to something else without supporting it. The kinds of evidence you need to support a major point are statistics, quotations from other published works, facts, examples, comparisons and contrast in views, expert opinion, and description. These are the specifics that will support your points. If you make statements and follow them up with generalities you will not convince your reader that your main point is true. Use what you have collected on your cards to support your points. Here is an example of the steps you can take to develop a major point.

1. State your point clearly.
   Gardening is an enjoyable avocation.
2. Develop the point beyond a brief statement.
   Faced with the pressures of modern living, many people turn to working with plants to relax themselves and become absorbed in the living world around them. For some people gardening may absorb every spare moment.
3. Support with quotes from authorities, statistics.
   Organizations that serve gardeners are growing rapidly. In the past two years garden clubs and other horticultural organizations report significant numbers of new members. An estimate of gardeners actively affiliated with these organizations numbers in the millions, according to James Jones, executive director of Gardeners, Inc.
4. Illustrate with examples.
   One organization, the American Horticultural Society, has purchased an estate for its new headquarters to serve a membership that has tripled in the last 18 months.
5. Interrelate with other main points.
   In addition to joining general gardening organizations, gardeners who specialize can join societies for those interested in growing irises, primroses, daylilies, African violets, orchids, and other garden favorites. Most of these groups have grown, too, as a result of the increased general interest in growing plants.

Be sure that all the main points are supported about equally with this kind of evidence. If you can't find enough evidence to support one point, perhaps it's not a major one. Then you need to reorganize the structure to include it under one of the other major points.

Avoid padding. You may be tempted to add extra words or rephrase a point in several ways to make the paper seem longer. This sort of padding is very obvious to the reader, who's looking for logical arguments and good sense in your paper. If you haven't enough evidence to support a statement, leave it out or get some more information to use. But don't think that you will improve your grade by padding with excess words that say nothing. Padding shows.

Make a clear copy. The first draft is usually rough—full of deletions, additions, and directions that are understandable only to the writer (see Figure 14-2). If you leave it in this state for even a day, you may lose a lot of time trying to recall exactly how you meant to blend in some of the notes hastily written between lines. Furthermore, if you retype or rewrite the material while it is still very fresh, some spontaneous revision may take place. The result, in any case, will be a clear copy that will be ready for revision after a "cooling off" period of a day or so.

Now put it on the back burner. What you now have is a first draft, organized in the order it will appear in the final paper, without a completed introduction and without a conclusion. You'll need both of these as well as a title. But they can come later after you've set the paper aside for a day or so. (Start early!)

The "cooling off" period is important. During the writing stage your mind is so full of associations with the words you have written that you are likely to see clarity and step-by-step sequences where these do not, in fact, exist; that is, your mind fills in and bridges the gaps.

When you read your manuscript after your mind has dropped some of these associations, you will have to read the words themselves to gain the meaning. You can now easily spot the glaring errors—you can be critically objective.

The "cooling-off period" has another advantage. When you're not thinking too hard about a paper, you may come up with a good introduction and conclusion (they should be related) and maybe a good title. You now have most of the paper written and you can relax a little, so that your brain will do work for you that you are unaware of. Suddenly you may come up with a good idea for the introduction and conclusion when you've been thinking of something else.

If this doesn't happen, you still gain a lot by setting the work aside so you can look at it freshly the next day. You were probably tired when you stopped writing and small errors of grammar or spelling will be clearer when you look at it later. Awkward sentences and unclear paragraphs show up more clearly then. Finally, when you reread your paper after letting it sit for a day or so, look carefully to be sure that you have stayed with the main points, that you haven't strayed off into some area that's interesting but not important to the paper.

REVISING THE PAPER

Revising or editing your written work is one of the most important skills you can learn in college. It involves the ability to view your own production with enough

Figure 14-2 Page from a First Draft.

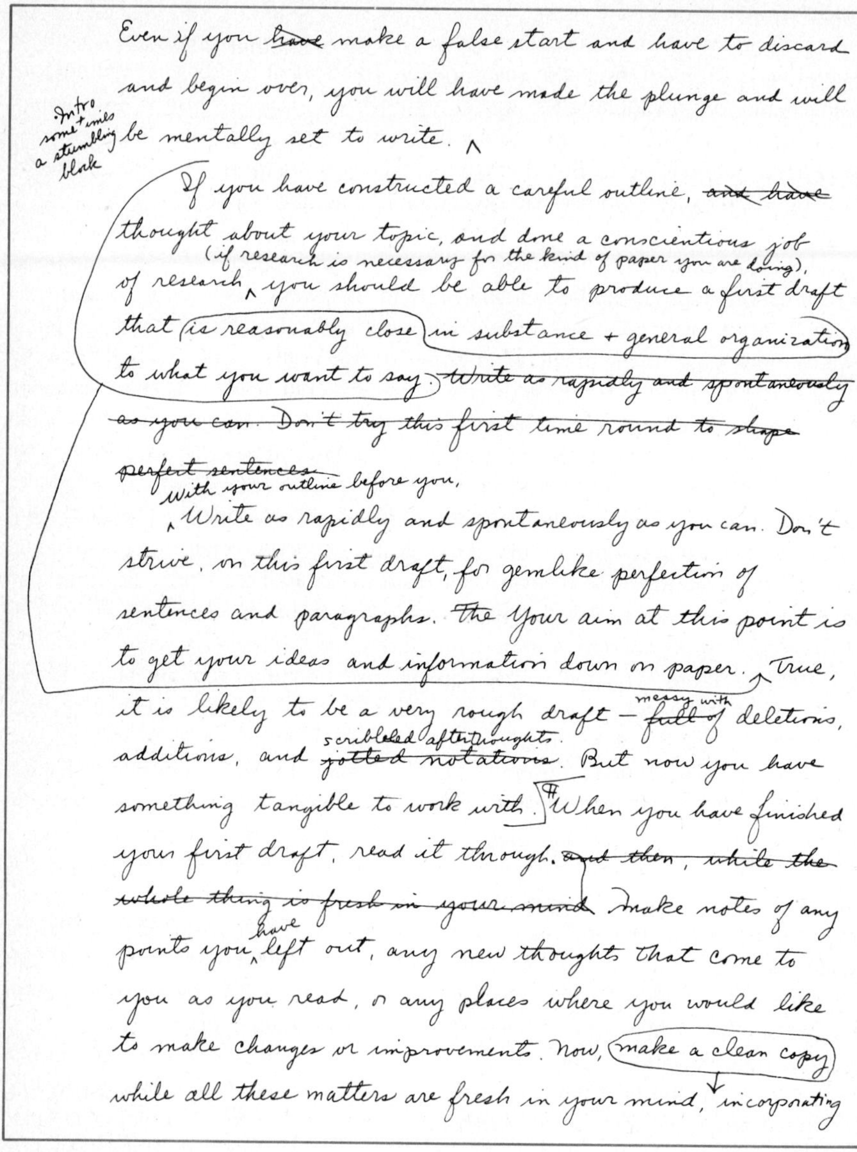

Even if you ~~have~~ make a false start and have to discard and begin over, you will have made the plunge and will *(Intro some times a stumbling block)* be mentally set to write. ∧

If you have constructed a careful outline, ~~and have~~ thought about your topic, and done a conscientious job *(if research is necessary for the kind of paper you are doing),* of research, you should be able to produce a first draft that (is reasonably close) in substance + general organization to what you want to say. ~~Write as rapidly and spontaneously as you can. Don't try this first time round to shape perfect sentences.~~ *With your outline before you,* ∧ Write as rapidly and spontaneously as you can. Don't strive, on this first draft, for gemlike perfection of sentences and paragraphs. ~~The~~ Your aim at this point is to get your ideas and information down on paper. True, it is likely to be a very rough draft — *messy with* ~~full of~~ deletions, additions, and *scribbled afterthoughts.* ~~jotted notations.~~ But now you have something tangible to work with. #When you have finished your first draft, read it through. ~~and then, while the whole thing is fresh in your mind~~ make notes of any points you *have* left out, any new thoughts that come to you as you read, or any places where you would like to make changes or improvements. Now, (make a clean copy) while all these matters are fresh in your mind, ↓ incorporating

courage to anticipate (and be concerned about) the potential reader's reaction. This means polishing and boiling down ideas, struggling to say things more clearly, and even, if necessary, writing three or four drafts.

Technical Details

Here are some technical details that you must have under control if your paper is to make a good impression on the reader.

1. Transitions. In writing your paper you need to consider how to help your reader move easily from one main point to the next. If he feels that there's no connection—that you simply jump from one point to another—he will find it hard to follow the logical sequence of events or argument that you have (or should have!) so clearly established in your own mind. To tie one idea to the next you need words like *first, second, next, in addition, finally, consequently, as a result, on the other hand.* Transitional words and phrases will help your ideas flow smoothly and make your paper easier to follow. Check carefully after you have done a first draft to see that there is some sort of transitional device leading from each paragraph to the next. Other chapters in this book discuss the use of transitions in greater detail.

2. Grammar. Students who use the English language correctly get their ideas across to other people more clearly and forcibly than those who fumble every sentence. Moreover, students who apply the rules of grammar in their papers get better grades. If you are unsure about these rules or careless with them, your meaning may get lost. That would be a pity after all the research and organization you have done. If you feel that you could use a review of grammar, there are good texts that give you the elements of English grammar by a programmed method. Some of these textbooks are even fun to read. You may be wise to get one and study it.

3. Spelling. If your spelling problems are not severe, you will find a dictionary helpful. If your spelling is very bad, look for one of the paper-backed books that list the most commonly misspelled words. They're often written for secretaries. If you cannot recognize that you are spelling words incorrectly, one of the best ways to solve the problem is to have someone who is good at recognizing spelling errors read your paper and mark the words that are wrong. Have the person mark them, *not* correct them. Then you can look the words up and write them in correctly. If you do this conscientiously over a period of time, you will improve your spelling. Make a list of the errors you make, and see whether you habitually misspell some of the same words. Then work to spell them correctly the first time.

Plagiarism

What is plagiarism? It's a kind of stealing. It means stealing other peoples' words and ideas and making them appear to be your own. If you paraphrase something from already published material and do not give the reference, you're guilty of plagiarism even though you have no intention of stealing! It need not be as blatant as copying whole passages without giving credit. Simply rearranging sentences or rephrasing a little without crediting is still plagiarism. Your paper will gain in authenticity if you quote an author and then draw your own conclusions.

Those who grade papers are quick to note a change in style of writing from one of your papers to another or from one part of your paper to another part. Your writing is like your fingerprints—individual. This is your style. If you try to use another's work, his style will not match the rest of your paper, and the difference

Figure 14-3   One Way to List Footnotes.

1. Leon Dallin, <u>Listener's</u> <u>Guide</u> <u>to</u> <u>Musical</u>
   <u>Understanding</u> (3rd ed.; New York: William
   C. Brown, 1972), pp. 112-114.

2. George Leland Bach, <u>Economics</u>: <u>an</u> <u>Introduc-</u>
   <u>tion</u> <u>to</u> <u>Analysis</u> <u>and</u> <u>Policy</u> (7th ed.; Englewood Cliffs, N.J.: Prentice-Hall, 1971),
   p. 101.

will be obvious. Instructors compare your papers and your work on exams if they think you have plagiarized. The instructor may possibly give you the benefit of the doubt if he cannot prove where you got the plagiarized material. But if he can—and it's usually not difficult—it's grounds for expulsion from college. In a world where the written word is the major product, stealing it from someone else is a serious offense.

Footnotes and Bibliography

Material from other sources must be credited. You may include a reference right after the quoted material within the body of the paper such as (Jones, 1965, page 264). This refers to the work by Jones listed in your bibliography. (More about that later.) Or you can use a subscript (1) and cite the full source at the bottom of the page or in a complete listing at the end of the paper.

Footnotes are used to give credit for quoted or paraphrased material. They are listed in the order in which you use the source material in your paper. Figure 14-3 shows a format for listing your footnotes at the end of the paper. Other forms are given in hand-books on English usage.

The *bibliography* includes the sources you used in your footnotes and may include other books or published material you read as background for the paper but did not quote in the paper.

A bibliography is just that—not "notes," "endnotes," "sources," or any other title. It's a listing of books you used in preparing the paper and you should use the correct title for this listing. When you write the bibliography, use the cards you prepared earlier. Each should have complete information about the author's name, title of book, publisher, date, and edition (if this applies).

These books should be listed alphabetically by author. There are several different bibliographic forms that are used in different fields. Either select a standard form from a handbook on English usage, or follow the form used in one

Figure 14-4   A Useful Format for a Bibliography.

Bibliography

Dallin, Leon. <u>Listener's Guide to Musical Understanding</u>.
3rd ed. New York: William C. Brown Co., 1972.

Harris, Marvin. <u>Culture, Man and Nature: An Introduction to
General Anthropology.</u> New York: Thomas Y. Crowell Co.,
Inc., 1971.

Hayakawa, S. <u>Language in Thought and Action.</u> 3rd ed. New
York: Harcourt Brace Jovanovich, 1972.

Jones, Kenneth L., Shainberg, Louis W., and Byer, Curtis O.
<u>Health Science</u>. 2nd ed. New York: Harper and Row. 1971.

Whaley, Donald L., and Malott, Richard W. <u>Elementary Principles of Behavior</u>. New York: Appleton-Century-Crofts,
1971.

Zobrist, Albert L., and Carlson, Frederick R., Jr. "An
Advice to a King Chess Computer," <u>Scientific American,</u>
228:6 (June 1973): 92-105.

---

of the journals that pertains to the subject you are writing about. No matter what form you use, it is most important to follow it consistently in every single entry in your bibliography (see Figure 14-4).

For newspaper sources you need the paper's name (underline titles of all periodicals); date of issue (March 27, 1973); author's name, if it was a by-lined article; and title of article (headline). If there was no by-line, then you just use the title of the article.

The Title

It's often a good idea to wait until you've written the paper before you decide on a final title. The title should reflect the content of the paper, but it can have an interesting twist, or perhaps make use of part of a quote if you think it's especially appropriate to the paper. A straightforward title is fine if you can't come up with one you think is especially good. In some cases, reports on scientific subjects for example, a straightforward title telling what the paper is about is best.

Introduction

You already have a general statement of the purpose of the paper—this is the basis of your introduction. Now in revising the paper, you can write the introduction in its final form. It should briefly state your purpose in writing the paper and how you are going to carry out that purpose. It might include a quotation that is particularly suitable or an interesting example or anecdote. Choose any of these devices carefully; they must be right on target. If you're not sure they will add to the paper, then settle for a straightforward statement of purpose and general method.

The introduction, the title, and the conclusion should have some continuity, something in common.

Conclusion of the Paper

Don't leave the paper without a concluding passage. If you do, the reader will be left dangling, wondering what happened to you and the rest of the paper. Let him know he has come to the end.

Usually the conclusion summarizes or restates the purpose described in the introduction. It can draw a conclusion or state your opinion that something should be done about the situation. Or it can predict what is in store for the future, drawing on what you've written in the paper. The kind of conclusion you draw will depend on the kind of paper and the subject. Just be sure you do have one. It need not be long or involved.

MAKING THE FINAL COPY

All the time and energy you have spent on your research paper should be reflected in the appearance of the final copy. Make it look neat, clean, and attractive. Then the reader will be psychologically prepared to appreciate all the other good qualities of your paper. Here are some hints.

1. Use only one side of white paper. Although few instructors will specify precisely what size paper to use, the most commonly used paper measures 8½ x 11 inches.
2. Type your paper or have it typed. Handwritten papers are difficult to read, and may not be accepted in some courses.
3. Leave a generous margin at the top and bottom of each page and a margin of one and one-half inches on both sides to provide room for the instructor's comments.
4. Type your paper without any strike-overs (erase errors thoroughly and neatly) and be sure to double-space.
5. Set up long direct quotations (five or more lines) in "block" style; that is single-space and indent the lines from both sides about a half-inch or five typewriter spaces. You omit the quotation marks when you block a quotation in this way, because the block set-up shows that you are quoting.
6. Proofread your final copy. Go over it carefully to catch spelling errors, typing errors, and other minor flaws. This is a very important step that is too often neglected.
7. Hand in the paper on time. It is not uncommon for instructors to deduct points for late papers.

What should be on a title page? Figure 14-5 shows a typical format. The format for an inside page of the paper is shown in Figure 14-6.

Figure 14-5   The Title Page of a Research Paper.

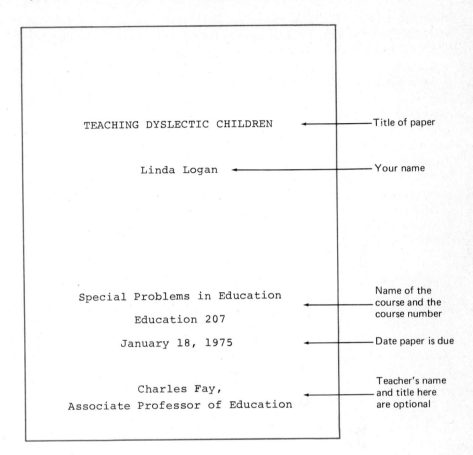

TEACHING DYSLECTIC CHILDREN ◄───── Title of paper

Linda Logan ◄───── Your name

Special Problems in Education
Education 207 ◄───── Name of the course and the course number

January 18, 1975 ◄───── Date paper is due

Charles Fay,
Associate Professor of Education ◄───── Teacher's name and title here are optional

Figure 14-6   Format for Inside Pages of a Research Paper.

```
L. Logan                    -5-
Teaching Dyslectic Children
Education 207
January 18, 1975
```

THE VALUE OF WRITING RESEARCH PAPERS

Now that you have finished all these steps and turned the paper in, you will feel a sense of relief. After you complete your first two or three papers, the whole process will seem much easier. You will have acquired a skill that will continue to serve you.

Moreover, you will have learned about a topic in depth. It's a good way to learn, and you may discover that you have developed a long-lasting interest in the subject.

15

RESEARCH PAPERS: ADDITIONAL POINTERS

In the last chapter we saw how writing a good paper is a step-by-step process. In this chapter we shall expand two of those steps because they are so important to a successful experience with a research paper that they deserve more extended discussion. These two steps are (1) choosing a topic and (2) doing library research and taking notes.

Then we shall see how all the techniques for writing a good paper are put into action when Joe, our friend from Chapter 1, tells us how he managed to get through the freshman English course he was dreading so much.

CHOOSING A TOPIC

Since finding a topic is often the biggest stumbling block in writing a paper, it is essential that you know how to choose one easily and efficiently.

Basically, there are three steps to follow in selecting a topic for a research paper:

1. Choose a subject that interests you.
2. Narrow your subject.
3. Find a focus.

Choose Your Subject

Choose a subject that interests you. The outstanding American expert on Tibet spends half of his time in Washington as an adviser to governmental agencies, yet

Adapted from an article by Walter Pauk, "The Research Paper: Time and Technique," *Journal of Reading,* Vol. 13, No. 1, October, 1969.

he has never traveled beyond the boundaries of the United States. His knowledge has come entirely through reading about a country that fascinates him. Similarly, you can use your interest in a subject as a springboard for action: in this case, writing a research paper.

Suppose that you have long been interested in the medical profession and would like to write a paper about it. Good! You know what you are interested in, and that is a big plus. But what a huge subject! It includes the training of doctors, their career patterns, their patient relations, the best way to build up a practice, foreign-born doctors, the shortage of doctors, and scores of other topics. How can you do justice to all of them? Obviously you cannot. You will have to narrow your subject.

Narrow Your Subject

The most common criticism of research papers is that the topic is too broad. You may well wonder, "Well, how can I know when I have narrowed my topic enough?" A Cornell professor of English suggests this sure-fire method: Put your subject through three or four significant narrowings, moving from a given category to a class within that category each time.

For example, here is a sample narrowing for a paper of 10 to 15 pages:

General Topic:	*The Civil War*
1st Narrowing:	The Crucial Battles of the Civil War
2nd Narrowing:	The Crucial Battle of Chancellorsville
3rd Narrowing:	Lee's Tactics at Chancellorsville
4th Narrowing:	"Stonewall" Jackson's Attack at Chancellorsville

Or suppose that after considering many different aspects of the medical profession, you feel that you are most interested in the shortage of doctors. The subject seems to be a natural one, because you immediately begin to speculate about it: Why don't the medical schools accept more medical students? But more students would mean more professors and enlarged facilities. Then why not shorten the number of years of training? Or why shouldn't the government stand the entire cost of medical training? All these ideas springing into your mind shows that you have a natural interest in the topic; in fact, any of these ideas could be the focus for your paper.

Let us pause at this point to sum up the topics you have considered, and the amount of narrowing that has been done. Here is what the summing up looks like:

General Topic:	*The Medical Profession*
1st Narrowing:	The Shortage of Doctors in the U.S.
2nd Narrowing:	Overcoming the Doctor Shortage
3rd Narrowing: (Alternative)	Overcoming the Doctor Shortage by Accepting More Medical Students

3rd Narrowing: Overcoming the Doctor Shortage by Shorten-
(Alternative)   ing the Term of Training

3rd Narrowing: Overcoming the Doctor Shortage by Gov-
(Alternative)   ernment Subsidies

Since the shortage of medical doctors is a subject of current concern, many articles have been written about it in newspapers, magazines, and journals. If, at this juncture, you think of going to the library to dig for more ideas in the *Readers' Guide to Periodical Literature,* you are well on your way toward finding the right topic.

Now, with the *Readers' Guide* in hand, you would probably try first to find your information under the caption *Doctors*; but all you would find there would be a note telling you to look under another caption, *Physicians*. Under *Physicians,* you find a long list of titles of articles. After looking through the entire list, however, you are dismayed that you did not find even one article on any of the three topics of the third narrowing. After looking through several more volumes of the *Readers' Guide* and finding only one or two titles on each topic, you decide to abandon the three topics because of the lack of material.

Going back to the current volume of the *Readers' Guide,* you begin looking for another topic with an emphasis on the shortage of doctors. The list of titles on the page looks somewhat like this:

PHYSICIANS
1. Family doctor: Medicine's newest specialty
2. Dilemma in Dyersville: doctors needed
3. Let's give foreign doctors a fair shake
4. Curing the doctor shortage: apprenticeships
5. Never marry a doctor
6. Medical assistant; the health team approach
7. Who is the doctor's doc?
8. Medical shortages abroad, too

As you look down the list, your eyes stop at title 4, "Curing the doctor shortage: apprenticeships." You intuitively sense that this topic could lead to an exciting paper. You imagine that this article might take the approach that the doctor shortage could be cured by having select students learn how to become doctors by actually working under the supervision of practicing physicians. You can also imagine the arguments that would inevitably follow. Some people would argue about the lowered quality of medical care, while others would argue about the dramatic increase in quantity. You feel that you have found an exciting topic that would make your paper both interesting to write and equally interesting to read. Your thesis could be on the side of apprenticeship, arguing that through careful selection of students, placed under the tutelage of "master" doctors, new doctors of high quality could be produced. Of course, you need to find articles that would support this view.

As you finish looking down the long column, you realize that there are no other titles on the topic of apprenticeship training. After searching through several volumes under the caption *Physicians,* you emerge with a total of four articles. Since four articles is hardly enough material for a good paper, you reluctantly drop what seemed, only a short time ago, a promising and exciting topic. So you begin searching for another topic.

During the exploration, you find a reference that leads you to another caption, *Medical.* Under this new caption, you find something like this:

MEDICAL assistants
Medical assistant: the health team approach
Physician's assistant: new help for the sick
MEDICAL delusions
Great bracelet fad: newest health fad

Desperately seeking a topic and a theme about doctor shortages, you contemplate the "medical assistants" approach; but before becoming excited about this new topic, you first check the availability of material. After a thorough search, you again decide that there are not enough articles available to write an interesting and meaningful paper. Although it may appear at this stage of the search that you are wasting time, you are actually saving time by not making a false start into a topic that cannot be finished adequately.

Continuing to turn the pages of the *Readers' Guide,* you find the caption *Medical electronics.*

MEDICAL ELECTRONICS

1. Costly machines to save lives
2. Dizzy machine; electronystagmograph
3. Mechanics of medicine: a 200-mph surgical drill
4. Mini-eye on blood pressures
5. Push-button pain reliever
6. Someone to watch over you (for 2¢ a day)
7. Will electronics solve the doctor shortage?
8. Engineers apply skills to medical devices
9. Medical devices: an unhealthy situation
10. Electronic first-aid for the busy doctor
11. Move over, doc
12. Medical electronics takes a deeper look

As your eyes move down the list of titles, you instantly know that you have found enough material to support both a topic and a point of view. You are particularly interested in the number 9 title, "Medical devices: an unhealthy situation." It indicates that there may be both positive and negative aspects to the use of medical devices. Volumes of the *Readers' Guide* for other years reveal that there are many more articles under the heading *Medical electronics.* You have finally found your topic.

Provide a Focus

To avoid making your paper a mere accumulation of facts, you must crystallize a genuine question, and your facts must then be used to answer this question. Whether it can be *definitely* answered or not is unimportant. The important thing is to focus all your research on answering a broad question, so that your paper will have direction and purpose.

If you have narrowed your topic to medical electronics, your focus might be expressed by the following question:

> In what ways do electronic machines help a doctor in his practice of medicine?

Or, more pointedly,

> Do electronic machines help or hinder a doctor in the practice of medicine?

The answer to the second question could make extremely interesting reading. You may even discover, after you have done all your research, that you are willing to take a stand on the question. Then your facts could be organized around your point of view.

A word of caution about taking a stand on your subject: Do not become so biased that you either consciously or unconsciously pick out the strongest arguments for the side that you want to win, and consequently ignore or minimize the evidence on the other side. Remember, you are not writing the research paper to win an argument. Your task is to inform both yourself and your readers. This does not mean that your guiding idea or point of view cannot be the essence of your organization. But be fair. Present both sides of the argument.

At this point, you have finally found a manageable topic and you have found a focus by asking a good question about it. You do not yet know the answer to your question, but you are ready to start your research.

TAKING LIBRARY NOTES

Taking *two* sets of notes is a useful variation on the system of note-taking presented in the last chapter. The first set of notes is your bibliography: one card for each book, magazine, or other source of information. The second set of notes consists of the detailed information that you gather from each of your sources.

This system may sound time-consuming. "Why bother to write all that information down twice?" you may ask. But you won't be writing the same information twice. You'll be gathering *more* information with *less* writing. Here's how the system works.

Select a Working Bibliography

As you do the research for your paper, you need to know what books and magazine articles you are going to consult. Not all of them will prove to be useful, of course, but you need to check them out anyway. This list of "references to look up" is your working bibliography.

Make your working bibliography from the more promising articles and books you find in the card catalog and the *Readers' Guide*. Be generous: it is better to check out a few references that do not help you than to miss the one outstanding book on your topic just because its title doesn't appeal to you. Write down everything that sounds as though it relates to your topic.

An efficient method for making a working bibliography is shown in Figure 15-1. The different parts of each slip are explained below.

A. On the front of a 3 x 5 slip, record the name of the library where the reference is located. Many universities have special libraries located in separate schools on campus. Later, if you should need the reference for additional material, you will be able to find it directly, without going back to the card catalog. If your college has only one library, you can omit part A.

B. Record the short title of your subject. This will be important when working on current and subsequent papers.

C. Record the library call number. You will not have to refer to the card catalog whenever you want to use the same book again.

D. Accurately record the full reference in exactly the same form that you plan to use in the bibliographical portion of your paper. This ensures your including all the essential parts of the reference; also, using the correct form now will make typing your paper much easier.

E. On the back of the 3 x 5 slip, briefly record your opinion of the reference. You may write, "Not useful—does not discuss principles," or "Excellent case studies of poor readers at the secondary-school level."

Do not stop with the card catalog and the *Readers' Guide*. Other valuable sources of information include *Poole's Index to Periodical Literature* and special indexes that list new books and articles for one field. Examples are the *Psychological Abstracts* for the field of psychology and the *Educational Index* for the field of education. Also check the general encyclopedias, such as the

Figure 15-1

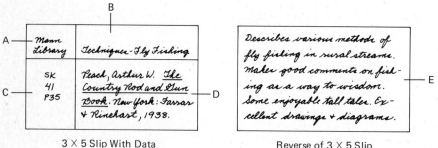

3 X 5 Slip With Data

Reverse of 3 X 5 Slip
With Comments

Figure 15-2   A Detailed Note Written on One Side of a 3 × 5 Slip.

Quine

Modern logic can be divided into three parts:
1. Truth functions
2. Quantification
3. Membership

(p. 2)

Britannica, the *Americana,* and the *New International,* and more specialized works like the *Encyclopedia of Banking and Finance* and *Who's Who in America.* Finally, there are the yearbooks, of which the *World Almanac* and the *Book of Facts* are notable examples.

One frequently overlooked source of information is the personal interview. Every campus and town has its share of experts and authorities. If possible, arrange for an interview and be prepared to take notes.

Take Detailed Notes

This stage is time-consuming; but if it is done with painstaking care, you will be well repaid for your effort, because your paper will be half written.

Each of these eleven suggestions will help you take better notes and produce a better final paper.

1. Use note paper of uniform size. The 3 x 5 paper slips are suggested because they are uniform, less bulky, and less expensive than cards. Never make a running list of notes on large paper; such notes are almost impossible to organize.
2. Use only one side of the slip, and record only one topic on each slip.
3. Identify the reference information on the note slips by writing the author's last name for the title of the reference in the top left corner of the note slip. The page number or numbers should appear in parentheses at the end of each item of information. Then you can quickly find the exact page again if further information is needed, and you have all the information you may need for a footnote (see Figure 15-2).
4. Just as in taking notes on a textbook, always skim the article or chapter you are reading before writing the notes.
5. Write notes in your own words. This will help you understand what you are

reading. Furthermore, you will be putting the information into a form that can be used in your paper. Always distinguish clearly between your words and the author's. Failure to do so might lead you unwittingly into plagiarism.

6. Notations should be concise, yet sufficiently detailed to provide accurate meaning.

7. Taking time to write notations neatly will avoid the time and frustration of later deciphering.

8. Use ink. Notes written in pencil will become blurred through handling and sorting.

9. If you need direct quotations, use only a few of the outstanding phrases or sentences. Most students tend to quote too much and too often.

10. Abbreviate only the common words; otherwise you will lose time figuring out unfamiliar "shorthand."

11. When ideas and insights occur, write them on separate note slips under the caption "my own."

Now that you have taken all the notes for your research paper, you are ready to organize them and write your paper, using the techniques described in the preceding chapter.

TECHNIQUES IN ACTION

You have been exposed to a number of steps for writing a research paper. Although these steps were easy to understand as you read them one by one, you might still find them not so easy to apply in actual practice. The following story is told to help you make the transition from "reading about it" to "applying it."

As you may recall from Chapter 1, Joe was worried about his freshman English class. He didn't know how he would have time to read all the assignments, and the teacher had a reputation for being very tough. Well, here is what happened to Joe, written in his own words.

MY FIRST RESEARCH PAPER

Registration was like a game of chess. The smart students made their moves early. They stood at the heads of long lines, not especially to get the best courses, but to avoid being "stuck" with one—the one taught by Professor Horst von Schliermann.

The chances of being forced into the 3:00 o'clock were very slim, but still too terrifying to take a chance. Professor Schliermann had, as the students said, "a special deal with the administration." He could hand-pick twenty freshmen for his class, but had to take another ten at general registration.

This unusual procedure was a compromise. It came about in this way: Professor Schliermann had taught only graduate courses before; but ten years ago, he decided that he would like to teach one freshmen section of English 105. So, in a German-accented voice (it was hard to account for the accent, for he was a third-generation American), Professor Schliermann suddenly proclaimed to the dean that he would take twenty freshmen and turn them into scholars.

The dean was faced with a dilemma. On the one hand, a negative answer might be taken as a rude rebuff by the proud and sensitive Schliermann. Also, the dean thought, "If he resigns, I'll have to answer to the president." Schliermann was eagerly sought after by other universities. He was the university's brilliant light. On the other hand, a positive answer would be a blow to the morale of the other members of the English department, who had no choice but to take their usual thirty-per-class; therefore, the compromise. Needless to say, I was one of the unlucky ten.

Right from the very first day in class, I could see how well Schliermann had chosen. The twenty were geniuses. I later found out that they all had straight A's in high school and all clustered close to 800 on the SAT. My verbal was a paltry 540, but my math a proud 720. This was, however, a course in English where math skills didn't count for much.

At first I thought it was just rumor, but after the first test I knew it was true. We unfortunate ten compared notes and found our grades in the 30's and 40's. But no one questioned Professor Schliermann's honesty or sincerity. Our papers were filled with notations, symbols, and helpful comments. We did, however, question his standards. They were not for us mortals.

Six transferred to other sections immediately; the other three transferred after the second quiz. Everyone knew that transfer was possible. The other instructors expected to get the ten of us in their classes. But in this way morale was preserved, because administratively, at least, all the classes started out with thirty students each.

Perhaps it was the lemming instinct in me or Schliermann's glittering eye, but I stayed like Coleridge's wedding guest. On the day after the last day for changing classes, I took my usual seat. The other twenty students, who usually chatted loudly until Professor Schliermann entered the door, were strangely silent today. You see, in all these past ten years, not one of the unchosen had ever stayed in Schliermann's class. Everyone knew this.

We could hear Schliermann's brisk but firm footsteps drawing closer to the open door. The pace was faster than usual. We saw the toe of his left foot puncture the blank space of the doorway. He was entering. The blood was pounding at my temples. I could hardly see. He always walked straight to the lectern, put down his notes, and said "good afternoon" to the class. Perhaps he would do the same today, but I *knew* today would be different. His right hand now swung into the doorway, and then his head emerged. It was turned in my direction. I knew it would be turned even before he entered. In my condition, I couldn't tell whether his lips parted a telltale bit, or compressed slightly. Schliermann didn't greet the class as usual. He just lectured, but more seriously. I couldn't keep my mind on the lecture. No one could. It seemed that I had spoiled the atmosphere. I wished I had been less foolhardy.

On Monday, however, the class resumed its normal pace and atmosphere. I was present but not accepted. The twenty sat in a solid square. I sat outside the square, alone but adjoining like an appendix. But that didn't matter, for I was really fascinated by Professor Schliermann. He was a great teacher.

I took good notes and studied the assignments. During discussions, I occasionally forgot myself and spoke out. I worked hard on quizzes and exams, but I always fell a bit short. It wasn't that I couldn't understand the ideas and concepts; rather, time always ran out. I needed more time to think. I was slower—much slower—than the rest. But, I wasn't discouraged. I was learning a lot.

It was just before the Thanksgiving recess that Professor Schliermann announced it. "It" was the research paper—fifty pages of it, and counting for one-third of the final grade. I should have been petrified because I couldn't write. I knew it, and now Professor Schliermann would have definite proof. Yet, I was glad. This was my chance—my only chance to raise my present hard-earned average of 62.7 to the necessary 70.

This would be the first instance where I'd have an advantage over the other students—I'd have the advantage of *time*. I needed time. Time is the great equalizer; time is democratic. We all receive the same amount of it every morning. No distinction is made between the genius and the plodder, the parsimonious and the profligate. This is what I told myself; it helped me feel a little better.

There shouldn't have been any excitement because everyone knew about *the Schliermann paper*. Then, too, it wasn't due until one week after the Christmas holidays—a long way off. But still, there were groans and whisperings. I could hardly hear the professor's caution against plagiarism. Very few paid attention to his second point about choosing a topic. I somehow caught, "The first topic you settle upon should be narrowed three to four times." What did he mean by this?

After the others had left, I edged up to Professor Schliermann, who was gathering up his lecture notes, and asked about the idea of narrowing the topic. He said, "If, for example, you choose as your topic the 'Civil War,' you would be almost sure to fail because you could not possibly do justice to such a large topic—dozens of books would be necessary to cover that subject, not a fifty-page paper. Remember, the title of your paper is a promise. It's like a contract in which you promise to deliver something specific. Even a second narrowing of the topic to 'The Battle of Gettysburg,' a single battle of the war, would still be too large; so by subjecting the topic to a third narrowing such as 'The Battle of Cemetery Ridge,' you'd have come closer to manageability, but the topic would still be too big; so perhaps a fourth narrowing such as 'The Tactical Importance of Cemetery Ridge' would be necessary. This would be a topic on which many data could be found and one on which a paper could be written in depth."

I was now excited about writing the term paper so I went straight to the library, eager and determined to find a good topic on which to use this new method of narrowing.

I was surprised to find the cavernous library so empty of students. But, of course, there would be time during the holidays of Thanksgiving and Christmas—there was no pressure yet. I went directly to the reference librarian, who smiled and seemed happy to have some business. She showed me where to find and how to use the various special reference books. Another librarian, who joined us, had an intriguing idea. She said, "If you choose an area carefully in your first year, and continue throughout your four years in college to research and to write on topics in that area, you could probably become quite an expert." This idea was overwhelming to me.

So, for the next three days I thought of nineteen areas, jotted them on a sheet of paper, and during the Thanksgiving holidays reflected on them. By the time I returned to school, I had rejected fourteen of them. The remaining five areas I decided to talk over with Professor Schliermann. He seemed happy to see me. In about five minutes we eliminated two. As far as the other three were concerned, he suggested that I talk about each with professors who were experts in the respective areas.

These talks were wonderful. I got to know three new professors from whom I received not only insights but also titles of the important books in each area as well. After thinking through the suggestions made by these three professors, I settled on the area that was most interesting to me.

So, with the topic both decided and narrowed, back to the library I went to start reading and collecting data. With the first week almost over I was still surprised to find no one else in the reference room. I gathered some books and began taking notes on sheets of paper. The reference librarian soon sauntered over and asked if I knew the advantages of recording my notes on 3 x 5 slips. Without waiting for an answer she said that unless I was able to categorize my notes, they would become unmanageable and burdensome. Her specific suggestions were these: First, record only one point, or a small cluster of several related points, on one card. Second, write a subject-matter label at the top of each card. Third, use only one side of the card. Fourth, each card should bear the author and page number of the source. Fifth, put all verbatim material in quotes. Sixth, almost all of the notes should be in your own words. Seventh, whenever you have a thought or insight of your own, jot it down in the pertinent part of your notes and enclose it in brackets to signify "my own."

Seeing that I had no slips, she darted to her desk, pulled out the bottom drawer and thumped on my table several rubber-banded stacks of cards. "These are old reference cards," she said, "used on one side. I knew I'd find a use for them someday."

After spending more than a week in the reference room gathering data, I felt that I was ready to write the first draft. After clearing a large table, I set about to put a shoebox full of cards into categories. The librarian was right. Having a title or caption on the top of each card, and having notes on each which pertained to only one item permitted me to place the cards in separate categories. If I had put two different notes on one card, I would have had to rewrite the items onto two cards now. I was glad that I had a system. It was like playing cards. As I dealt the cards onto piles, I could see that on my next paper, I would try to caption my cards even more specifically.

I didn't have a written outline. I had tried to write one just after selecting my topic, but I couldn't anticipate the material that I would find. However, although I didn't have an outline, it would be unfair to say that I selected the material for my notes haphazardly. I selected material that I thought had a bearing on my specific topic. Once I immersed myself in the topic, I began to sense what was relevant and what was not.

So, with the cards in categories and sub-categories, I started to follow the second step of the librarian's advice. I began to shift the little piles of cards into an order which seemed logical for my paper. It took several hours of shifting, thinking, re-shifting, but by the time I went to bed that night, the physical existence of an outline was on my table top; admittedly, it was rough and crude, but it was better than what I could have done with paper and pen at the very beginning.

With the categories spread out before me, I began to make a detailed outline on paper to see with greater precision where I stood. As I wrestled with topics, sub-topics, and supporting materials I began to see where I had gaps in data and weak spots. My detailed outline revealed plainly the areas in which my paper lacked balance and completeness. My work for the next few days was cut out for me; I knew that I must look for the specifics that the paper presently lacked. I was glad each card bore a reference to the source, so I could go back not only to the book, but to the page as well.

After a few days of using my spare hours in the library, I was ready to add additional 3 x 5 cards to existing categories and to make several new ones. I felt that the more complete I could make my stacks of cards, the more meaningful would be the first draft. It is much easier to rearrange whole stacks of cards than to rearrange paragraphs already written down.

Finally, I was satisfied with my outline. Then I began writing the first draft. It surprised me to see how easy it is to write a long paper once the material is placed in order. I actually enjoyed the process. I now understood better the meaning of Schliermann's words: "If you don't gather enough first-class material, you will have trouble writing a long paper." It took four days of writing in my spare time to complete the paper. On each day I concentrated on writing one of the four major parts of the paper. When I finished, I immediately read it over and it sounded good to me—so good that I knew that I'd be able to enjoy my Christmas holidays. A wonderful reward. So I banged out a clean copy on my typewriter and left it on my desk to cool while I went home for the holidays.

On the very last day before we departed for the Christmas holidays, Professor Schliermann did his duty as a teacher to remind the class to work hard on our papers because they were due on January 10—five days after our return to campus. The students fidgeted, a nervous laugh or two mingled with some of the spontaneous whispering, but no one said anything. At the moment, I thought to myself that I hadn't seen any of the chosen twenty in the library; but then they could have been there at other times. Also, the thought struck me that they loved to discuss every moot point in class and to write creative papers—information they already had in their heads; but perhaps a *research* paper which demanded hard and dogged work was just too much for their creative souls. Well! I just thought these thoughts and was a bit ashamed.

Even though I was failing Professor Schliermann's course, the good feeling generated by my completed research paper provided the tone I needed to enjoy my Christmas holidays. I had a good rest.

I arrived back on campus on Friday to avoid the weekend traffic and rush. That evening, feeling proud of myself, I casually picked up my completed paper and, to extract the fullest amount of satisfaction from my accomplishment, I began reading. By the time I finished page 3, my smile had vanished, and by page 14 fear had gripped me. My theme, which sounded so smooth upon completion, was now disjointed, repetitious, disorganized, and some paragraphs were almost meaningless. How could that be?

I quieted myself after the initial shock by realizing that I still had seven days, while many of the other students in the class had not even started their papers, nor would most of them arrive back on campus before Sunday. That would leave them but a scant five days. As I thought about how to approach the job of fixing up my research paper, I realized, for the first time, the truth of the words which I had discarded automatically as "teachers' preachings": "No paper should ever be handed in unless you have revised it. For the revision to be effective, you must always put your paper away for a few days, or a week, so that you will lose some familiarity with it. Then, when you reread it, you will be better able to spot the rough portions. Once these are spotted, revise, revise, revise."

My paper was rough, and how! I recalled the steps for revising: first, look through the material to make sure the facts are understandable and supported by details and examples; second, make sure the organizational plan for the paper is clear and the topics are in logical sequence; third, check for consistency of style; and fourth, make sure the mechanics of spelling and hyphenating are correct. I found that I had scattered throughout the paper bits of interesting material—interesting but not always pertinent. I placed some of this misplaced material into the introductory portion, and the rest of it I threw out. It was hard to throw away these gems that I worked so hard to extract from the reference books, but I heard ringing in my ears: "good writers don't put down everything that is interesting. Remember the iceberg with its seven-eighths underwater and only one-eighth showing! This submerged part—your background—gives the iceberg its strength and power."

After weeding out the extraneous material, I concentrated on the plan of the paper and found that it, too, was a bit hazy—parts of the general statement which should have been at the beginning were in the body of the paper. So I sharpened the beginning by stating the general theme, then broke it down to the five main points that I had planned to prove and support. By the time I got through with that, I really knew for the first time what I was trying to do. I was shocked to realize that my own concept of what I was trying to do hadn't been clear! By the time I went to sleep Sunday evening, I had hammered out a clear statement of what I was trying to prove and support.

Monday rolled around all too soon. The vacation was over. There was a lot of hustling on campus as student's went into a faster tempo of study. Papers were due, final exams imminent, and most plans to complete work during the holidays had fallen through.

Schliermann reminded the class of the Friday deadline. There was no whispering this time, just grim silence. I, too, contributed to the silence. I had to write not only a passing paper, but a paper good enough to earn an 85 if I were to raise my average to the passing grade of 70. I had perhaps counted too heavily on time and technique. Time was running out, and technique wasn't holding up. But I still had a chance. Most of the chosen twenty, I was sure, hadn't started.

During my study period, I worked hard to strengthen the main body of the paper by aligning my main topics in the same order as in the statement of purpose at the beginning of the paper. I made sure that each main topic led off with a general statement. You might call it a topic sentence. Then around each main topic I grouped the supporting materials. I was surprised that some of the supporting materials were rather widely scattered even though I had carefully laid out a sequence when I grouped my 3 x 5 cards. By bringing related materials into their proper blocks, I was able to avoid repetition. I re-worked each main topic, especially those that seemed vague or hastily done. Since I had more material than I used originally, I dug back into my 3 x 5 cards whenever an idea needed additional support.

On Tuesday I worked and reworked the material into a summary that was not repetitious, synthesizing the thesis and key points in such a way as to show mastery of the material.

The next day was Wednesday, and soon it was Wednesday night, but I hadn't finished the revision, and after that, there were over fifty pages to type, and I was not a fast typist. At least, I finished a good draft late that night.

After the nine o'clock class on Thursday, I was free to give the whole day to my paper. I first read the entire paper aloud, checking for style. By reading aloud I could better detect vague words, redundant words and awkward sounding sentences. I corrected every sentence so that it read smoothly and naturally. As a result, I spent a fair amount of time with a dictionary to find more precise words. Also, I worked on internal transitions to give my paragraphs and sentences better cohesion. Reworking the paper in detail took longer than I thought it would, and I worked and typed far into the night.

This was it. This was the day! In class, I never heard such an outpouring of incidents to a professor from frantic, frightened freshmen who had tried so hard to look and act sophisticated. "The reference room is so full, you can't find a table to write on." "Two other people are working on the same topic that I am, so I can't get hold of the reference books." "Someone ripped out of the reference book the entire article I am researching." (This is an example of what ordinarily honest students will do when under pressure.) "I'll need more time, because all the typists in town are busy, and they can't get to mine until after this weekend."

Schliermann was calm, but exceedingly serious. He looked around the room making no attempt to answer any of the excuses. After a moment, he held up his hand for quiet and went on with his lecture as if nothing had happened. There was deep silence that hour. Professor Schliermann was always good, but he was especially good that day. He talked hard and earnestly. Most of the students sat glumly, looking straight ahead with jaws set. Only a few had the discipline to take notes. For some reason, the professor's words seemed to be aimed at me. He was trying hard to make scholars of us, as well as mature men and women. About half the students handed in papers that day. Spurred by the announcement, "Five points a day will be deducted on all late papers," the rest were in on the following Monday. I was happy that mine was on time.

With only a week and a half to go, Professor Schliermann lectured hard and fast, saying all that he had to say. By now, I had reconciled myself. Though I still wanted to pass the course, I wasn't too worried about it. I was just glad to have had the opportunity to hear and learn in Professor Schliermann's class.

On the following Monday, the last day of class, in strode Professor Schliermann with our research papers. "Before I hand them back to you," he said, "I want to talk about them both generally and specifically." He continued, "A few of the papers were excellent, a few very bad, and most mediocre. The excellent ones were creative and imaginative in their use of technique; but the poor ones seemed as if they were put together artificially and mechanically with scissors and paste."

That last remark hit me. Of course, I should have known that Professor Schliermann would be quick to see the artificial way my paper was put together: how I took notes on cards; distributed them in piles; mechanically shifted stacks of cards around; made an outline last, not first; filled gaps by digging out more material; mechanically revising, looking up words, reading aloud to detect faulty intonation—all done like a "hack" in mechanical and piecemeal fashion. The rest of the class had real talent—they were truly gifted. In four or five days, they were able to write down their thoughts directly, almost full-blown, like true artists. And like true artists they made good with one chance, whereas I had dozens of chances to write and rewrite.

As Professor Schliermann continued to talk about "scissors and paste," he suddenly picked up a paper to illustrate a point. I was shocked. I could tell it was my paper. I just couldn't stand the embarrassment. All I wanted to do was to get out of that room, fast! Then I suddenly realized that though I knew it was my paper, no one else did. So I steeled myself. Professor Schliermann read one paragraph after another. He jumped to the first part of the paper for a paragraph, then to the end for another. Then I noticed that the rest of the class was listening attentively, and though Professor Schliermann's voice was excited, it was kindly. As I pulled myself together to listen, I heard, "This is what I mean by scholarship. The technique is discernible? Yes! But put together with a scholar's love, and care, and time."

P.S. You guessed it! I passed the course.

V

THE SPECIALIZED SKILLS

16

HOW TO STUDY MATHEMATICS

HARRISON GEISELMANN

Problems intrigue us, and most of us enjoy solving them. We demonstrate this again and again when we accept the challenge to solve a problem such as the following:

> At exactly 2 o'clock, two bacteria are placed in a growing medium. One minute later there are four bacteria, in another minute eight bacteria, and so on. At exactly 3 o'clock, the growing mass of bacteria measures one gallon. At what time was there one pint of bacteria?*

As you saw, the preceding problem involved only careful reasoning and a knowledge of arithmetic. Now try this geometry problem!

■ A window at a store was a yard square. The owner decided that the window let in too much light. So he boarded up one half of the window, but left it in the shape of a square, and it was still a yard high and a yard across. How did he do it? ■

Doing mathematics is actually a form of problem-solving using the most efficient methods developed over the centuries. Once you recognize the practical-ity of mathematics, its usefulness in solving all sorts of problems, you will study and learn it more surely and enthusiastically.

*The answers to all problems are found at the end of the chapter.

FROM ARITHMETIC TO MATHEMATICS

College work in mathematics is merely a continuation of a program that begins in the elementary grades with the first operations of arithmetic and continues through the junior and senior high schools with algebra, geometry, and trigonometry. No other subject in the curriculum has so long-sustained and cumulative a development, for at each stage in the program you must be prepared to use all the mathematics you have studied previously. When you have difficulty with mathematics, it is almost always because you have not fully mastered some of the principles and processes, so that whenever you're called on to use these, you're in trouble.

HOW TO REMEDY A WEAK BACKGROUND

If your background is shaky, what can you do about it? A thoroughgoing review is hardly feasible on top of your regular course load. There are, however, two practical ways to strengthen weak spots and fill in gaps.

First, you can attack each particular difficulty as it arises. Whenever you run into a need for a process or formula or principle that you don't understand, clear up that point so that it won't bother you the next time. The fact that you have an immediate need for the material will give you an incentive to master it. This is a good way to get the mathematical review you need for physics, chemistry, biology, astronomy, economics, and courses in the social sciences and education where statistical techniques are used. It is also a practical plan of attack if you are experiencing only occasional difficulties in your college mathematics course.

To accomplish spot review work of this kind, you should have at hand textbooks covering arithmetic, algebra, geometry, and trigonometry—preferably those you used in secondary school and are familiar with. Naturally, when you are reviewing, you should make every effort to understand the underlying process involved. For example, when you're reviewing a formula, you should understand how it was derived. Try to do the problem in Figure 16-1.

The second way to overcome weak spots in your background is a preventive measure: a systematic diagnosis of your mathematical competence. For this purpose, provide yourself with a "self-help" review book (your instructor can recommend one) and work your way through it to discover what topics you need to study and to practice on.[1] By drill work with examples and problems in your particular area of difficulty you can forestall real trouble at a more advanced level.

The most common areas of weakness in arithmetic are fundamental operations with decimals and fractions, ratio and proportion, and percentage; in algebra, they are evaluation of expressions, fractions, fractional and literal equations, factoring, quadratic equations, and word problems; in trigonometry, identities and logarithms.

[1] A good review workbook is *Basic Mathematics*, by M. Wiles Keller and James H. Zant (Boston: Houghton Mifflin Company; Form B, 1956; Form C, 1964; Second Series, Form A, 1970). Each Form covers arithmetic, algebra, and trigonometry, and contains diagnostic tests from which the student can determine his strengths and weaknesses.

Figure 16-1   Understanding the Basis for Mathematical Operations: the Pythagorean Theorem.

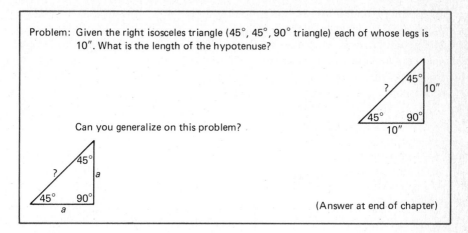

Problem: Given the right isosceles triangle (45°, 45°, 90° triangle) each of whose legs is 10″. What is the length of the hypotenuse?

Can you generalize on this problem?

(Answer at end of chapter)

DEVELOPING GOOD STUDY HABITS

In no field of study is the change from secondary school to college greater than in mathematics. In high school you probably did most of your drill work in class, under supervision, or as homework to be passed in for correction and credit. In college, however, you will have to get the equivalent of this drill by working out numerous exercises on your own—practicing those manipulations and operations which one masters only by doing them over and over again. And most of this "homework" you will not hand in for correction and credit. Your reward will be the proficiency that comes through hours of self-paced study, hours spent in working out exercises and problems and thinking your way to understanding.

As we suggested earlier, there is a good reason for learning to be self-propelled in studying mathematics. In the context of modern life, mathematics is a very practical subject: it is all applied, or applicable. In an advanced course or in a job situation, there won't always be a teacher or a textbook at hand to tell you what process or formula to use. Mathematics can provide you with some powerful tools; but like all tools, they will be useful only if you know how to use them without having someone else guide your hand.

Keeping Up to Date

We have seen that mathematics—like a foreign language—is a cumulative subject in which you must be prepared at any point to use anything or everything you have previously learned; and further, that it is a subject in which drill and practice are required for the mastery of essential operations. For these reasons, it is absolutely necessary to keep your work up. If you fall behind, you'll find it terribly hard to catch up again, because you will have to take time from the drill work which ensures competence and understanding.

Taking Notes in Class

The general principles of note-taking discussed in Chapter 9 apply also to lectures and class discussions in mathematics.

There are, however, some special things to keep in mind. First, keep notes to a minimum. In courses involving quantitative relationships, the very process of note-taking hinders the student in following the instructor's line of argument. Record main ideas, but don't try to take down all the details and examples.

If the lectures are closely related to the textbook, you may find it helpful to read ahead before the lecture; you can then tell to what extent the lecture repeats and to what extent it supplements the text, and can take notes accordingly. You might even keep your textbook open and write supplementary or clarifying information right on the book page. But first check with your instructor to see whether he has any objections to your reading ahead or referring to the text during the class period.

If you lose the thread of a lecture or class discussion, or if you fail to understand a line of reasoning or a mathematical procedure, ask the instructor for clarification. Even if it's only a minor point at the time, failure to clear it up may lead you into major difficulties later. You'll have to do *your* part, though, by doing your advance preparation and giving the instructor your full attention during the class period.

To provide the maximum reinforcement for classtime learning, study your notes and the related text material and problems as soon after class as possible. But don't attempt any problems until you are sure you understand the material. Working at an assignment before you are ready for it wastes time—and, worse, may set you off on faulty procedures and interfere with understanding.

Studying for Examinations

The best way to study for an examination is to keep your daily work up throughout the term. Then at examination time you can concentrate on polishing up what you have already learned.

Start early to review the problems you have had in assignments and previous tests, paying special attention to the more troublesome ones. This will give you a chance to ask your instructor for help if you are still unsure of some procedures.

You may find the 3 x 5-inch card system useful for memorizing important formulas and principles which you will not be able to look up in the textbook during the examination (see Figures 16-2 and 16-3). Record one item to a card, and carry the cards around with you to study at odd moments. Be sure, however, that you understand the *meaning* of information which you memorize in this way, so that you could still work the problem even if you forgot the rote words and symbols. Consider a formula a convenience or short cut, not an end in itself.

Whenever you get back a test or examination, rework the problems on which you made mistakes and find out what you did wrong. Correcting your errors is one of the most valuable learning experiences you can have and is sure to have a bearing on your performance in subsequent tests.

Figure 16-2   Example of the 3 X 5 Card System for Memorizing Formulas.

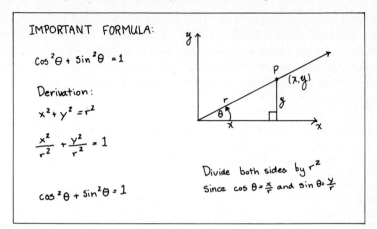

IMPORTANT FORMULA:

$$\cos^2\theta + \sin^2\theta = 1$$

Derivation:

$$x^2 + y^2 = r^2$$

$$\frac{x^2}{r^2} + \frac{y^2}{r^2} = 1$$

$$\cos^2\theta + \sin^2\theta = 1$$

Divide both sides by r^2
Since $\cos\theta = \frac{x}{r}$ and $\sin\theta = \frac{y}{r}$

Figure 16-3   Example of the 3 X 5 Card System for Memorizing Principles.

IMPORTANT PRINCIPLE:

The sense of an inequality is not changed if both members are multiplied or divided by the same positive number.

Symbolically   if $a > b$ and $c > 0$,
then $c \cdot a > c \cdot b$ and $\frac{a}{c} > \frac{b}{c}$

Examples: Since $10 > 8$
then $3 \cdot 10 > 3 \cdot 8$ or $30 > 24$
and $\frac{10}{2} > \frac{8}{2}$ or $5 > 4$

PRACTICAL SUGGESTIONS FOR PROBLEM-SOLVING

Solving a mathematical problem is basically a two-part operation. First, you have to analyze it, then you have to compute it. If you fail to size up the problem correctly, of course, you can't compute your way to the correct solution. On the other hand, an error in calculation—whether from carelessness or from inadequate understanding of basic operations—can cancel out even a brilliant piece of analysis.

Set Up the Problem

To avoid the tendency toward trial-and-error and manipulation to get an answer, read the problem twice, carefully. Note what things are *given*, what principles and relationships are stated or implied, and what is to be found or proved. It may help you to jot these essentials down on a piece of paper. Now set the problem up. Don't think yet about computing it; concentrate first on analyzing it.

For example:

PROBLEM: How many minutes will it take a pump delivering 2.75 gals. per stroke and making 88 strokes per minute to pump 500 barrels of oil? (One barrel = 31.5 gals.)

Suggested set up:
   Analysis:
      (1)   2.75 gals. per stroke × 88 strokes per min. = 2.75 × 88 gals./min.
      (2)   How many gallons of oil to be pumped?
            500 barrels × 31.5 gals./bar. = 500 × 31.5 gals.

Suggested set up:
            Let M = minutes required to pump 500 barrels of oil

$$M = \frac{500 \times 31.5}{2.75 \times 88} \quad \frac{\text{gals./min.}}{\text{gals.}}$$

$M \approx 65$ minutes.
(Note: $\approx$ means "is approximately equal to.")

Setting up the complete problem gives more opportunities for canceling, combining numbers, short-cut arithmetical processes, and other simplifications than you have available when you do a problem in piece-meal fashion. In addition, some instructors give partial credit on examinations if you can demonstrate your ability at least to set up the problem, even if you do not solve it correctly.

Draw a Diagram

By drawing a careful diagram you can often clarify facts, principles, and relationships that are less evident from words alone. To illustrate:

PROBLEM: A pulley, 7 inches in diameter, is turning a belt and is rotating at 60 revolutions per minute (rpm). How fast is the belt moving in feet per minute? (Assume no slipping between the belt and the pulley.)

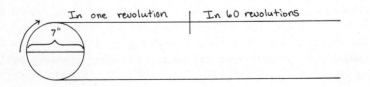

ANALYSIS OF DIAGRAM:

When the pulley turns around once (1 rpm), it moves the belt a distance

$$C = \pi D = \frac{22}{7} \cdot \frac{7}{12} \text{ ft, or } \frac{11}{6} \text{ ft.}$$

In 60 revolutions, it would move the belt $\frac{11}{6}$ ft. times 60, or 110 feet in a minute.

The complete set-up, then, and the solution, is:

$$\frac{22}{7} \cdot \frac{7}{12} \cdot 60 = 110 \text{ ft. per minute.}$$

Notice the advantage of setting up the entire problem, simplifying and doing the calculation at the end, instead of computing as you go along.

Apply Your Knowledge of Arithmetic

In algebra you can often use your knowledge of arithmetic to test a procedure about which you have doubts. Is it possible to cancel as shown in the following?

$$\frac{a + b}{b} = a + 1 ?$$

And does $\sqrt{a^2 + b^2} = a + b$? By substituting several pairs of numbers for a and b, you can see that these statements are not generally true.

When the numbers involved in a problem are so large, so small, or so complicated that they interfere with your analysis of the problem, try temporarily substituting simpler numbers. In this way the nature of the problem is often more clearly revealed. For instance:

PROBLEM: If the mass of an electron is about 9×10^{-28} grams, and the mass of a proton is about 1.62×10^{-24} grams, approximately how many times the mass of an electron is the mass of a proton?

ANALYSIS: If you are hesitant about the operation you are to perform, make up numbers that are easier to grasp: Let the proton weigh 16 grams, and the electron 2 grams.

Obviously, the proton will weigh $\frac{16}{2} = 8$ times as much as the electron. Hence the proton will weigh $\frac{1.62 \times 10^{-24}}{9 \times 10^{-28}} =$ about 1800 times as much as the electron.

Another effective technique, especially in word problems leading to equations, is to choose an answer *first* and from this to figure out the arithmetic procedure involved. For example:

PROBLEM: An alloy of copper and zinc is 10% zinc, the alloy weighing 400 lbs. How many pounds of pure zinc should be added to this alloy to make an alloy which is 20% zinc?

ANALYSIS: To discover the arithmetic procedure, let us add 100 lbs. of zinc. (See if you can draw a diagram representing this problem.)

Then the new mixture of 500 lbs. contains the original 40 lbs. of zinc plus 100 lbs., or 140 lbs. The fraction of zinc is $\frac{140}{500}$ which reduces to $\frac{28}{100}$ or .28, or 28%. In our problem we do not know how much zinc to add, but we do know that the per cent of zinc is 20%. So, letting x = no. of lbs. of zinc to be added, $\frac{40 + x}{400 + x} = \frac{20}{100}$.

Compare this equation carefully with the arithmetic performed above. Solving, $x = 50$ lbs.

Still another technique is to make an "educated guess" at the answer. When you are required in a problem to find the numerical value of some quantity, it is a good practice to guess at, or estimate, the answer in advance. A little slip in the mechanical work may cause a large error and give you an obviously absurd result, and the preliminary guess may enable you to catch and correct such an error. On the other hand, you may find that your guess is way off the mark; but through such experiences you will improve your mathematical intuition. All good scientists and mathematicians have to be good guessers, able to set up workable hypotheses out of their thorough knowledge of processes and calculations.

Check Your Results

Get in the habit of checking your results by one or more of the following methods: (1) substitute your answer for the unknown in the problem, to see whether it agrees with the given information and satisfies the given conditions; (2) re-work the problem by an alternate method; (3) estimate the answer before attacking the problem, and use it as a measuring stick. Checking can reveal errors both of analysis and of computation, and it reinforces understanding. Checking is *not* a duplication of effort and a waste of time, but it is an important and constructive process.

Use Short Cuts

Your efficiency in all mathematical operations will be improved if you are constantly alert for opportunities to use short cuts. For instance:

PROBLEM: A chemical mixture calls for 2.5 cc of element A to every 5.5 cc of element B. If this is cut down to 1.5 cc of element A, how many cc of element B should be used?

ANALYSIS: The usual way of solving this problem in direct proportion is to let b equal the no. of cc of element B. Then,

$$\frac{2.5}{1.5} = \frac{5.5}{b},$$

and by using the principle of a proportion, that the product of the first and fourth terms (extremes) equals the product of the second and third terms (means), we solve the equation:

$$2.5b = (1.5)(5.5),$$
$$b = \frac{(1.5)(5.5)}{(2.5)}$$
$$b = 3.3 \text{ cc.}$$

However, a more efficient procedure is to note that you "cut down" element A by a factor of $\frac{1.5}{2.5}$. Hence element B will be reduced by the same factor.

$$\frac{1.5}{2.5} \times 5.5 = 3.3 \text{ cc.}$$

Using short cuts also implies doing as much mental mental arithmetic as you can. Here are a few examples of calculations that you can easily do without resorting to pencil and paper.

To multiply a two-digit number by a one-digit number, such as 34×4:

$$(30 + 4)4 = (30)(4) + (4)(4) = 120 + 16 = 136.$$

To multiply a number by 25, divide it by 4 and multiply by 100 (i.e., append two zeros); for example, 25×32:

$$32 \div 4 = 8, \text{ with two zeros appended} = 800.$$

Here's another example. In evaluating a quantity such as

$$\frac{.00056 \times .25}{.00007},$$

take advantage of the fundamental principle that multiplying the numerator and the denominator of a fraction by a number (not zero) will not change the value of the fraction. In this case, multiply numerator and denominator by 100,000. Also, since $.25 = 1/4$, the entire quantity reduces to $\frac{56 \times 1/4}{7}$, or $8 \times 1/4 = 2$.

Learn to Use the Slide Rule

A widely circulated item of student folklore is that the slide rule is only for engineers and scientists and is difficult to use. This simply is not true, as junior high school students of average intelligence can and do demonstrate. Essentially, the slide rule is a device consisting of a fixed rule and a sliding one, both marked with graduated logarithmic scales. Calculations are made by suitably juxtaposing one scale against the other and reading the result. There are numerous models, ranging from simple ones on which relatively uncomplicated processes are computed, to elaborate ones for very complex and difficult processes. Unless you are planning to go on to advanced courses in the sciences or engineering, you should probably get one of the simpler and less expensive models, at least to start with. You will find it extremely useful in multiplication and division—and special cases of these, such as finding percentages, calculating ratios, raising to powers, extracting roots, and other time-consuming operations. Although at first, while you are learning to use it, you will find the slide rule less accurate and more time-consuming than computation "by hand," the tremendous time-saving that results when you have mastered it will far outweigh any temporary inconvenience.

THE PROPER ROLE OF MEMORY

In the study of mathematics most students rely entirely too much on memory. Competence in mathematics is not, to any great extent, a matter of remembering things. To take a very simple example, a child in the early grades memorizes his multiplication tables. This gives him a convenient mathematical tool and contributes to his speed in performing arithmetical operations. But it is much more important for him to see how these multiplication tables are made up by addition. Suppose he has forgotten the product 7 times 9. If he happens to know that 5 times 9 is 45, he can, by adding 9's quickly, deduce that 6 times 9 is 54 and 7 times 9 is 63. Or he may know that 10 times 7 is 70 and find, by subtracting 7, that 9 times 7 is 63. He should not be completely helpless when he has forgotten a particular product. This means, of course, that he should build up his own table for 9 times 1, 9 times 2, 9 times 3, and so on, by adding 9's before he tries to memorize the results.

This kind of thing is important throughout the study of mathematics. Algebra students memorize the formula for solving the general quadratic equation, $ax^2 + bx + c = 0$.

$$x = \frac{-b \pm \sqrt{b^2 - 4ac}}{2a}$$

But if they have not used the formula for several years, they have probably forgotten it. They may remember the general appearance of the formula but have forgotten, say, whether the sign under the radical is plus or minus. How can they now solve an equation such as $3x^2 - 10x + 2 = 0$? One way to overcome the difficulty is shown in Figure 16-4.

Memorizing the formula is a *convenience*; but an understanding of the process of completing the square, by which the formula is derived, is much more important. (See page 235 for the derivation of the quadratic formula.) Students always seem to remember the formula $\sin^2 x + \cos^2 x = 1$, but they forget the similar formula connecting $\tan x$ and $\sec x$. If they know the meaning of the trigonometric functions $\sin x$, $\cos x$, $\tan x$, $\sec x$ (even for acute angles x), it is a trivial matter to recover these formulas when they have been forgotten (see Figure 16-5).

A practical reason why mathematical ability does not have to depend very largely on memory is that textbooks and handbooks are usually available in which to look up the forgotten rule or formula or number. You can usually remember that $\sin 30° = 1/2$, and it would be convenient if you could remember all the numerical values given in a table of sines of angles from 0° to 90°. But it would clearly be foolish to attempt such a memory stunt. When you want a numerical value for $\sin 41°$, you simply look it up in a table. True, if you have not studied calculus, you will have to accept the value of $\sin 41°$ on the authority of the table. So far as you can, however, you should learn the underlying processes and computations on which formulas and tables are based, rather than rely on memory or authority. This way, when memory fails or a textbook is not at hand, you will not be completely helpless; you can reconstruct the needed formula or value for yourself.

Figure 16-4   The Proper Role of Memory in Mathematics: Using an Old Formula to Solve a New Equation.

The equation $3x^2 - 10x + 2 = 0$ is of the form $ax^2 + bx + c = 0$, where $a = 3$, $b = -10$, and $c = 2$. Using the general formula for solving equations of this type, we have

$$x = \frac{-b \pm \sqrt{b^2 - 4ac}}{2a}, \qquad x = \frac{-(-10) \pm \sqrt{(-10)^2 - 4(3)(2)}}{2(3)},$$

$$x = \frac{10 \pm \sqrt{100 - 24}}{6} = \frac{10 \pm \sqrt{76}}{6} \approx \frac{10 \pm 8.72}{6}$$

$$x \approx 3.12 \text{ or } 0.21$$

Figure 16-5   Using a Basic Understanding of Trigonometric Functions to Recover a Forgotten Formula.

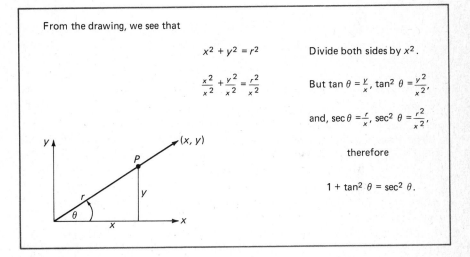

From the drawing, we see that

$$x^2 + y^2 = r^2 \qquad \text{Divide both sides by } x^2.$$

$$\frac{x^2}{x^2} + \frac{y^2}{x^2} = \frac{r^2}{x^2} \qquad \text{But } \tan \theta = \frac{y}{x}, \tan^2 \theta = \frac{y^2}{x^2},$$

$$\text{and, } \sec \theta = \frac{r}{x}, \sec^2 \theta = \frac{r^2}{x^2},$$

therefore

$$1 + \tan^2 \theta = \sec^2 \theta.$$

SKILLS ARE IMPORTANT—UNDERSTANDING IS ESSENTIAL

In the study of mathematics, then, there are two objectives: to develop skill and accuracy in certain formal processes, and to acquire a clear understanding of the meaning of these manipulations and the reasons for them. Too many students put all their effort into the first of these objectives. They learn rules and formulas, depending almost entirely on memory. This way is "right," that way is "wrong," with teacher or textbook being the authority for "right" and "wrong." Students too seldom ask *why* this is right or that is wrong. Following the rules that have been given them, they go through a process and obtain a correct result, but often have little understanding of the real meaning of the process or the result. The student in calculus can differentiate x^2, by rule, and obtain $2x$ as the derivative

Figure 16-6   The Improper Use of Memory in Mathematics: Obtaining the Derivative of x^2 by Rule Alone.

Since $y = x^2$ (1)

$y + \Delta y = (x + \Delta x)^2 = x^2 + 2x\,(\Delta x) + (\Delta x)^2$ (2)

Subtracting (1) from (2), we obtain

   $\Delta y = 2x(\Delta x) + (\Delta x)^2$

Dividing both sides by Δx, we have

$\frac{\Delta y}{\Delta x} = 2x + \Delta x$

$\frac{dy}{dx} = \lim_{\Delta x \to 0} \frac{\Delta y}{\Delta x} = 2x$

without any understanding of *why* he writes the 2 as a coefficient and reduces the exponent to 1, and without knowing what the derivative 2x means when he has obtained it (see Figure 16-6).

If you should memorize and reproduce correctly the sounds which constitute a sentence in the Russian language without knowing anything of their significance, you would not be speaking Russian—you would merely be making Russian noises. And if you manipulate mathematical processes correctly without understanding their meaning, your work is not mathematics at all—you are merely making mathematical marks. The vast shorthand symbolism that has been invented to record and communicate mathematical ideas is only the *language* of mathematics, and language is a doubtful asset to anyone who has no ideas to communicate. It is, for example, a convenience to memorize the formula,

$$\frac{d}{dx}(x^n) = nx^{n-1},$$

but this symbolism is *mathematics* only for the student who understands something of the meaning of a derivative and why this formula gives the derivative in this particular case. (See any standard calculus text for the derivation of this formula.)

PRECISION IN THE LANGUAGE OF MATHEMATICS

As you progress in mathematical insight and understanding, the language of mathematics becomes increasingly important. You must know the *exact* meaning of mathematical words and symbols: such words as "factor," "slope," "proportion," "logarithm," "prime," and "identity"; and such symbols as $=$, $<$, $(\ )$, Σ, $!$. If you have trouble remembering any special terms or symbols, write out a definition of each one on a 3 x 5 card. Then you can use the cards for review at odd moments. Table 16-1 shows the kind of brief definition that is needed.

TABLE 16-1 DEFINING MATHEMATICAL TERMS AND SYMBOLS

Words

---

1. Factor: when two or more quantities are multiplied together, each quantity is called a factor of the product. Example: In $3 \cdot 4 = 12$, 3 is a factor of 12 and 4 is a factor of 12.
2. Slope: The rate at which a curve rises or falls per horizontal unit. The slope of a nonvertical line is expressed in terms of *coordinates* of any two points. For example, slope $= (y_2 - y_1)/(x_2 - x_1)$.
3. Proportion: a statement of equality between two ratios. Example: $\frac{3}{4} = \frac{6}{8}$
4. Logarithm: the exponent to which a given base is raised to yield a given number. For example, since $2^3 = 8$, we may write $\log_2 8 = 3$.
5. Prime: a number is prime if it has exactly two divisors, itself and one. For example, 3 is prime (with divisors 1 and 3), but 4 is not (it has divisors 1, 2, and 4).
6. Identity: an equality that is always true, i.e., is true for all values of the variable concerned. Examples: $2 + 3 = 5$, $4x - 3x = 1x$, and $\sin^2\theta + \cos^2\theta = 1$.

Symbols

---

1. $=$ "is equal to," or names the same quantity; the properties of equality are: (1) Equality is *reflexive*: $a = a$. (2) Equality is *symmetric*. If $a = b$, then $b = a$. (3) Equality is *transitive*. If $a = b$ and $b = c$, then $a = c$.
2. $<$ "is less than." For example, $5 < 8$.
3. $(\ )$ is a grouping symbol. For example, $3 \times 2 + 4 = 10$, but $3 \times (2 + 4) = 18$.
4. Σ is a summation symbol. For example, $\overset{3}{\underset{1}{\Sigma}}\ x^2$ means to sum the squares of the counting numbers from one to three: $1^2 + 2^2 + 3^2$, or 14.
5. $!$ is the factorial symbol. For example 5! means the product of the first 5 counting numbers, $1 \times 2 \times 3 \times 4 \times 5$, or 120.

It would seem that the word "equal" and the corresponding symbol, $=$, are easy to understand, yet students will sometimes say that one equation is *equal* to another, or write: $x + 1 = \frac{y}{2} = 2x + 2 = y$.

What the student means, of course, is, given the equality,

$$x + 1 = \frac{y}{2},$$

if we multiply both sides of the equality by two, we have a new equality,

$$2x + 2 = y.$$

The student who writes the first set of equations possibly *means* something which is correct, but he *writes* something which is incorrect and does not express what he means. Such carelessness with the language of mathematics is not uncommon even among the better students. A student whose mathematical *thinking* is sound is often unable to communicate his ideas. When the instructor asks him a question, he may know the correct answer but give the wrong words. Or he may misinterpret the words of the question and thus go astray.

Learn the language and symbolism of mathematics, and learn to use these words and symbols precisely. Only then can you fully and accurately communicate with others, orally or in writing, in the realm of mathematics.

SUMMARY OF IMPORTANT STEPS IN STUDYING MATHEMATICS

■ 1. Most everyone who is willing to exert a sincere effort can do mathematics and can find pleasure in solving problems.
2. Make sure that you attack and clear up each difficulty in mathematics as it arises!
3. Keep your daily work up throughout the mathematics course!
4. In problem-solving make a practice of estimating the answer first, then setting up the problem before the calculations.
5. Keep memorization to a minimum; rather, aim at understanding concepts, principles and formulas.
6. Learn to use the special language and symbolization of mathematics precisely. ■

Developing your grasp of mathematics as a way of thinking will be one of the most important skills in your total education.

ANSWERS TO PROBLEMS

1. *Answer to Problem, page 221.*

Since every succeeding minute the number of bacteria doubles, every *preceding* minute there are one-half as many, and hence they occupy one-half as much volume. Therefore, at 2:59 there are 4 pts. of bacteria, (1/2 of 8 pts.), at 2:58, 2 pts. of bacteria, and at *2:57* there is one pint.

2. *Answer to Problem, page 221.*

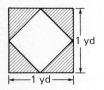

3. *Answer to Problem, page 223.*

Letting x = the hypotenuse, and using the Pythagorean Theorem,

$$x^2 = 10^2 + 10^2$$
$$x^2 = 200$$
$$x = \sqrt{200} = \sqrt{100} \cdot \sqrt{2} = 10\sqrt{2}.$$

Generalizing:

$$x^2 = a^2 + a^2$$
$$x^2 = 2a^2$$
$$x = \sqrt{2a^2} = \sqrt{2} \cdot \sqrt{a^2} = a\sqrt{2}.$$

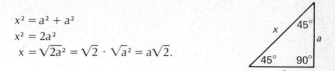

4. *Completing the square, and its use in deriving the "quadratic formula." (See page 230.)*

    If we square several binomials, we note that (1) we always obtain a trinomial, and (2) the third term is related to the coefficient of the second term; that is, if we take one-half the coefficient of the second term and square it, we obtain the third term. Therefore, we can "build up" a perfect trinomial square, given the first two terms.

    (a) $(x + 3)^2 = x^2 + 6x + 9$
    (b) $(x - 5)^2 = x^2 - 10x + 25$
    (c) $(x + h)^2 = x^2 + 2hx + h^2$

    In (a) $\left(\frac{6}{2}\right) = 9$, in (b) $\left(\frac{-10}{2}\right)^2 = 25$ and in (c) $\left(\frac{2h}{2}\right)^2 = h^2$.

    For example: what should be added to $x^2 + 8x = ?$ to make it a perfect trinomial square? Answer: $\left(\frac{8}{2}\right)^2 = 16$ or $x^2 + 8x + 16$. This is equal to $(x + 4)$.

    Now, in the general quadratic equation:

    $$ax^2 + bx + c = 0$$
    $$ax^2 + bx = -c$$
    $$x^2 + \frac{b}{a}x = \frac{-c}{a}$$

    In order to make the left side a perfect square, we square one-half of the coefficient of the second term $\left(\frac{b}{a}\right)$ and add it to both sides of the equation:

    $$\left(\frac{b}{2a}\right)^2 = \frac{b^2}{4a^2}$$
    $$x^2 + \frac{b}{a}x + \frac{b^2}{4a^2} = \frac{b^2}{4a^2} - \frac{c}{a}$$

    Then we take the square root of both sides and simplify, to derive the "quadratic formula."

    $$\left(x + \frac{b}{2a}\right)^2 = \frac{b^2 - 4ac}{4a^2}$$
    $$x + \frac{b}{2a} = \frac{\pm\sqrt{b^2 - 4ac}}{2a}$$
    $$x = \frac{-b}{2a} \pm \frac{\sqrt{b^2 - 4ac}}{2a}$$
    $$x = \frac{-b \pm \sqrt{b^2 - 4ac}}{2a}$$

17

STUDYING SCIENCE: AS A SCIENTIST SEES IT

KENNETH GREISEN

Man is born a feeble little organism in the midst of a vast, unknown universe, at a moment long after evolution began and long before it will cease. Here he exists in a tiny span of space and time. Science is the game he plays of trying to find out what is going on: where he is; what time it is; what has happened before, both here and elsewhere; and what will happen afterwards. In the beginning he does not even know what questions to ask, or with what words to formulate them. He is like Don Quixote attacking the windmills. Science is his brazen challenge against the unknown.

The fantastic thing about this quest is the extent of its success. Men can now trace their own history back for a million generations. They can describe with considerable reliability what is going on in the interior of stars. They have information about the structure and content of the universe out to a distance of 40,000,000,000,000,000,000,000 miles, and can analyze the detail of its parts down to a fine structure of 0.000,000,000,000,01 inch. They can measure changes as gradual as the slowing of the earth's rotation on its axis or as sudden as the excitation and decay of a nucleus, which may occur in 0.000,000,000,000,000,000,000,01 second; they can measure speeds as slow as continental drift or as fast as that of light.

If the excitement of this game fires your imagination, you may throw away these suggestions on how to study; your own enthusiasm will be your best guide. All too often, however, the beginning of study of an unfamiliar subject is difficult and painful, and many students turn away from a potentially pleasurable subject in discouragement. The following notes are assembled out of the writer's experience as a student and as a teacher of science, in the hope of easing the way for some of the students in the new generation.

CRITICAL ATTITUDES, GOOD AND BAD

Unquestioning acceptance of every word read in a textbook (or in a scientific journal or other reference) and every word heard in class is not conducive to either the understanding or the retention of new knowledge. It leads to the situation aptly described as words flowing in one ear and out the other. Knowledge must make sense in order to be understood and filed logically in the brain. Each new bit of information should be challenged with the questions, "Is this consistent with what I have learned before? How is it related to the structure of my past experience and knowledge? Is it a logical consequence of what I have already accepted? Or is it new and independent, but plausible, and established on good authority? Is it something to be accepted temporarily on faith? Or does it seem implausible, illogical, inconsistent with what I know or otherwise doubtful?"

Ordinarily these questions need not take up much time to answer, because a good textbook or lecture or scientific article will proceed in a systematic manner, and will point out the bases for acceptance of new information. Sometimes, however, it is desirable to interrupt the even flow of reading or listening to question an apparent gap or weakness in the argument.

At this point one may distinguish two types of critical attitude, one negative and the other positive. The negative one is obstructive and harmful. In approaching new material heard in a lecture or read in a textbook, it is not wise to be continually seeking to find fault, or to be unwilling to accept anything temporarily on faith. There are students who characteristically interrupt and challenge an argument before making a sympathetic effort to hear it through and comprehend it thoroughly. Usually such a student is so preoccupied with formulating objections that he fails to hear or see the essential points in the exposition. He is convinced in advance that what he is about to hear or read is wrong. This is not a mood that permits learning, especially when the new material is difficult.

The positive attitude is one in which the student expects to be convinced. Instead of making every effort to reject each new bit of information, he makes every effort to fit it into his framework of logical thought and thereby to accept it. When the new bit doesn't fit, he questions not only the teacher or author, but also his own understanding. He then makes inquiries, not with determination to prove the teacher wrong, but in search of more insight and information. Not infrequently, of course, a teacher or other reference *will* be found in error. The positive approach will uncover these errors with more reliability than the negative one. But above all, the positive critical approach is enormously more efficient in learning.

In short, your effort should be directed primarily toward comprehending rather than toward attacking the source of information. But this does not mean you should hesitate to raise questions or to call attention to statements that seem wrong—or that you should accept information without supporting evidence.

HOW IS SCIENCE DIFFERENT?

Perennial Concern with Problems

Science consists of solving problems or at least trying to solve them. So does any scholarly subject. But in science the problems are almost invariably quantitative.

Qualitative description and classification play a part in the beginnings of some sciences, but are supplanted by quantitative calculation as the subject matures. A student of science, therefore, cannot escape mathematical problems (see Figure 17-1).

A familiar complaint heard by every science teacher from about 50 percent of his students is: "I understand the subject but just can't do the problems." This statement is never true. The reverse is occasionally correct: one can sometimes do the problems correctly without understanding the subject well. But one cannot really understand a science and still be at a loss when faced with the problems accompanying the course of instruction. Difficulty with the problems is a sure sign that you are hazy on basic principles, or weak in the mathematical background that you are assumed to have, or both.

The Need for Precision in Language

Science is continually struggling to make its terms both precise and consistent to avoid ambiguity and error in communication. Most English words have many different meanings, depending on the context in which they are used. But in scientific usage it is unsatisfactory to rely on context for meaning.

Old words may have new meanings.   In the field of physics, for example, many words and terms, unfortunately, were taken from our everyday language. That in itself is not bad, but what makes for confusion is that new scientific definitions have been attached to them. These scientific definitions are usually operational in the sense that they imply a method of measuring a designated quantity and assigning a number to it. Consequently, a new student of physics is faced with a double job: to pry loose the traditional definition and to attach to the same word a new scientific definition.

Biology coined new words.   In the field of biology, whenever a new process or thing (organ or part of the body) was discovered or under special consideration, the experts would turn to old Latin and Greek word forms and put together a new word which would henceforth mean just that one precise process or thing. For example, the word *endocardial* means "situated within the heart." The word is made up of *endo* meaning "within," and *cardia* meaning the "heart." This system provided a built-in safeguard against imprecision. But such was not the way in physics.

The confusing foursome.   According to experienced teachers, the four words in physics used most frequently with imprecision or in downright error are the following:

word		technical meaning in physics
force	:	agency causing acceleration
momentum	:	mass × velocity
energy	:	ability to do work
work	:	force × distance

Figure 17-1   Quantitative Calculation

Determining the speed of a bullet
by the ballistic pendulum

If a bullet of mass m and unknown speed u is fired into a nearby pendulum bob of mass M, so that the bullet buries itself in the bob, the impact is then inelastic and the two colliding bodies move together after impact with some common speed v. Since no external forces are called into play during the interaction, the total linear momentum after impact is the same as that before, and therefore

$$u = \frac{(m + M) v}{m}$$

Thus determinations of m, $m + M$, and v are all that are needed to calculate u, the speed of the bullet.

In each subject, one must make an effort to learn the special language and use the words with as much precision as possible. Misuse of a single word can often make a statement completely wrong or meaningless.

FACTS MUST FIT TOGETHER

The outstanding lesson is that you should not try to learn a science as a collection of isolated facts, for two reasons: first, isolated facts have little meaning or usefulness, and second, they are so numerous that they pose a monstrous task of memorization if you do not put them into some unifying pattern.

Therefore, as each new bit of information is read or heard, what should you do with it? What should your mental filing system be like? You should not try to become a walking encyclopedia. You should ask, "How does this fit together with what I know already?" If there is a clear connection or niche into which the new bit fits, there will be no difficulty in retaining it. Such a discipline will increase your ability to assimilate further knowledge. If the new information seems to contradict what is known, closer examination is called for, because a fault in the pattern is indicated; something is either wrong or misunderstood. If the new bit of knowledge has no apparent relation to anything you know, and is not the beginning of a new subject you intend to study further, do not bother to try to remember it; you would not remember it for long anyway.

When trying to absorb large quantities of new information and knowledge, as you are when studying a new subject, you can vastly increase the capacity of your mental "filing cabinet" by "chunking." Chunking is done by placing ideas, concepts, facts, and details into categories. In other words, you create large packages of knowledge, and in this way, remembering is greatly enhanced and retrieval facilitated.

The highest kind of category is a specific law or principle. The law of gravitation, for example, eliminates the need for remembering tables of weights and distances. All you need do is apply the law:

■ Every portion of matter attracts every other portion of matter, and the stress between them is proportional to the product of their masses divided by the square of their distance. ■

LEARNING FROM LECTURES

In some courses the lectures will be found to be highly organized and clearly intended as the primary source of information. The outside reading will then serve to supplement the lectures, amplify some of the discussion, and clear up some of the sticky points. In other courses a textbook will be followed closely and will be the main source of systematic information. The classes may then serve to illustrate the reading material with lecture demonstrations, or questions and answers, or discussion of the reading assignment.

Taking Lecture Notes

In a lecture, take notes on ideas, not words.   Do not attempt to get a verbatim version of the lecture. Too much concern with catching and writing *all* the words will usually get in the way of your seizing the ideas. After all, the objective of taking notes is to have a record of the main ideas of the lecturer so that you can study them later in the privacy of your own room, either for deeper understanding, review, or preparation for examinations. Good notes may be saved as a permanent record for future reference.

Be systematic.   Use the Cornell system for taking notes, as illustrated in Figure 17-2. This systematic format makes possible a natural sequence of additional steps without laborious re-copying. After writing the notes in the main space, you have the left-hand space in which to *label* each idea and detail with a key word. These two steps make possible the use of the *recitation* technique described in a previous chapter.

In your time schedule, budget a regular period as shortly as possible after each lecture to put your notes in order: by filling in missing steps in the arguments, by detecting and correcting any errors, and by connecting this new portion with the previous lecture.

Make master sheets.   Periodically (in preparation for tests or at other spaced intervals) arrange to re-organize your notes on separate sheets of paper by clustering the ideas and details under main topics and categories. The activity of constructing this kind of framework and fitting the ideas into place will fix them in your memory with maximum comprehension and accessibility.

Figure 17-2   Format for Taking Classroom Lecture Notes as well as Notes Based on Textbook Reading.

ends stronger
 	
like = repel
 	
unlike = attract
Earth - magnet
   poles
   compass
Experiment
   iron filings
 	
Theory:
  not sure
  molecule
    arrangement
	February 26 (MON.) - Physics 101 - Prof. Lassiter ①
	
	I. Polarity of Magnets
	  1. Magnetism is stronger at ends than middle
	  2. Like poles repel each other
	    Ex. Two N poles when brought together, fly apart when released. Same for "S" poles.
	  3. Unlike poles attract each other
	  4. Earth is one big magnet
	    a. Magnetism strongest at poles
	    b. Compass needle aligns N to S
	  5. Experiment to show stronger ends
	    a. Place bar magnet under glass
	    b. Pour small iron filings on glass
	    c. Tap glass & filings arrange selves showing lines of force
	
	II. Theory of Magnetism
	  1. Not sure what causes it
	  2. Believe: way molecules are arranged

Use of Questions

Do not let gaps in your understanding persist. These will be indicated by difficulties in achieving clarity in your construction of your framework of topics and ideas, by difficulty in solving assigned problems, and by difficulty in completing the laboratory experiments satisfactorily. When such gaps are evident, start asking questions. These are appropriate in the following situations.

Questions asked of the teacher at start of class.   These are usually the best questions, because they can be well considered. Doubtful points arising from the previous lecture or in the reading assignment can have been thought about, cleared of trivialities, and reduced to essential elements. Something that presented difficulty for you probably did the same for other members of the class; so well-considered questions will in many cases form the most profitable focus for class discussion.

All too often, a student assumes that only he, of all the students, is lacking in adequate understanding, or else he is afraid to reveal ignorance. Such timidity is bad. It underestimates both the teacher and yourself, misjudges the purpose of the course, and makes it harder for the teacher to keep in touch with his class.

According to experienced professors, the most fruitful *type* of question is exemplified by the following:

■ "Did I use the right strategy in attacking this problem? Are there other strategies that I could have used?" ■

This type of question opens up the channels of thinking toward processes, approaches, and methods of attack more than any other type of question.

Unfortunately, the usual type of question asked by students is as follows: "How do you do this problem?" This type of question holds almost no future. It simply seeks specific ways to solve specific problems, and generally implies a mind that imposes upon itself the self-defeating task of trying to remember by rote too many isolated instances.

Interrupting a lecture.   Do not be bashful. Often it is helpful for the whole class to have a lecture slowed down, or brought to a halt for a while, especially if some point is obscure. Moderation in lecture interruptions is advisable, but not abstinence.

Questions asked of the teacher between classes.   A good teacher's interest in his subject and his students continues between classes in spite of many other duties. In most cases you will find that he actually enjoys a discussion with an individual student, because that is the most favorable of all teaching situations. But remember one reservation: you must show some sign of having done (or tried) the assignments and of having thought about the problems for yourself, before asking for assistance. Private sessions between teacher and student are for supplementation of your own work, not spoon-feeding. The main job of learning is an individual process and must be done alone.

Questions asked of other students.   Discussions with other students can be of great assistance. Because friends learning a subject together share the same difficulties and need not hesitate to contradict each other, they can enlighten each other very effectively.

READING A TEXTBOOK IN SCIENCE

In some ways, studying a science textbook is like studying any other textbook (see earlier chapters in this book for details). You should take notes using the Cornell format, review them using the recitation method, and from time to time make master sheets. It should be obvious that studying a textbook is also similar to learning from lectures.

However, there are special techniques that will help you get the most out of a science textbook.

Using Mental Visualization

James Clerk Maxwell, a famous British mathematical physicist, recognized that different people, as they read and study science, mentally visualize or reconstruct concepts and ideas in personal ways which are equally acceptable and intellectually respectable.

He said that "there are some minds which can go on contemplating with satisfaction pure quantities presented to the eye by symbols, and to the mind in a form which none but mathematicians can conceive."

But he fully recognized that there are those who find more enjoyment in following geometrical formulations, and there are still others who are "not content unless they can project their whole physical energy into the scene which they conjure up."

Maxwell, therefore, recommends that "for the sake of persons of these different types, scientific truth should be presented in different forms, and should be regarded as equally scientific, whether it appears in the robust form and vivid coloring of a physical illustration, or in the tenuity and paleness of a symbolic expression."

Professor Maxwell is implying that the concepts and ideas in a textbook can be lifted out of it and placed in one's mind only by the unique process of mental visualization. Of course, different people have different ways and abilities to visualize; but, they all visualize to varying degrees. And the process can be initiated, facilitated, and heightened by the way an author presents his material.

Fortunately, most textbooks and articles in science are heavily illustrated with diagrams to aid the process of visualization. Learn to use illustrations and text to complement one another. When there is no diagram to illustrate a process or idea, make your own. Your own diagram will stick in your mind long after the descriptive words are forgotten.

For example, the following paragraph describing one of Faraday's experiments was not accompanied by a diagram.

> In 1831, Michael Faraday, one of Britain's greatest scientists, did the experiments which completely demonstrated the close relationship between electricity and magnetism. One of his famous experiments was to take a coil of wire and connect the ends across an instrument capable of measuring tiny currents. By quickly pushing a bar magnet through the coil he was able to produce a small current in the coil and to measure that current. What he was really doing was to *change* the strength of the magnetic field in the coil by inserting and removing the magnet. The more rapidly he changed the field the more current he could generate.[1]

Figure 17-3 is an example of how a reader can easily convert a descriptive paragraph taken from a textbook, such as the paragraph above, into an actual diagram, thus enabling him not only to understand the described process better, but to visualize and remember it as well. This is the first special technique in studying science.

Learning New Terms

A second important technique is learning new terms. You will find that your science textbooks are crowded with terms that are new to you. Since these terms

[1] J. D. Jukes, *Man-Made Sun* (New York: Abelard-Schuman Ltd. 1959), p. 33.

Figure 17-3   A Descriptive Paragraph Diagrammed.

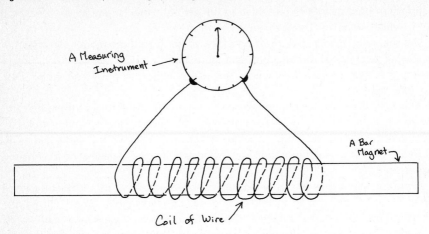

A Measuring Instrument →

A Bar Magnet →

Coil of Wire →

stand for essential concepts, you must know precisely what they mean if you are to understand the subject matter. Again, the textbook writers will have anticipated your need and provided help. The important new terms are usually emphasized by italic or heavy type at their first occurrence and specifically defined at that point or in a glossary at the end of the book. Put extra time and attention on memorizing these terms and learning what they mean. Put these terms on 3 x 5 cards and master them as you would any desirable vocabulary word.

An Important Tool: the Language of Measurement

Third, learn the language of scientific measurement: the metric system of weights and measures and the Centigrade, as well as the Fahrenheit, temperature scale. Learn to think meaningfully in these quantities and measures so that you will not be reading mere words and symbols.

For example, you should know that the word *metric* comes from *meter*, which is the principal unit of measuring length in this system. It was developed by French scientists in 1799 and is now used everywhere in the world for scientific work. Table 17-1 compares some of the metric units with English units of measurement.

You will want to know the background of the different temperature scales, too. Gabriel Daniel Fahrenheit, a German physicist, developed the Fahrenheit thermometer scale. He substituted mercury for alcohol in the tube to make the thermometer more accurate. This thermometer is used mainly in the home. The Centigrade thermometer, however, is used for scientific purposes.

Both thermometers look alike and have the same-sized tubes, and the mercury rises and falls to the same levels. They differ in the way the scale is graduated. On the Centigrade thermometer, the point at which water freezes is marked 0 (zero), while on the Fahrenheit thermometer it is marked 32. On the Centigrade scale, the boiling point is 100, while on the Fahrenheit, it is 212.

On the Centigrade thermometer, the space between the freezing point (zero degrees) and the boiling point (100 degrees) is divided into 100 equal spaces or degrees. On the Fahrenheit thermometer, there are 180 spaces between freezing and boiling points.

To change readings on the Centigrade thermometer to the Fahrenheit scale, the centigrade reading is multiplied by $\frac{180}{100}$, or $\frac{9}{5}$, and then added to 32.

To change Fahrenheit reading to centigrade, subtract 32 from the Fahrenheit reading and multiply by $\frac{5}{9}$.

A Final Word

Finally, don't skip over the problems. Work them out! This is so important that we have devoted a special section to it.

Different sciences call for different attacks and emphases in the reading. In a general way, we may say that biology and geology place relatively heavy emphasis on key terms and definitions; physics and astronomy, on measurement and mathematics; biology and chemistry, on manipulation; physics and chemistry, on visualization. Adapt your study methods accordingly.

WORKING SCIENTIFIC PROBLEMS

The Value of Practice

The most successful way to solve a problem is to remember how you solved a similar problem previously. This is true even in research, but especially true of

TABLE 17-1 COMPARISON OF CERTAIN METRIC AND ENGLISH UNITS OF MEASUREMENT

Metric system		English system	
Length			
Meter	= 1.093 yard	Yard	= 0.9144 meter
	= 3.281 feet	Foot	= 0.3048
	= 39.370 inches	Inch	= 0.254 meter
Kilometer	= 0.621 mile	Mile	= 1.609 kilometers
Weight			
Gram	= 15.432 grains	Grain	= 0.0648 gram
	= 0.32 troy ounce	Troy ounce	= 31.103 grams
	= 0.0352 avoirdupois ounce	Avoirdupois ounce	= 28.35 grams
Kilogram	= 2.2046 pounds avoirdupois	Pound	= 0.4536 gram
Metric Ton	= 2204.62 pounds avoirdupois	Short ton	= 0.907 metric ton
Carat	= 3.08 grains avoirdupois		

problems encountered in tests, when time is limited. When we first attempt a new kind of problem, it is natural to be hesitant, to make false starts, to be temporarily stymied—in general to waste time. With each succeeding problem of a similar nature, we learn to go at it more quickly and surely. Besides, each problem usually has some feature not present in previous ones. Therefore as we go on, the range of material with which we are familiar steadily expands. Gradually we build up a capability of competent attack on a wider and wider range of problem types.

Complex problems are usually made up of many simple parts. If these elementary steps are so familiar that they are automatic, we can concentrate on how they fit together in the problem as a whole, and proceed from start to finish without confusion. But if each elementary step presents difficulty, we usually get so involved in and confused by the details that we cannot find the right path to a solution.

Most people who seem to be wizards at problem-solving have just had a lot of practice. Like woodsmen who have followed many a trail before, they have learned to recognize the signs, they see familiar steps, and they can follow the trail of logic to a solution of a new problem with ease. Practice means experience; it is the source of good judgment; and its value cannot be overemphasized.

In studying a science, therefore, one should do not only the assigned problems, but all problems related to the material under study that one can find time for. If your own textbook does not have many, look for examples in other books on the same subject. Best of all, try to *make up appropriate problems for yourself.* Making up good ones is harder than solving them, but it is an excellent exercise, and particularly fine sport for two students who are studying together.

While engaging in this sport, it is especially useful to try to imagine the problems a teacher will make up for your tests. With practice, you can become rather expert at this.

Procedure on New Problems

A student who does his work faithfully should encounter strange, novel problems only in homework. A recommended approach to such unfamiliar problems is as follows:

1. First, study and organize the relevant text material and class notes from your framework of main topics and supporting ideas.
2. Distinguish and list carefully what knowledge is given in the problem, and what is to be discovered.
3. Try to conceive a chain of logical steps leading either forwards from the known quantities to the unknown one whose value is to be found, or backwards from the unknown to the given quantities. If necessary, work from both ends to the middle, until a logical connection is established.
4. Express these steps of logic in the form of equations.
5. Combine and solve the equations for the desired answer.
6. Check the answer by inquiring whether it is reasonable in magnitude (i.e., agreeing with experience or with a rough solution of the problem). If unsure, substitute the answer into the original relations and see whether it fits consistently.

Discussion Questions

These questions appear occasionally in quizzes and examinations. The chief trick is to comprehend the purpose and point of view of the person asking the question. Learn to put yourself mentally in his place. Ask yourself how the question is related to subjects under recent discussion in the class or in reading assignments; what principles it is intended to bring out. Then if you can visualize the framework of topics and ideas which you have made, the nature of your answer should no longer be in doubt. The remaining task is to express your answer in clear language, using the technical words accurately.

Practice is needed for skill in answering discussion questions as well as mathematical problems. This skill can be developed, in time, by taking vocal part in discussions of the subject with your friends; by participating in classroom discussions; and by giving attention to careful expression not only in English composition courses, but every time you have occasion to write anything, in school and out of it. The most serious of common faults are not in grammar, but in vocabulary, logic, and effective ordering of steps in an argument.

WORKING IN THE LABORATORY

Keep in mind that the laboratory is the front line and that the techniques of problem-solving that you are learning on a modest scale are the same as those that achieve the great breakthroughs in science. Here are some hints on good attitudes and habits for laboratory work:

1. Do not trust memory. Write down everything you think may be pertinent. Some things observed in the laboratory may strike you as being so clear at the time that there seems to be no point in writing them down. But memory fades; and if the experiment is not completely written up in the same period in which it is performed, you may not be able to recall important items. These may include identification and properties of the instruments, ranges and units of the scales on the meters, dimensions and schematic diagram of apparatus, sensitivity of a balance, headings and units for columns of data, quirks of performance of equipment, need for repetition of measurements, and numerous other details. Figures 17-4 and 17-5 show these features and others that are mentioned in this discussion.

2. Make a permanent record of observations. Follow the practice of professional scientists in keeping a full record of all your calculations, observations, and results in a special notebook; don't ever write anything down on separate scraps of paper—not even your arithmetical calculations. If you make mistakes, cross them out and go on from there, but keep everything as part of your complete record. Start your record of each experiment or laboratory session on a new page, headed with the date. In this way you will have a permanent log of all your data and mental processes pertaining to any problem on which you have worked—all the raw materials for your final report.

Figure 17-4   A Diagram of Loading Jig Apparatus, Shown Here as Part of a Laboratory Report.

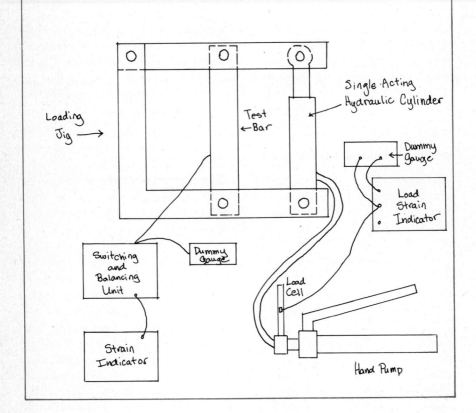

```
Experiment #3053 - Strain Measurements
October 27th

     The purpose of this experiment is to determine stress
sustained by a rectangular bar by means of wire resistance
strain gauges. Six of these gauges are taped onto different
positions on the bar, then strain readings taken, during
both loading and unloading processes, and the results con-
verted to stress by using appropriate equations.
```

3. Organize the recording of data.   Arrange them so that they will be clear and fully labeled for later reference. The few extra minutes you take to make neat and orderly records during the laboratory period will save you time that you would otherwise have to spend later in deciphering and arranging haphazard notes. (See Figures 17-6 and 17-7).

4. Do not trust yourself or the apparatus too much.   It is an unwise practice to record a lot of untested numbers, dismantle the apparatus, and leave the laboratory, intending to analyze the data and deduce the result of the experiment

Figure 17-5   Headings and Units for Columns of Data, Shown Here as Part of a Laboratory Report.

Experiment #3057
Measurement of displacement,
velocity, and acceleration

FREQ (CPS)	Displacement				Velocity			Acceleration			Graph Freq. for Peak Accel.
	Traveling Microscope			Vibration Meter	Oscilloscope		Vibration Meter	Vibration Meter		Graphs	
	Reading 1 mm	Reading 2 mm	Δ mills	Δ mills	Volts	in./sec	in./sec	in./sec²		in./sec²	
40	16.176	13.58	102	97	15.5	27.1	29.2	9300		9040	41
30	16.21	13.15	96.8	98	11	19.3	21.9	5700		5390	31
20	16.09	13.69	94.5	100	7.5	13.1	14.9	2950		2845	21.2
10	16.07	13.63	96.3	102	3.5	6.12	6.9	1020		788	11.2

Displacement, velocity, and
acceleration of the vibrating
table were measured at different driving frequencies
and the data were used to
analyze the effect of the
spring-damper system put on
the vibrating table.

at a later time. It is much better to carry out at least an approximate analysis (including rough graphs) of the data while they are being taken, so that one has a chance to detect anything that is going wrong in time to do something to remedy the situation—such as readjusting the apparatus, checking or repeating an observation or asking an instructor for advice and assistance.

5. Baby the apparatus. Another skill, often invisible to those who do not possess it, is the ability to manipulate delicate apparatus and distinguish small variations in its behavior. It is sometimes amazing what consistently accurate measurements can be coaxed out of laboratory apparatus by unusually sensitive

Figure 17-6   A Page from a Student's Record Book Showing Raw Data Gathered Directly from Measurements Made by Instruments.

Experiment 3057 – October 27

Measurement of displacement, velocity and acceleration
EQUIPMENT: (a) Linear Variable Differential Transformer; (b) an Oscilloscope; (c) an accelerometer; (d) an Analyzer-Recorder; (e) a Vibrating Table.

Raw Data

FREQ(CPS)	DISPLACEMENT	VELOCITY	ACCELERATION
40	Micro (mm) $\left.\begin{array}{l}1.6176 \\ 1.358\end{array}\right\}\Delta = 101.9$ mils VIB. MTR. 97 mils	VIB. MTR. $29.2 \frac{in}{sec}$	V.M. $9300 (in/sec^2)$
30	Micro (mm) $\left.\begin{array}{l}1.621 \\ 1.375\end{array}\right\}\Delta = 96.8$ mils VIB. MTR. 98 mils	VIB. MTR. $21.9 \frac{in}{sec}$	V.M. $5700 (in/sec^2)$
20	Micro (mm) $\left.\begin{array}{l}1.609 \\ 1.369\end{array}\right\}\Delta = 94.7$ mils	VIB. MTR. $14.9 \frac{in}{sec}$	V.M. $2950 (in/sec^2)$
10	Micro (mm) $\left.\begin{array}{l}1.607 \\ 1.363\end{array}\right\}\Delta = 96.3$ mils VIB. MTR. 102 mils	VIB. MTR. $6.9 \frac{in}{sec}$	V.M. $1020 (in/sec^2)$

hands and eyes; or what can be seen in a microscope or telescope by some students and not by others. People are not born with such skills, rather they develop them by conscientious, loving effort.

Poor performance in a laboratory is often due to carelessness, but may also be the result of a pessimistic or uncooperative attitude: being too ready to say an apparatus doesn't work, or to accept unnecessary limitations on its capability. The

Figure 17-7   A Page from a Student's Record Book Showing Steps, Observations, and Notes.

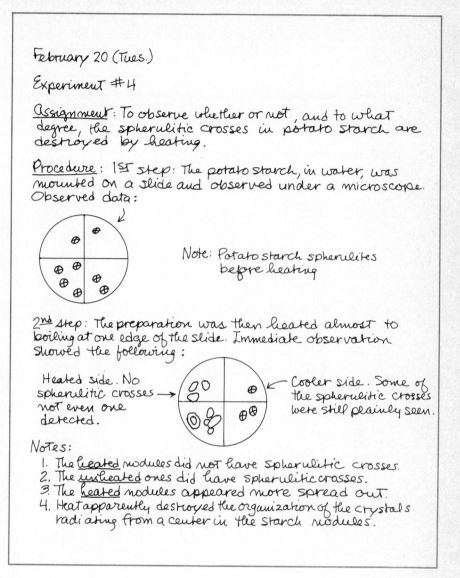

February 20 (Tues.)

Experiment #4

Assignment: To observe whether or not, and to what degree, the spherulitic crosses in potato starch are destroyed by heating.

Procedure: 1ST step: The potato starch, in water, was mounted on a slide and observed under a microscope. Observed data:

Note: Potato starch spherulites before heating

2nd step: The preparation was then heated almost to boiling at one edge of the slide. Immediate observation showed the following:

Heated side. No spherulitic crosses → not even one detected.

Cooler side. Some of the spherulitic crosses were still plainly seen.

Notes:
1. The heated nodules did not have spherulitic crosses.
2. The unheated ones did have spherulitic crosses.
3. The heated nodules appeared more spread out.
4. Heat apparently destroyed the organization of the crystals radiating from a center in the starch nodules.

trick is to regard the apparatus as your friend, not your opponent; the rest follows naturally, with practice. So, treat it tenderly, and coax out of it all the resolution and accuracy of which it is capable. Make notes of its limitations and the expected accuracy of the measurements. And watch the apparatus like a hawk for signs of strange behavior. No real equipment is quite like the ideal version pictured in a textbook or laboratory manual. Typically, each piece of apparatus has an individual personality.

Figure 17-8 A Student's Abbreviated, Work-Type Lab Report.

Experiment 34

A.   PURPOSE: To observe the increase in birefringence of nylon by increasing the orientation of fibers through stretching, despite the thinning of the nylon by necking.

B.   PROCEDURE
(a) A narrow strip of thin transparent nylon sheet, stretched in some spots and not stretched in others, was observed between crossed polarizers with low magnification.
(b) About 1 mm diameter as-extruded nylon monofilament was stretched and the necking observed.
(c) Textile-grade nylon fiber was observed as-extruded and stretched. The diameters and polarization colors of each region of the fiber were noted.

C.   RESULTS
(a)

unstretched nylon; polarization colors: 1st order white.

stretched nylon; polarization colors: 3rd order red and green.

(b) Nylon monofilament necked abruptly, rather than breaking, when pulled:

(c) 16 mm objective, 1 eyepiece micrometer division = 16.0 μ

	Diameter	Converted diameter	Retardation
Unstretched	4.3 div.	68.8 μ	200 μ
Stretched	1.9 div.	30.4 μ	1850 μ

	Birefringence
Unstretched	0.003
Stretched	0.059

D.   CONCLUSIONS
Unstretched nylon fiber exhibited a 1st order white polarization color, i.e., showed very low birefringence. The birefringence was calculated to be about 0.003.
   When pulled in tension, the nylon fiber necked abruptly. The stretched portion of the sample showed 3rd order and higher polarization colors, despite decreased thickness. This was due to a marked increase in birefringence, to about 0.059, resulting from the parallel orientation of fibers effected by stretching.
   Without polarizers, the nylon fiber appeared slightly greyed or opaqued where stretched. Orienting the polymer fibers leads to a decrease in clarity. Also, the stretching results in mechanical discontinuities which would tend to scatter the light.

6. Keep purpose in mind.   Try to know the purpose of the particular laboratory work in which you are engaged, which varies a great deal from case to case, and keep it in mind. Doing so can save much expenditure of useless effort, and prevent overlooking the main point of the exercise.

7. Write up your reports clearly, legibly, and concisely, and in the prescribed form.   The style should be impersonal; in technical reports it is customary to use the passive voice, more than in other writing. The conventional form of a laboratory report, with minor variations, is approximately as follows (see Figure 17-8):

Purpose (Object): A thesis statement to explain what the problem is.

Theory: The background for the problem and the justification for your method of attack.

Apparatus (Equipment, Materials): A listing and brief description of essentials, often including a sketch of the apparatus.

Procedure: A step-by-step report of what you did.

Results: A step-by-step record of your observations.

Conclusion: A summary of your findings and an assessment of their accuracy to show how they succeed or fail in resolving the problem with which you started.

Above all in writing a report, remember that your purpose is to make your findings understandable to a reader and that the principles of good written communication are not something to be "popped" into a pigeon-hole labeled "English courses" but are among the most essential tools of today's scientists.

18

HOW TO SPEAK EFFECTIVELY

JAMES A. WOOD

In college you will almost certainly be called on to give speeches or other oral presentations from time to time. And if the prospect doesn't exactly kindle you with joyful anticipation, you are not alone. Yet the ability to speak effectively before a group is not a difficult skill to develop, and it is one that will serve you well, whatever your sphere of activity, all your life.

It should hearten you to realize that even the experienced and successful speaker may feel apprehensive before giving a speech. But he has learned to convert nervous tension into constructive energy that actually helps him to be alert, vigorous, and effective in speaking. To make nervous energy work for you, rather than against you, you must be (1) fully prepared to do your job, and (2) motivated by a strong and sincere desire to communicate to your audience. This means knowing your subject well, taking ample time to think about and plan what you will say, evaluating your topic in terms of your intended listeners, concentrating on what you can give them of interest and value—in a word, being audience-minded instead of self-centered. This mental attitude will have a bearing on your speech at all stages, from planning through the moment of delivery.

THE PLAN FOR THE SPEECH

The ideal finished plan for a speech or oral report is a very detailed outline, usually containing 30 to 50 percent as many words as the actual speech. It is thus much fuller than an outline for a written paper, but far from being your speech word for word. From it you can see the order and relationship of ideas, distinguish main ideas from supporting materials, and note where the major junctures or transitions come. It enables you to learn the speech as a complete, organized pattern of ideas, and thus to avoid the rote memorization which often results in a parrot-like delivery.

Basic Parts of the Outline

The outline may conveniently be divided into four basic parts: introduction, purpose statement, body, and conclusion.

1. Introduction. In the introduction you seek to win the *good will, attention,* and *interest* of your listeners. Your means to this end are a pleasant, confident delivery, and such devices as a striking example, statistic, or quotation, an interesting but relevant narrative, or relating the topic to something the audience is already interested in. The introduction should also provide any *background information* the audience is likely to need, such as definitions of important terms, or appropriate historical or social context.

2. Purpose statement. Your statement of purpose tells your audience just what ground you intend to cover. In addition to stating your topic, you may list the main points you intend to cover, or otherwise explain your basic strategy in the speech, so the audience can more readily perceive the structure and key points as the body of the speech unfolds. This statement provides a focus for the entire speech. Phrase it clearly and precisely in direct language that you can use in the presented speech. Usually the purpose statement comes at or near the end of the introduction.

An example of a relatively full purpose statement follows. After an introduction in which you remind the audience that they have studied the way various film directors prepare to shoot films and that Ingmar Bergman is a major current film director (linking topic to audience and supplying background material), you might state your purpose as follows:

■   **"Today, I will explain how Ingmar Bergman prepares to make a film. I will consider three main points: how he gets his initial ideas, how he plans the scenario, and how he selects cast and locations. On each of these three points I will contrast his methods with those of other major directors we have studied."**   ■

---

3. Body. The body or main part of the speech should comprise between 65 and 90 percent of the whole. Here you develop the topic presented in your purpose statement. The main points listed in your purpose statement, if you so pre-outline, then become the main heads in the body.

4. Conclusion. The conclusion is essentially a summary of the main points made in the body of the speech. Many confusing speeches have been saved by a summary which brings key points into sharp focus for the audience. The conclusion also gives you an opportunity to round off the speech smoothly by referring to something mentioned in the introduction, by suggesting broader implications of the topic or by specifically relating speech to audience.

Components of the Speech

A speech may be thought of as a fusion of main ideas, supporting materials, and transitions. A good speaker gives deliberate attention to each of these components separately and in combination.

1. Main or key ideas. A shrewd speaker will not expect his audience to remember a welter of details. Rather, he has a few key ideas he wants to convey (for example, the four main stages in building a house, or five characteristics of Hemingway's prose style), and he constructs his speech so as to help the audience grasp and remember them. He may hope some of the audience will note and remember subordinate points also, but he regards these primarily as means of making his key ideas clearer and more memorable.

You must first, then, have a precise idea of the main points you wish to put across and the best order in which to present them. On these points you build your outline, making sure that every item in the body of the speech contributes to developing a particular main idea. In this way you insure against confusing your audience by digressing or backtracking.

2. Supporting materials. Supporting materials help your listeners to understand, accept, and remember your main ideas. They provide evidence for the main points, relate the subject to the knowledge and experience of the audience, and maintain interest. They are used in greater quantity and variety in speaking than in writing to give the audience a chance to absorb and accept the main points; for unlike the reader, the listener cannot stop to ponder or look back.

Whereas main ideas are likely to be general statements, supporting materials should be specific: *factual data,* such as names, dates, places and events; *examples,* ranging from brief references to detailed anecdotes, which can be either real occurrences or ones you make up to illustrate your point; *vivid description* of how things look, feel, sound, smell, taste; *comparison and contrast* with things familiar to the audience; *expert testimony or opinion,* cited or quoted; *literary quotations,* when they are apt. *Statistics* can be useful, but must be handled with care since they are harder to take in by ear than by eye. If they can be translated into concrete or pictorial terms, so much the better; thus, in addition to stating the estimated gallons of water wasted by a community's leaky plumbing over a period of time, you might cite the number of homes that could be fully supplied by this wasted water.

A special type of supporting material is the *visual aid,* which covers a wide range of materials, including blackboard or chartboard drawings, poster-type materials displayed on an easel, three-dimensional models, specimens, and films. Visual aids are useful in holding the audience's attention and in presenting statistical relation-ships (as in graphs) and complicated structures or processes which are hard to explain in words alone. Though experienced speakers sometimes draw or write as they talk, a beginner would be wise to prepare in advance and to practice with any aids he intends to use and thus avoid having to think about two things at once.

3. Transitions. Transitions help emphasize your main ideas and enable your audience to move mentally with you from one point to the next. If your transitions are not unmistakably clear, your listeners will become confused. Inexperienced speakers often fail to realize that oral presentation requires far more transitional material than writing does and that oral transitions must be more obvious and repetitive than those used in writing.

Oral transitions may take a number of forms. First, you may emphasize main ideas by *restatement,* saying them twice, in different words. This gives your hearers a better chance, a little more time, to grasp these ideas and to see that they are relatively important.

Another transitional device is *pre-outlining.* Near the beginning of your speech, perhaps within the purpose statement, you may tell your audience the main points you intend to take up. Similarly, at the beginning of each major section, after stating the main idea, you may outline the ground you intend to cover.

If you have several sections of parallel nature and importance, you may make use of *listing:* either *enumeration* ("First, . . . ," "Second, . . . ," etc.) or a *key phrase* repeated with the introduction of each main idea, or a combination of both ("The first type of jet engine is . . . ," "The second type of jet engine is . . .").

Connective transitions tell your audience that you are moving on to a new section of your speech and indicate how it is related to the previous one; for example, "Now that we understand the problem that faced the engineer, let's see how he solved it," or, "Since we now know the history of this riot, let's attempt to identify its underlying causes."

Finally, in *internal summaries* you can condense and restate some or all of the points you have presented up to that point in the speech.

We see then that skillful use of restatement, pre-outlining, enumeration, key phrasing, connective transitions, and internal summaries all help to emphasize key ideas and enable the audience to follow your structure. (You have just been treated to an internal summary of the preceding section! Incidentally, the ability to spot such transitional material in your reading can greatly increase the efficiency and thoroughness of your mastery of textbook material.)

MAKING YOUR OWN SPEECH PLAN

Choosing a Topic

Many speakers get off to a bad start by selecting a topic that is too broad. Remember that in ten minutes of speaking you can cover the equivalent of only five to seven typewritten pages, and that supporting materials and transitions should take up a proportionately larger part of an oral presentation than of a written one. Usually a speaker should not try to get more than three or four main points across in a short speech of ten or fifteen minutes. It is the depth of perceptive explanation, interpretation, and illustrative detail, rather than the amount of ground covered, that determines the value of a speech.

Consider the interests of the audience and the demands of the occasion, but also pick a topic you are really interested in. Your interest, or lack of it, will be sensed by your listeners and will influence their reception of what you have to say. Also, you will find preparation of the speech more enjoyable if you are really interested in the topic and if you anticipate that your audience will be.

Phrase your topic in one simple sentence, to serve as a tentative purpose statement, and analyze it to see if it is clearly focused. Avoid such vague phrasing as, "I am going to talk about speech preparation and how it makes things easier"; instead, rephrase this as, "This morning, I will explain five steps for the efficient preparation of a speech."

Preliminary overview

Ransack your mind for information, ideas, opinions, and bits of supporting material on the topic and for ideas about further sources of information. List all these items, and use the list as a guide in gathering further information. If you start from what *you* know and think, your own personality will emerge in the speech and thereby provide some original flavor and perhaps even a fresh outlook on the topic.

At this stage you may also discuss your topic with friends or experts, and you may survey library or other resource material available on your topic. This will give you a clearer idea of the scope and potential points of your topic.

Break your subject down into the main areas or ideas you want to cover. Your topic statements for each of these will become the tentative main headings in your outline for the body of your speech.

Research

From the list of items you made in your preliminary overview, you can decide what material you must obtain from the library or other sources of information. If you have performed a survey of bibliographical materials available, you can select the most promising ones to go to first. Don't overlook your own experience and imagination as resource, especially for such supporting materials as analogies, comparisons, and actual or hypothetical examples. Always keep the needs of both your topic and your audience in mind.

Preparation of final outline

The purpose statement, as the focus, should be at least tentatively planned at an early stage of your preparation. The introduction and conclusion are usually planned after the body of the speech—unless you get an inspired idea while you are doing research or working on the main part.

The outline for the body of the speech should be taking shape around your main headings while you are doing your research. When you have all your material together, plan the exact phrasing of your statements of main ideas, sub-ideas, and transitions. Phrase these in oral style, just as you intend to say them in the presented speech. For example, say, "As my last point, I will explain the great care Bergman uses in selecting his cast and locations," rather than, "Bergman takes great care in selecting his cast and locations."

Now insert your supporting materials as sub-entries under the appropriate main headings, but don't write them out in full as you did the main statements and transitions—a few words of reminder are enough. If you muddle main ideas or transitions, your whole structure may come crashing down. But if you slip up on a supporting detail or two, the consequences are not serious; and your delivery will have a more spontaneous quality if you develop supporting detail from notes as you speak rather than from pre-planned sentences.

At least two days before you are to give your speech, go over your outline to put it in final form and make a final check on structure and phrasing. Many speeches fail to achieve their full potential just because the speaker does not take the trouble to see that supporting materials are adequate in quantity and clearly relevant to main ideas, that irrelevant material is deleted, that sufficient and clear transitions are planned, and that key ideas are clearly and forcefully phrased.

PREPARING TO DELIVER THE SPEECH

Learn Your Ideas Thoroughly

First, read your outline through several times, both silently and aloud. You aim is to learn the pattern or sequence of ideas, not to memorize words and sentences. To fix the pattern in your memory, test yourself with such questions as, "What are my main points?" "How do I explain my third main idea?" "What transition do I use after the section on . . . ?"

Next, say your speech aloud a few times, referring to your outline when necessary. Time yourself to be sure you meet the required time limits. Keep thinking in terms of ideas, not of set phrases and sentences. Remember that oral speech patterns are more conversational and less formal than written ones.

In order to maintain more spontaneity and contact with the audience in delivery, you may plan on using conventional speaking notes—a very much abbreviated outline of words and phrases, typed or written on 4 x 6 inch cards. These notes will help you keep to your plan but will not tempt you into reading, as your full outline might.

The Practice Delivery

With your speech plan well in mind, and your notes in hand, you are ready to practice delivering your speech. Try to duplicate the actual speaking situation as closely as possible. Ideally, you should practice your speech in the room or hall where you are to give it, with a few friends serving as audience. At least rehearse the speech standing up and aloud. This is your chance to anticipate the physical "feel" of speech-making. Pay conscious attention to your gestures and voice; think about what you are going to do with your hands; use your speaking notes so you will be accustomed to them; speak loud enough to be heard at the back of the room; assume an alert and confident bearing. Practice sessions are the time to attend to these mechanics of delivery; when you actually present the speech, you will want to concentrate on getting your ideas across to your listeners.

Go through the speech from beginning to end. If you make mistakes, keep right on going—you can give special attention to troublesome parts later. Some students can get by with one or two trial runs; others need ten or a dozen. Practice is more valuable if spread over two or three days. Even for a simple class report, avoid the temptation to practice only at the last minute or not at all. Remember that practice is what produces confident and effective delivery.

FACING THE AUDIENCE

No matter how much you practice, there are some things that can be worked out only in the actual speaking situation. An effective speaker is sensitive to the response of his listeners and responds in turn to them. He is both stimulated and cued by his audience, alert to the need to make minor adjustments in his presentation; for example, he will slow down and insert internal summaries if his hearers seem confused, or omit some supporting material and get on to the next point if they seem restless.

An important element in delivery is good eye contact with the audience. You should appear to be in a genuine two-way relationship with your listeners, and this is impossible if you are examining the ceiling or the floor, or staring fixedly at your notes or your hands. When you talk with an individual, you look directly at him; and you should do the same with your audience. Though you should have some eye contact with all the audience, your confidence will be increased if you maintain eye contact mainly with your more attentive and responsive listeners.

Your physical bearing has a direct effect on your audience's response. If you sag or lean against a desk or speaking stand, you will suggest apathy and dullness to your listeners. If you fiddle with a pencil or a ring or your note cards, their attention will be diverted from what you are saying. Stand erect, and convert nervous energy into expressive gestures and movement. Be free to gesture and move, but avoid excessive, pointless movement. (Remember that the time to develop effective gestures, movement, and posture consciously is during practice sessions.)

Effective use of voice can do much to enliven your delivery. First of all, you must speak loudly and clearly enough to be heard and understood. Vary your rate and pitch to hold the attention and interest of your listeners. If you clip rapidly along in an even, monotonous tone of voice, you will suggest that your main aim is to get the whole thing over as fast as possible and that what you have to say is of no particular interest anyway. As a rule, you should speak more slowly and formally when you are giving main ideas or difficult material, and more rapidly and conversationally when you are citing examples or narrating anecdotes. Don't be afraid of a pause. If you forget what comes next, take time for an unhurried look at your notes. Avoid filling up time with "uh, uh" and other vocal fillers. Good speakers, in fact, make deliberate use of pauses to emphasize important points or to recapture an audience's wandering attention.

AN ORAL PRESENTATION OF A WRITTEN REPORT

In some classes you may be asked to make an oral presentation of a paper which you are also to hand in as a written report. This can present a problem for two reasons: (1) oral discourse, as we have seen, differs from written discourse in several significant ways; and (2) the required length of a written report may be incompatible with the amount of class time available for giving it orally. There are three ways of solving the problem:

1. You can write your paper and then use it as source material to prepare an oral report. This solution can produce an effective oral presentation, but it requires you to prepare two distinct reports, one written and one oral.
2. You can write the paper with the idea of oral presentation primarily in mind. But this has disadvantages too. For one thing, *writing* oral discourse is a rather specialized skill. Moreover, the very things that help make the oral presentation a success—the restatement and repetition, the numerous and obvious transitions, the relative amount of space given to the supporting materials, the personal quality and conversational tone—may be criticized as flaws in the formal written report. (Study the illustration in Figure 18-1.)

Figure 18-1   Contrasting Written and Oral Discourse. Notice how the lecturer restates and repeats his points, and how he uses more obvious transition to help his audience move from point to point.

	Writer	Speaker
Beginning	Nothing in English history contains such tragic overtones as the Battle of Hastings.	Last hour we discussed the political events that led to the Battle of Hastings. Let us turn now to the tragedy itself.
Thesis	But a divided England was less the cause of downfall than Norman lances vs. English axes.	Thus the English had to fight without the army that was still in the north. More important the Normans wore armor and fought on horseback, while the English had no armor and fought on foot.
Transition	The Normans fought with propaganda too; the Pope was on their side.	Third, it is important to remember that the Pope favored William, and his standard on the field frightened many English from the battle.
Conclusion:	Everything lent William power and conspired to change the fate of England.	To sum up, then, a divided England, superior weapons, and the favor of the Church gave William the advantage in every area of the conflict.

3. Probably the best plan is to write the report as you normally would, and then *adapt* it to oral presentation. On a clean carbon copy, note down the supplementary supporting materials and transitions you intend to add when you give the report orally. By merely noting these items, rather than writing them out in full, you have a chance to work in some conversational spontaneity. Practice reading the paper aloud until you will be able to look up from it frequently to establish eye contact with your audience. Know exactly where the supplementary oral materials come, and practice moving smoothly from reading to speaking and back to reading again.

SUMMARY

Effective speaking requires that you be fully prepared to do your job and that you be motivated by a sincere desire to communicate with your audience.

The speech itself is divided into introduction, purpose statement, body, and conclusion, each part having its own distinctive functions. For the speech to be clear and interesting, the speaker must use a logical pattern of a few main ideas which are developed by varied supporting materials and which are linked together and emphasized with transitions.

To prepare a speech efficiently, you should (1) select a limited, appropriate, and clear-cut topic, (2) initiate the search for information, ideas, and patterns, by a preliminary overview, largely of your own thinking, (3) do research for further ideas and supporting materials, (4) prepare a final detailed outline which organizes all the material and which shows phrasing of key ideas and transitions, and (5) rehearse the speech in order to fix the pattern of ideas in your mind and to polish your techniques of delivery. Such preparation will lead to vigorous, direct, and confident delivery. Even oral presentations based on written papers should reflect both adaptation in content and practice.

If you perform these steps fully, you will find that presenting material to a listening audience can be an extremely satisfying, even exciting, experience.

19

HOW TO MASTER A FOREIGN LANGUAGE

WILLIAM G. MOULTON

Language teachers are constantly working on new methods to help students learn foreign languages as efficiently and thoroughly as possible. You will find their efforts reflected in the textbooks you use and in the type of classroom instruction you receive. But textbooks and teaching methods are only part of the story —usually, in fact, just about one-third of the story. For if we accept the traditional rule-of-thumb that a college student should average two hours of outside study for each hour of classroom work, this means that you are on your own for two-thirds of the time.

The following study hints are offered in the hope that they will help you to work more efficiently during the unsupervised two-thirds of your foreign language time. They offer no magic answer, no patent pill that will make everything easy and painless; they are merely meant to help you in your *work*. However, since most students approach the study of a foreign language from precisely the wrong point of view, at least some of the following remarks should be useful to you. There is no one set of suggestions which will fit all students perfectly, and experience will show just which techniques are most useful in your own particular case.

LEARNING TO SPEAK A FOREIGN LANGUAGE

You can't learn a language by "thinking" about it. Nearly all the non-language work which a college student does involves (or should involve) a large amount of thinking. Of course, you are asked to read a certain amount of material and to learn a certain number of facts; but this is only the beginning. The most important thing in most courses is for you to go home, sit down, and *think* about these facts:

263

organize them, analyze them, and interpret them. Most students are so accustomed to this "thinking" approach that they try to learn a new language in the same way; the results are always disastrous.

A Language Is a Set of Habits

All of us speak our native language with complete fluency. Since we learned this one language so extremely well, it is worth while considering just how we did it. It is obvious from the very start that we didn't do it by "thinking." We had almost completely mastered the sounds and structure of the language by the time we were five or six years old, and at that time we couldn't "think" anywhere near as well as we can now that we are adults with an expensive education behind us. Instead of "thinking," we just listened to other people and copied what they said. By doing this over and over again, we eventually built up the complicated sets of habits which now let us talk our native language with complete ease. The "thinking" which we now do when we talk is concerned almost entirely with *what* we are going to say (the content), rather than with *how* we are going to say it (the language). We don't "think" about saying *he works* (with an ending *s*) but *they work* (with no ending); nor do we "think" about pronouncing the word *the* as *thee* before words beginning with a vowel ("the apple, the orange"), but as *thuh* before words beginning with a consonant ("the peach, the banana"). Complicated things like this have become completely matters of habit. Most of us don't even know we do them until somebody points them out to us.

You've got to listen and imitate. As adults trying to learn a foreign language, we face much the same job that we did as children learning our native language. We can't use quite the same methods, but the general approach will still be the same; we've got to listen to someone who knows how to speak the language, and we've got to imitate him as exactly as we can. In one way we're worse off than children; they start with a clean slate, whereas we're going to find that our native language habits get in the way all the time. But in another way we have a distinct advantage: since we already know one language, we can be told how the new language is put together, how it works, and how it differs from our native language. These directions ("grammar") can speed up the learning process considerably. Their only use, however, is to help us imitate more successfully; they are not an aim in themselves.

You've got to memorize. If a language is a set of habits, the only way to learn the language is to learn these habits. And you don't learn habits by "thinking"; you learn them by practice, practice, practice. In all your other courses you are asked to go home and organize, analyze, and interpret factual data; in your language course you will have to go home and practice the material you've heard in class over and over again until it becomes second nature. It's as simple—and as hard—as that.

Study Out Loud

One way to memorize the new material would be to read it over silently, again and again. That would be pretty ridiculous, of course, since you would then be learning not the language itself, but only the way it is symbolized on paper. In addition, it would be enormously inefficient. In reading silently, you would be using only your visual memory. If you study out loud, on the other hand, you first double your efficiency by adding auditory memory; then, by adding motor memory, you at least quadruple it, because motor memory is the most efficient of all. (Motor memory, you may recall, is the memory of what you do with your muscles. Proof of its efficiency is the fact that nobody ever forgets how to ride a bicycle, even though he may have had a terrible time learning it in the first place.) So do your language studying out loud. Of course, your roommate is going to think you're crazy when he walks in and finds you mumbling to yourself. But pay no attention to him; he probably has some peculiar habits too.

Divide the Material into Small Units

As children, we were all good at memorizing; as adults we have had most of this memorizing ability educated out of us. Hence a few comments on the technique of memorizing may be helpful. First of all, don't try to memorize a large body of material at once. Break it up into small units, memorize each of these units separately, and then string them all together.

Divide your study time into small units.   If you spend two uninterrupted hours trying to memorize the material of a new lesson, you will do a poor job of memorizing and will probably go stark, raving mad in the process. Use a saner study technique. Start off with twenty minutes to half an hour at the most; then turn to some other work; then come back for another twenty minutes; and so on. Two hours divided into small bits like this will produce far better results than 120 straight minutes of agonizing study.

Go from the easy to the hard.   Start off by reading the foreign language aloud right out of the book; generally you will have little trouble remembering how the new words sounded or what they meant. As soon as you have read a sentence in this way, look away from the book and say it again. Only after you have practiced a section of material like this several times should you go on to the really hard part: looking at the English and then trying to say the foreign language without peeking. If you have trouble saying a whole sentence in this way, try breaking it into smaller pieces, say each of them individually, and then string the pieces together.

Make Full Use of Class Hours

Smart students pack fifty minutes of practice into each class hour. When somebody else is reciting, they are mentally reciting right along with him, and hence have new material half memorized even before they go home to study it. If you just sit back and daydream until you are called on, you are not only wasting the class time you're paying for, but you are needlessly piling up extra future hours of study and review on the very materials that are being covered in class. (P.S. Don't let this get around, but we've known students who got through the course solely on the basis of what they learned during class hours, without doing a lick of outside work. We don't recommend this, and we don't consider such people very smart; but at least they weren't so dumb as to waste class time.)

Don't Fall Behind

Even though steady, day-by-day work is the best way to learn any subject, it is true that in many courses you can get yourself out of a jam by some high-pressure, last-minute cramming. Not so with a language. Cramming for a language exam would be about as sensible as cramming for a swimming test; you just can't learn habits that way. Furthermore, language learning is a highly cumulative process. It is like making a tower out of blocks: you keep building on top of what you did the day before. If you don't keep at the job steadily, pretty soon you're trying to put new blocks on top of empty space. So don't fall behind. Once in a while, of course, you won't have time to prepare an assignment. It happens—occasionally—in the best of families. But when it does happen, for heaven's sake don't be so bashful as to stay away from class. If you do, making up the work will be twice as hard. Go to class, tell the instructor you're unprepared, and learn as much as you possibly can from the classroom work.

Do You Ever Need To "Think"?

Yes; but in a very special way. Memorizing new material can hardly be called "thinking." But you will help yourself enormously if, as you memorize, you think about the grammatical explanations that go with each set of new material. The grammatical section of a new lesson may tell you, for example, about verb endings. After you have read this section, and have spoken the examples out loud, start memorizing the new material; and every time you say a verb form, fit it mentally into the the scheme that has just been explained to you. This ability to think about the structure of the language is the one big advantage you have over a child; make full use of it.

LEARNING TO READ A FOREIGN LANGUAGE

How NOT To Read

The following method is guaranteed to waste a maximum of time and to produce minimum results. Start off with the first sentence of the assignment, read along until you come to a word you don't know, and look it up in the vocabulary. Then read along to the next word you don't know, look *that* up in the vocabulary, etc., ad nauseam. By following this method you will need about four hours to cover the assignment, and by the time you're through you will have looked up so many different words that you will probably not remember a single one of them.

Translating Versus Reading

The goal you should aim for is the ability to pick up a foreign language book and understand what it is all about. You will never reach this goal by doing only word-for-word translation. Some of you may have had the experience of translating Latin in high school. The writer of these lines always got "A" in his high school Latin, and always delighted the teacher with his splendid translations. But at the end of four years he discovered that, though he could translate with the best of them, he was totally unable to sit down with a Latin book and read it for content. The reason was, of course, that nobody had ever made him *read* (as opposed to *translate*) Latin, and he was too stupid to realize that he should have done it for himself.

Intelligent Guessing

If you are ever going to learn how to read for content, just about the most important skill for you to acquire is that of intelligent guessing, that is, figuring out what a word means from the context in which it is used. We do this all the time in English. All of us know how to read a lot of words which we never use in speaking, or even in our own writing.

To deduce the meanings of words from their contexts—or, for that matter, to remember the meanings of words which you have looked up in the vocabulary —you will have to read them more than once. Let's suppose that you have six pages to read, and that on each page there are ten words which you don't know. If you go through the six pages just once, and look up each of the sixty words, you certainly won't be able to remember more than ten of them. Instead of that, look up only thirty (a more manageable number) and make intelligent guesses for the remaining thirty. Then, with the time that you have saved in this way, re-read the six pages at least two more times (preferably at intervals of several hours). In this way you may be able to remember as many as twenty-five of the thirty words which you looked up; and you will also have a pretty good idea of the meaning of the thirty which you did not look up. Score this way: twenty-five certain and thirty probable. And that's a lot better than only ten certain.

How To Get Started

When you begin to do some reading in any foreign language, the cardinal rule to follow is this: *Never look a word up in the vocabulary until you have read the immediate context in which it occurs.* There is no sure way of knowing just how far you'll have to read to get the immediate context; it will vary from case to case. It would be idiotic to look up a word before reading through the whole sentence in which it occurs; some people prefer to read a whole paragraph, others a whole page or more. Perhaps the best over-all suggestion is this: read through the first sentence; and then keep on reading until you get lost. You may be able to follow along for a paragraph, or a page, or even the whole assignment.

Let's assume that you've read through a paragraph before getting lost. Now go back to the beginning again, and read along until you come to the first word you can't reasonably guess at. Underline the word (so you can find it again quickly); look it up in the vocabulary; find the English translation which fits this sentence; put a pencil dot in the vocabulary margin beside the word (to show you've looked it up once); and then, turning back to the text, re-read the phrase in which the word occurs, trying to fix its meaning as you do so. Go through the first paragraph this way, looking up only the words you absolutely have to and making intelligent guesses at the others. Then tackle the following paragraphs in the same way, until you have read about half the assignment. At this point you will want to take a short break, if only to relieve the boredom. Lean back and stretch; and then, *re-read the pages you have just finished.* This will use up only part of the time you have saved by making intelligent guesses, and it will do wonders. (The reason for doing it at this stage is that the whole section is still fresh in your memory, and a re-reading now will really tie down the loose ends. If you wait until later on, much of it will have grown cold.) Then go through the second half of the assignment, ending up with a re-reading again.

Trouble Spots

Aside from words that you don't know, there are two other problems you will run up against. First, there are the so-called "idioms": groups of words that mean more than the sum of their parts. Handle these just as you do single words; underline them and look them up in the vocabulary, putting a pencil dot beside them there. Secondly, despite all the help that a vocabulary gives you, there will be passages here and there which you just won't understand. The most important thing to remember here is: *don't waste time on them.* If you can't understand such a passage the first time through, put a vertical line in the margin beside it and read on ahead. Quite often you will pick up a clue later on, and the difficulty will be cleared up when you do the re-reading. But don't waste time on it even then. If, after a second honest try, you still can't figure out what it means, put a second vertical line in the margin, and ask your instructor to explain it to you when you go to class.

Nuisance words.   The above method, besides helping you to read efficiently, carries with it a number of interesting by-products. The underlinings automatically furnish you with a list of the words and idioms you had to look up; the single vertical lines in the margin show you which passages caused trouble the first time through; and the double vertical lines indicate the passages you had to ask your instructor about. All of this is extremely useful for reviewing later on. But perhaps most important of all are the dots you put in the vocabulary margin each time you look up a word. It is a well-known phenomenon that every reader has his own private set of nuisance words: words that he just can't seem to remember, and has to look up again and again. The dots in the vocabulary margin will automatically furnish you with a list of your own nuisance words. After you have read fifty pages or so of the book, run through the vocabulary and make a list of all the words that have more than two dots beside them. There won't be many such words; and if you spend a little extra time on them, you will save yourself a lot of vocabulary-thumbing later on.

Don't Do It the Hard Way

The method outlined above is not the only way to read a foreign language, but it is probably the most efficient one. Traditionally, students have used three other general methods. The first is to write out a full English translation of everything. This is so wearisome a process that, fortunately, it has been followed by only a few of the over-eager. The second method is to make a list of all the words that have been looked up, together with their English translations. This is highly recommended for students who have time to kill and don't enjoy bridge or the movies; but, again, the sheer mechanical labor involved is out of all proportion to the benefits received. The third method is to write an English translation over each word that has been looked up in the vocabulary. This cuts down considerably on mechanical labor, but ultimately it defeats its own purpose: when you re-read such a passage, your eye will run along the printed line, skip up to read the translation, and never even see the foreign word that you are trying to learn in the first place. If you *must* write down the translation, at least do so in the margin, not between the lines of the text. This will certainly do no harm; but we doubt that it is worth the time and effort involved. However, you can suit yourself on this point.

IF YOU STILL HAVE TROUBLE . . .

In the long run, foreign language study boils down to a constant process of learning, forgetting a bit, re-learning, forgetting a little less, and relearning again and again, until you begin to develop in the foreign language the same kinds of habits and skills that you already possess in English. The study hints given above should help you develop these habits and skills as efficiently as possible. As an added help, the textbooks you use will probably call for a considerable amount of review, and your instructor may add on some more. All of this should enable you to speak and read the language with reasonable fluency. If you still have trouble, the best suggestion we can make is that you do even more reviewing. Continue doing a conscientious job on each lesson as it is assigned; then spend a little extra time going over the material of past lessons. Quite often a little extra reviewing like this is all a person needs to catch up with the rest of the class.

A SUMMARY OF DO'S AND DON'T'S

Learning to Speak

1. You can't learn to speak a language by "thinking" about it. You've got to use it. And that means practice.
2. Don't worry if at first the language sounds "queer." It's supposed to. After all, it's a FOREIGN language. Imitate as exactly as you can.
3. Don't study silently. Quadruple your learning efficiency by saying everything OUT LOUD.
4. Don't try to learn a whole lesson all at once. Break it up into smaller units.
5. Don't study for long periods of time. Four half-hour periods of study will produce far better results than two uninterrupted hours.
6. Don't close off your mind when somebody else is reciting in class. Recite mentally with him—and get half the learning job done that way.
7. Don't fall behind. Language learning is cumulative. Lesson 11 is built on lesson 10, so you have to know 10 before you can learn 11.
8. Don't stay away from class if you're unprepared. You'll fall still farther behind. Tell your instructor, and learn from the classroom work.
9. Don't learn grammatical explanations as such. Learn to APPLY them. If you can't apply them, they're of no use to you.

Learning to Read

1. Don't look up every single word you don't know. Learn the art of intelligent guessing.
2. Don't look a word up in the vocabulary until you have read at least the whole sentence in which it occurs.
3. Don't just translate. Learn to read for meaning. English is what you are trying to get away from.
4. Don't read the assignment just once. Save time by intelligent guessing, and then use this time for re-reading.
5. Don't try to cover the whole assignment in one sitting. Break it up, re-read each part, and then re-read the whole.
6. Don't agonize over passages you just can't understand. Ask your instructor. That's one of the things he gets paid for.
7. Make a list of your own particular nuisance words—words you have to look up again and again—and spend special time on them.
8. Except for such nuisance words, don't write out lists of words you had to look up—unless you think you have time to waste.
9. Don't write English translations over the words you look up. If you have to write translations, write them in the margin.

INDEX

DATE DUE

MR 13'90	MAR 27'90		

DEMCO 38-297